DONALD WINNICOTT
AND
JOHN BOWLBY

DONALD WINNICOTT
AND
JOHN BOWLBY
Personal and Professional Perspectives

Judith Issroff

with contributions from
Christopher Reeves and Bruce Hauptman

KARNAC
LONDON   NEW YORK

First published in 2005 by
H. Karnac (Books) Ltd.
6 Pembroke Buildings, London NW10 6RE

Copyright © 2005 by Judith Issroff
Chapters 2, 5, and 6 copyright © 2005 Christopher Reeves
Chapter 3 copyright © 2005 Bruce Hauptman

The rights of Judith Issroff, Christopher Reeves, and Bruce Hauptman to be identified as the authors of this work have been asserted in accordance with §§ 77 and 78 of the Copyright Design and Patents Act 1988.

All rights reserved. No part of this publication may be reproduced, stored in a retrieval system, or transmitted, in any form or by any means, electronic, mechanical, photocopying, recording, or otherwise, without the prior written permission of the publisher.

British Library Cataloguing in Publication Data

A C.I.P. for this book is available from the British Library

ISBN: 1–85575–308–1

10 9 8 7 6 5 4 3 2 1

Printed in Great Britain by Hobbs the Printers Ltd, Totton, Hampshire

www.karnacbooks.com

Our desire to pay tribute to the memory and achievements of Donald Woods Winnicott and John Bowlby will be obvious to those who share what we write herein in honouring them. I would like to remember Bob Rodman and grieve his inability to enjoy what would surely have engaged him.

CONTENTS

ACKNOWLEDGEMENTS ix

ABOUT THE AUTHOR AND CONTRIBUTORS xi

Introduction
    Judith Issroff   1

CHAPTER ONE
Winnicott and Bowlby: personal reminiscences
    Judith Issroff   13

CHAPTER TWO
Singing the same tune?
Bowlby and Winnicott on deprivation and delinquency
    Christopher Reeves   71

CHAPTER THREE
Reflections on Donald Winnicott and John Bowlby
    Bruce Hauptman   101

CHAPTER FOUR
Bowlby and Winnicott: differences, ideas, influences
    Judith Issroff   115

CHAPTER FIVE
A duty to care:
reflections on the influence of Bowlby and Winnicott
on the 1948 Children Act
    Christopher Reeves   179

CHAPTER SIX
Postscript: from past impact to present influence
    Christopher Reeves   209

APPENDIX A	217
APPENDIX B	218
APPENDIX C	219
APPENDIX D	220
APPENDIX E	222
REFERENCES AND BIBLIOGRAPHY	229
INDEX	275

ACKNOWLEDGEMENTS

I am indebted to John Mallinson, generous friend and gentleman, for patiently solving far too many baffling computer glitches and breakdowns; to my friends Antonia Shooter and Mario Marrone, whose comments have been so helpful, and to my doughty 98-year-old mother, Phoebe, whose ever critical eagle eye discerned errors the rest of us had overlooked. I single out for special thanks Tatiana Orloff-Davidoff for making the final hours of combing for errors constructive fun rather than tedious, Ruth Rigbi, whose English mentoring has helped me immeasurably over many years, and Stanley Cohen for cogent and much-needed criticism that enabled me to re-shuffle the structure within which to share the welter of cloud-like, constantly changing thoughts that untidily spring to my naturally undisciplined, adjective-laden, drifting and changing mind. For remaining deficiencies neither Stanley nor Tatiana is responsible. I am grateful, also, to Christopher Reeves and Bruce Hauptman, who may have preferred a different book, but without whose contributions this one would have been much depleted. I regret time constraints that precluded other contributions, notably from George Allyn in Paris.

ABOUT THE AUTHOR AND CONTRIBUTORS

JUDITH ISSROFF is South African-born, British, and Israeli, a quintessential product of the Tavistock Clinic, School of Family Psychiatry and Community Mental Health, and the Independent British psychoanalytic tradition. She is a specialist child, adolescent, and family psychiatrist who was John Bowlby's registrar in the Department of Children and Parents and a consultant in the Adolescent Unit, 1970–1977. She is qualified also in the analysis of children, adolescents, as a group analyst, and in conflict management. As a consultant in the Tavistock Adolescent Unit between 1971 and 1977, she ran training groups for H.M. Prison Service senior personnel. Her experience with survivors of trauma and in cross-cultural and social psychiatry in the Middle East and elsewhere is extensive. After many years of full-time psychoanalytic practice, she founded and ran an NGO devoted to finding professional non-violent ways to ameliorate conflict and, funded by UNICEF, consulted in post–civil-war-devastated Mozambique. As a consultant psychiatrist in child and adolescent psychiatry she has worked in the United Kingdom and Northern Ireland in many CAMHS NHS placements. Following her mentors, Winnicott and Derek Miller, she has supervised and lectured in a variety of situations and published on many topics. Her interests, poetry, and writings cover a range of diverse areas.

BRUCE HAUPTMAN is a child, adolescent, and family psychiatrist who runs the Harvard-connected Community Therapeutic School in Boston for handicapped and complexly disordered youngsters that he founded after his Tavistock-based studies in London with Bowlby and Winnicott. He also works in Alaska with Inuit communities.

CHRISTOPHER REEVES is a retired child psychotherapist. After studying psychology and philosophy at Oxford, he trained in the Department of Children and Parents at the Tavistock Clinic, during John Bowlby's tenure as Chair of the department. For two years he attended clinical seminars run by Donald Winnicott. He was President of the Medical Section of the British Psychological Society and, from 1980 to 1982, Editor of the *Journal of Child Psychotherapy*. He has written widely on clinical issues in child psychotherapy and therapeutic education, as well as on philosophy and the history of ideas.

DONALD WINNICOTT
AND
JOHN BOWLBY

Introduction

Judith Issroff

This book is the product of an invitation extended to me by Mario Marrone, co-Founder and then President of IAN, to talk about John Bowlby and Donald Woods Winnicott at the first international meeting of the International Attachment Network (IAN) in Birmingham and, later, in Barcelona. At the time, as a peripatetic locum consultant in child, adolescent, and family psychiatry, I was working in North Staffordshire. My supportive obligatory "supervisor", a Jungian psychotherapist, Karl Woolliscroft, and I would explore the surrounding countryside and canal-side paths while co-counselling. He was curious to hear about Winnicott and Bowlby. And so, reminiscing and thinking as we walked one lyrically lovely summer afternoon, my talk was conceived. This book grew from the interest and enthusiasm with which it was received after Cortina and Marrone decided it did not fit into their book (2003).

Later, talking with Pearl King, I discovered that I, too, had achieved the status of what she calls "living history"—a repository of memories that might interest a few others now and/or in the future. For years, as works building on or relating to Winnicott and Bowlby have appeared, I have been reading them, interested and sometimes delighted in new insights and constructions generated, in the growing supportive evidence-base for their theories, glad their ideas were being made use of, even if not always grasped accurately in the case of Winnicott's—that is, in the way I understand them to have been conceived. That is the fate of words as they are metabolized.

Even as limited an apprenticeship as my own with individuals of the stature of Winnicott and Bowlby becomes a part of one in that one takes certain theories and ways of working for granted almost without realizing that one's approach is perhaps not universal, or how and from whom it is derived. Each of us is different in what we use and how we use it. It was an almost unthought decision I swiftly made that it would be more enriching and interesting—to me, at least, and so to any reader—to contact those still alive among those who studied with both Bowlby and Winnicott to join me in a personal and critical tribute to these two men who so profoundly helped us to find our own ways and thoughts in our professional lives. The immense importance of their respective contributions is already well appreciated. I hoped to indicate how their work affected the professional development and interests of their students. We, the privileged who were in direct contact with both of them simultaneously, well recognized how their personalities and contributions differed. I contacted everyone I could of those who were students of both Winnicott and Bowlby between 1965 and 1971 to tell them about the intended collection of papers. Victoria Hamilton and Juliet Hopkins both felt they had already said what they wanted to say (Coates, 2004; Hamilton, 1982, 1987a, 1987b, 1988, 1995, 1996b; Hopkins, 1990, 1996, 2002). I recommend that these valuable contributions be read along with the material included here, which they richly augment. For instance, Victoria Hamilton remembers that Bowlby believed two things necessary "for winning acceptance for new ideas: a strong belief in one's own convictions and a long life" (Coates, 2004, p. 588). When he has time to complete it, I hope Paris-based George Allyn's non-includable thoughts will be published elsewhere. Others among those still alive regretted being unable to contribute for diverse personal reasons. Only Christopher Reeves and Bruce Hauptman were able to join me, so the book is very different from the one originally conceived. But the material is new, even for those who already are familiar with the work of these two individualistic masters, pioneers and leaders in their fields, men who surely deserve their places not only in psychoanalysis, but in social history and the history of ideas.

Winnicott and Bowlby were both thinkers and scientists, but with different approaches: comparing them leads straight to the perennial questions about the nature of the scientific enterprise in a clinical situation or with a field of observation where the sample population is as complex as a human being, with a human life span, and with an inner imaginative world accessible to consciousness as well as a postulated unconscious realm and innate tendencies to duplicity not open to objective scrutiny. The question of the overlapping areas of sciences and arts and the nature of the construction of reality is also always lurking in the background.

How did Winnicott's and Bowlby's respective life strategies and communicative styles succeed—or fail? Both made revolutionary and evolutionary contributions to the fields of psychoanalysis and also crossed over into many other areas—among them child development and the understanding of the needs of children and their carers for continuity of experience and quality of care. They were among the forerunners in perinatal, community, and forensic paediatrics, child and family psychiatry, psychiatric classification, and preventive psychiatry. They delineated criteria of health and pathogenesis—in particular the effects of separation, loss, mourning, and other traumata. Their concerns included child-rearing and education, no less than children in hospital, understanding society, and social policy. Winnicott's work is widely read and used in fields such as literary criticism, art history, philosophy, and theology. Half a century before it was voiced by Biebel, both Bowlby and Winnicott recognized that

> the interaction between psychoanalysis and other disciplines and professions like biology, ethology, linguistics, semiotics, sociology, ethics, cognitive psychology, poetics, rhetoric and neuroscience is at a moment of fertile communicative possibility, but for this to come true, we must work on those factors that approximate the concepts, cognitive strategies, modalities of thought, and smooth out problems in communication, problems which are not only of theoretical order but also of biological, psychosocial and sociological orders. [Biebel, 1999; translated and quoted by Tutté, 2004, p. 909]

It is thanks to the work of psychoanalysts like Bowlby and Winnicott that neuroscientists like Panksepp (1999, p. 35), who is searching, as Bowlby did, "for a new consilience . . . among the many disciplines that are honestly seeking to reveal the deeper layers of human nature", can emphasize that "there should be a major scientific role for psychoanalytic approaches in such endeavours, for the currents of mind run deeper and in more complex patterns than any one of our methodologies can adequately probe" (Panksepp, 1999, p. 35).

Allan Schore's monumental overarching integrative studies in many fields have placed child psychiatry, and psychiatry in general, at the turning point of a much welcomed paradigm shift. A descriptive Kraepelinian nosology has allowed for the pharmaceutical-industry-funded symptom-relief-led attempt to use ICD-10/DSM-IV diagnostic appellations such as ADHD (attention deficit hyperactivity disorder), which medication might alleviate, to be treated as if they were real diagnoses, when they amount to no more than, say, the term "headache", which might be relieved by administration of an analgesic without much attention to delineating or dealing with its underlying cause. This has now been replaced by the basis for more substantial delineation, treatment, and prevention of psychiatric, psycho-social, and personality disorders. For this necessary revolution we are indebted to John Bowlby, whose reformulations of psychoanalytic theory in terms of cybernetics and systems theory, with the focus on attachment bonding, and the research his work has inspired, along with technological innovations and consequent research in the neurosciences, have enabled Schore's important formulations. With well-evidenced better understanding of aetiology and the pathogenesis of psychiatric and personality disorders in multi-faceted ways that make sense also within traditional psychoanalytically studied experience, psychoanalysis, psychiatry, and the neurosciences reinforce recognition of the central importance of affect regulation within inter-human interplay: Freud, Bowlby, and Winnicott remain major pillars of contemporary theoretical construction.

Winnicott and Bowlby aimed to make their ideas accessible to everyone, and both succeeded in that their works are enduringly useful and exciting to ordinary readers, from interested parents, child-minders, and nursery teachers to the most sophisticated of psychoanalytically aware, erudite, and trained philosophical and scientific minds. Their ideas are as relevant today as they were three quarters of a century ago, and as seminal a source for further exploration for those who encounter their respective *écriture* as were Darwin and Freud for them.

My chapters in this volume are personal, anecdotal, aimed at those interested in learning more about what these two men were like and how very different they were, even though their areas of interest overlapped. I think this is clear in their respective written legacies. I try to bring them alive as I experienced them in their authenticity and humanity and to compare and contrast them in a smorgasbord kind of way.

I compare them in a descriptive, conversational, opinionated, passing show fashion across a number of topics in order to try to make them live for those who did not have the privilege of personal acquaintance with these two powerful individuals to whom I am so deeply professionally indebted. Personally, I am also grateful to Winnicott, to whom I turned directly and from whom I gained so much informally on more than one occasion. My ordering of descriptions is of no particular significance. I digress freely and know that while possibly Bowlby might have frowned on my undisciplined meanderings, Winnicott would have enjoyed them indulgently. Bowlby was a believer in focus and discipline, Winnicott, a psychoanalyst's psychoanalyst, in the creative spontaneity of free associations and the discoveries thereby revealed. There are merits in both approaches. I have allowed myself to explore many side-themes while looking back at two men whom I was fortunate to encounter and whose influences permeate my life and work.

I have quoted extensively from Winnicott's criticism of Bowlby's views because it helps us to understand how and why he took issue with the latter and how possibly each provoked the other to elaborate aspects of theory that are widely accepted today. They did react to each other—at times explicitly, at other times one can only guess how much of the other's opinions are not cited but lurking in the background of what was written. In other words, one wonders how great the—unacknowledged—influence of each was on the other? Winnicott and Bowlby are linked by many because they worked towards what seemed to be the same ends, and in similar and overlapping fields. But I hope the differences in their work, as in their personalities, will become clear further on.

A conceptual itinerary is not the aim of this book. I hope readers will be stimulated to search out references that will enable them to access sources and commentaries, and, accordingly, numerous publications that deal separately with both personal and professional aspects of both men and their contributions are referenced. The bibliography may seem extensive but is by no means exhaustive; however, it is enough to enable any interested reader readily to access Bowlby's, Winnicott's, their followers' and commentators' work in a way that is likely to lead back to the sources on the one hand, and, on the other, to the many fields of scholarship, research, and clinical practice that their work has generated.

Bruce Hauptman describes the opportunity Harvard afforded him when he returned to Boston to implement what he had absorbed from Winnicott, Bowlby, and others while in the United Kingdom: three decades ago he established a therapeutic community school where their ideas "permeate" the ethos and working practice for staff and parents alike. He reflects succinctly on Bowlby's and Winnicott's differing approaches to scientific, teaching, and clinical situations. Reading about Winnicott's influence on Barbara Dockar-Drysdale and her therapeutic community (1953, 1958, 1991, 1993), and her significance to Winnicott (Reeves, 2001, 2002), to Balbernie (1966) and the Cotswold Community, and to David Wills (1941) with Q-camps/Hawkspur supplements what Hauptman runs through in mentioning various Winnicottian ideas he has applied in this particular non-hospital investigative and therapeutic management-holding and educational situation, Barbara said that "Winnicott . . . was the most important person in my life" (Fees, 1995). George Lyward's school for highly gifted adolescent social misfits deemed "educationally unfit" was another special community that was important to Winnicott, and vice versa (Bridgeland, 1971; Burn, 1953; Lyward, 1958).

Christopher Reeves's thoughtful chapters lend weight and substance: they are an original and important contribution. In the first he considers Bowlby's and Winnicott's differences by looking at their approach to deprivation and delinquency. Following up on this, he undertook archival research to uncover the evidence they gave to the Curtis Committee, which enabled them to state their opinions in a way that could to some extent influence public policy in the window of opportunity offered in the immediate post-war period. He has recovered important material relating to their ideas and influence on public policy with regard to childcare. In his Afterword he discusses contemporary attitudes and legislation concerning "looked-after" children in a way that should be taken into account by academics, social workers, service providers, and policy-makers. Winnicott's and

Bowlby's views, as relevant today as they were over half a century ago, are perhaps under-appreciated, so I hope this book might help those who are not familiar with the full scope and applicability of their respective contributions to find their ways to this important legacy. Reeves's chapters should be read along with his publications that reflect on Winnicott in terms of transition and transience, leaving and dying (Reeves, 1996), his sagacious essay "On Being 'Intrinsical': A Winnicott Enigma" (Reeves, 2004), and his informative paper about Winnicott's and Bowlby's respective influences on the development of child psychotherapy in the United Kingdom (Reeves, 2003).

Christopher Reeves (2004, p. 427) writes: "One of the fascinations about Winnicott is his ability to surprise. It is not just that his writings are often paradoxical. They are often so unexpected." The "surprise" strand that Reeves explores is taken from Winnicott's autobiographical journal where he "made the following observation, almost as an aside, in the course of some private musings on death":

> so many of my friends and contemporaries died in the first World War, and I have never been free from the feeling that my being alive is a facet of some one thing of which their deaths can be seen as other facets: some huge crystal, a body with integrity and shape intrinsical in it. [quoted in C. Winnicott, 1990, p. 6)

In his fascinating paper Reeves declares that his quest is more personal than textual, his "interest the complex individuality of Winnicott rather than the inner coherence and continuity of his thought" (2004, p. 427). This remark applies equally to the chapters that follow.

Loss of friends, their "leaving and dying" (Reeves, 1996), played a major role in the prodigious achievements of both Winnicott and Bowlby: both were multifaceted and "driven" men whose lives had great integrity. Both in some sense experienced themselves as survivors in relation to their peers, were shaped in no small measure by their times, and introspectively were well aware of the social and personal events that had exerted profound influences on them and the development of their respective contributions, as will be evident.

Fifty years of Attachment Theory: The Donald Winnicott Memorial Lecture, given by Sir Richard Bowlby (2004), with recollections of Donald Winnicott and John Bowlby by Pearl King (2004), Brett Kahr, and Richard Bowlby, addresses important aspects of the professional and personal lives of these two great adventurous psychoanalysts, discoverers, and reporters, whose findings have made an actual difference to so many lives. Both John Bowlby and Donald Winnicott frequently pondered topics relevant to social and political issues, as Christopher Reeves's contributions herein underline. Bowlby ran a series of seminars deliberating where preventive psychiatry begins and where it overlaps with politics, which had a lasting influence on my forays into social and cross-cultural psychiatry. For many years he personally ran a weekly well mother and baby clinic. Although no believer in utopia, because he understood the turmoil and violence in the nature of man, Winnicott's preoccupation with the optimal society is evident, for instance, from his seminal 1950 paper "Some Thoughts on the Meaning of the Word 'Democracy'" and "The Place of the Monarchy" (1970), or his "Berlin Walls" (1969d). His acceptance of human nature in all its aspects was probably more realistic and less optimistic than the kinds of aspirations towards social engineering that Bowlby harboured. Social commentary is an important area where psychoanalysis could aspire to play a more influential role than it has achieved: neither Bowlby nor Winnicott was unaware of this, nor reluctant to speak up. I wonder what each might have said at this juncture in the affairs of mankind? (Issroff, 2004a).

Winnicott's Second-World-War radio broadcasts in his widely read and still well-selling *The Child, The Family and the Outside World* (1964a) have been translated into many languages but have possibly had less academic impact than has Bowlby's work in association with the World Health Organization (WHO) (Bowlby, 1951, 1966), which may be better known in certain academic spheres.

This book is intended to whet the appetites of readers, whether or not they are already familiar with the work of Bowlby and Winnicott. Our personal and professional appreciation of and indebtedness to them should be obvious. There is new material for those who already make use of their written heritage. I hope that the references will direct readers back to the source publications and to the—non-exhaustive—sample of the many and exponentially growing commentaries and publications about them and their work, as well as indicate the scope of their interests and personalities. Winnicott's and Bowlby's work can be appreciated by the intelligent lay public, not only students and professionals, in a plethora of fields—indeed, by anyone interested in almost anything that pertains to human nature, development, and creativity.

Those interested in further Winnicottiana—to use Brett Kahr's term—are directed to Peter Rudnytsky's special Winter 2004 edition of *American Imago* devoted to "The Unknown Winnicott", which includes Reeves's paper, "On Being 'Intrinsical': A Winnicott Enigma". What I discovered about what I think Winnicott considered important from what he selected to describe others, and another portrayal from how others have depicted him, will appear in *Something Short of Everything about Donald Woods Winnicott*. This is conceived as Part One, introducing "The Man"; I hope to follow it with a series of commentaries about the work of Winnicott and that of those who have expanded on and/or criticized it.

Although their differences are marked, as we show here, Bowlby and Winnicott shared certain common interests and professional trainings and undoubtedly did influence each other. Even had we not been fortunate enough to enjoy their tutelage, their works would have influenced us. It has been an exciting intellectual reconnaissance, re-reading and thinking about their work and what it has generated. It was immeasurably enriching to have studied with these two unusual, kindly, generous human beings—creative, dedicated men. We offer this in appreciation of their respective remarkable contributions and stature. Their heritage endures. Let us hope that eventually their ideas may bring about a significant positive change in awareness worldwide. For until the basic issue of better facilitated parenting and the need for reliable, sufficiently sensitive continuity of care during early human development is addressed—which itself requires peaceful and bounteous-enough social environments for caregivers—the kind of society that enables us to read and revel in their legacy will remain vulnerable and at risk of being damaged, even destroyed, by those whose parenting was not of the order of excellence that Richard Bowlby describes (2004).

Continuing their work

Various memorial institutions and lectures—such as IAN (International Attachment Network), CAPP (The John Bowlby Centre for

Attachment-Based Psychoanalytic Psychotherapy: www.attachment.org.uk) and the Squiggle Foundation in London—carry on the work of Bowlby and Winnicott, but only CAPP offers both training and a clinical service. Several centres established in the United Kingdom are named after Donald Woods Winnicott and continue his work. For example, Josephine Lomax-Simpson, a Winnicott-influenced psychoanalyst, set up the Messenger House Trust and named one of the communal homes "The Winnicott House" (Fees, 1998; Winnicott, 1966d); a day care centre and clinic was established by Dr Andrew Crowcroft at Queen Elizabeth Hospital in Winnicott's name; there are Winnicott Centres in Solihull, High Wykeham, and elsewhere. Residential and day therapeutic communities, educational and social workers influenced by Winnicott's work are discussed in the editorial postscript to Bruce Hauptman's chapter.

Bibliographic references

A comprehensive bibliography of Bowlby's works can be found in van Dijken's biographical journey into his early life (1998), and various tributes are listed in the Bibliography. However, since the publication of that biography, John Bowlby's boxed papers were discovered where he had buried them for safety in a barn in 1939 at the outbreak of the Second World War, when his family were selling a farmhouse in Wiltshire. These papers are now in the Wellcome Trust Archives in London, awaiting study.

Harry Karnac compiled a painstaking Bibliography of Winnicott's published works to date (Abram, 1996). There are large archives in London (British Psychoanalytical Society) and New York (Archives of Psychiatry, History of Psychiatry Section, Department of Psychiatry; and the Oskar Diethelm Library of the History of Psychiatry, Cornell Medical Center, New York) comprising thousands of unpublished, carefully documented case studies, limericks, poems, a large carton full of paintings, presumably more fragments than those published in *Psychoanalytic Explorations* (1989a), and many more unpublished letters. The Archive in Toddington of the Planned Environment Therapy Trust (PETT) Archive and Study Centre contains oral histories, unpublished letters, and memorabilia dealing with Donald and Clare

Winnicott's work with residential, therapeutic, and educational communities (Fees, 1995, 1998, 1999, 2002).

We eagerly await *The Collected Works of Winnicott* (in preparation) on which Jan Abram is currently working. There are 22 volumes of Winnicott. However, many of the late posthumous publications reproduce earlier papers and make them more accessible. Reminiscences, critical discussion, and papers building on Winnicott's work or utilizing his ideas accumulate apace. Perhaps Clare Winnicott did not, after all, burn the whole manuscript of Winnicott's autobiography shortly after his death, as I suspected she had when she told me that she had destroyed a drawerful of letters from his first wife, Alice, that, unbeknown to her, he had kept locked away. The provisional title that Winnicott chose was taken from T. S. Eliot's lines "costing not less than everything", but in my memory this was transformed into *Nothing Short of Everything* (Issroff, in preparation-c) when he spoke to me about it. It would be characteristic of him to "metabolize" and make these lines his own, transformed. Almost all we know about Winnicott has been filtered through Clare's biographical notes (1978). My interviews with two women who had lived with Donald and Alice for some years—whom I met through Marion Milner—gave a very different picture of that marriage from the one Clare has implied (Issroff, in preparation-a).

For a recommended list of readings by and about Bowlby and Winnicott, see especially those listed at the beginning of the References and Bibliography.

CHAPTER ONE

Winnicott and Bowlby: personal reminiscences

Judith Issroff

Intention of this personal communication

Here, after more than three decades of silence, I pay tribute in personal fashion: by reminiscing, I hope to share a glimpse of the men, their personalities, experience, wisdom, and ways of being in this world. Through my unabashedly subjective views I hope to awaken enthusiasm to pursue their respective *écriture* in those who may not be familiar with their works. As both were wont to do, I ask myself questions and allow myself to associate freely while trying to answer them. In no way is my attempt to be considered didactic. Because I choose this approach—a patchwork "meandering design", as Rycroft dubbed such essays (1992, p. 87)—there is no particular argument or linear structure, merely a series of topics and anecdotes comparing and contrasting them. Of course, I comment on areas of their work and their respective contributions. I have tried to separate personal memories from other comparative evaluations, although my chapter topics overlap.

How well did I know Bowlby and Winnicott? How well does one know anyone? To reminisce, I cannot but share some personal history. I am "expert" on neither Bowlby nor Winnicott, but a student, supervisee, and personal acquaintance, in particular between 1965 and

1970. Their contributions, personalities, and styles accompany me in my daily work and life; their wise adages reverberate along with the sayings of others from whom I was lucky to learn. The question "What were Bowlby and Winnicott like?" is answered as I recall my time with them. In their presence, as in their work, the two men were profoundly different.

Acquaintance with Bowlby

I studied at the Tavistock Clinic and School for Family Psychiatry and Community Mental Health (Dicks, 1969; Trist & Murray, 1999) from 1965, before its move to its present Hampstead location, and I worked there from 1966 to 1977. I was John Bowlby's registrar in the Department for Children and Parents between 1966 and 1968. We became acquainted when he was 61 years old, and soon I became the first senior registrar in the newly formed Adolescent Unit under Derek Miller (1969, 1973, 1983), working there at consultant level after Derek departed for the United States. During my time as trainee, Bowlby spent a sabbatical year in Stanford, so my formal weekly supervision with him lasted for only a year and a bit. I remember John Bowlby, with his fierce, quizzical eyebrows, in his red braces and sometimes a bow-tie, generally formal, polite, face crinkling into an absolutely sincere and genial smile. He was always most proper, somewhat diffident, and very careful in what he said or did not say. He took a lively, kindly interest in and directed and guided all my programmed activities. He invited me to observe during his weekly group with parents and children. I took part in a research group where, despite my own biochemical, laboratory-based scientific research background experience, I felt that my comments and suggestions were not welcomed. (I learned later from Dorothy Heard and Colin Parkes, who worked with him, that they often felt the same.) I attended all the seminars he gave, where, again, questions were not always warmly welcomed.

Bowlby was an enthusiastic teacher, and he steered me to a great deal of useful literature as well as a wide variety of learning-through-experience work and apprenticeship placements and situations with allied professionals. He made me aware of the importance of many areas and clearly had high hopes for the future of all his students and disciples. I was fond of him, liked and respected him, and felt that this was mutual. Although answers were not always forthcoming, nonetheless he always listened well. Years later we did share an intimate moment: while we both knew he had had strategically to maintain his focus of reading and writing for very good reasons, I nonetheless talked with him about my bewilderment that he had ignored the most articulate body of literature about loss, grief, and mourning—that of the *Shoah*, the Jewish Holocaust, a painful literature that he knew I had been studying steadily since 1967. I asked him why. It enabled me to explain to him that my reading had been stimulated by the very large number of cases of children of survivors that had come my way, both at the Tavistock Clinic and in the private practice I had inherited when Derek Miller left for the United States, together with the Tavistock Adolescent Unit consultant position from which I had voluntarily resigned most of my sessions, because I considered myself too young at the time. I explained to him how I had realized my good fortune in not having been in the position of those I had encountered and about whom I had read, and how I felt about the responsibility of having enjoyed the privilege of further education that my courageous and able refugee grandparents' and parents' efforts had permitted me while they denied themselves. These motives had led to my emigration, along with what I had absorbed from Winnicott (1950) about the critical $x{:}y$ ratio between the x number of relatively traumatized, handicapped, and dependent people a society could contain if it is to be able to operate democratically, for needy people depend on a sufficient y number of those enjoying a measure of health. He listened most attentively, and it was my impression that he was happy to learn why I had left the security of the Tavistock for the difficulties of life in Israel. I told him what a challenge that had been, and how enriching. I write about this to reveal and illustrate how easy it was to talk of personally significant matters with John Bowlby.

One felt that things Bowlby said were completely straightforward. Nonetheless, he was quite capable of side-stepping difficult issues in what were to him distracting, too challenging, or unimportant matters, or he might act in a transparently disingenuous way. For instance, he might agree to be one's referee when he was going to be on the appointments committee that already had decided to appoint a Maudsley candidate without discussing it, excusing himself, or warning one. Incidents like this ultimately led me to trust Winnicott more.

Despite my warm regard for Bowlby, I felt only superficially acquainted with him. In contrast, I have the illusion that I knew Winnicott quite well. In a way this may be less a matter of time spent together than of their respective ways of relating. Winnicott was capable of a kind of easy intimacy that played no part for John Bowlby. His son, Sir Richard Bowlby, has given me permission to quote him saying that his father displayed "an avoidant attachment style".[1] Bowlby kept his distance, although he was approachable. Winnicott invited and opened himself to intimacy—which may have been an illusory intimacy, in which he was personally distant. Never could Bowlby have triggered personal insights for me to the depth and extent to which Winnicott did so (Issroff, 1995a). Nonetheless, when Bowlby raised his dramatic eyebrows on meeting me at a party (I think it might have been in 1996, held to celebrate the completion of the publication of the Freud *Standard Edition*), elegantly shod in stiletto heels and wearing a recklessly low-cut, mini-skirted, black lace dress, I realized that while my self-presentation would be perfectly appropriate and unremarkable in Johannesburg in those days, or even in certain London circles, I was over-dressed for this collegial London gathering in the Adams rooms of Mansfield House.[2]

Bowlby was an avid ornithologist and ethologist, Winnicott a watcher of humans (Morris, 1967, 1970, 1978). While we drank our ritual tea, during which we were often silent—part of the deliberate "quieting" of me so I should experience his and my own profound "being-ness"?—Winnicott might begin one of my supervisions with something like: "I was walking down the Strand today, and there they were—all those nymphets. I thought, 'What do they want of a father?' And then it came to me they want to be eaten: loving is eating . . ." This seemingly irrelevant comment, delivered with his sage, offbeat charm, was, of course, pertinent to the case I was analysing with his supervision: that of a two-and-a-half-year-old girl who had never known a father and who, at that point, was functioning predominantly at some early oral stage developmentally—really pre-verbal, for all her apparent precocious ability to speak. Or, at another level, perceptively, he might have been relating to my personal need for fathering, and in this manner he might let me know that he was aware of this.

Richard Bowlby told me that John Bowlby's father was largely absent: away for four years fighting the War and otherwise a workaholic and an absent father. John identified with his grandfather. So Richard is not surprised that John neglected to explore the other—colour—figure of the primary attachment spectrum: namely, the highly significant bond to the father. A 22-year-long study of fathers carried out in Germany (Grossman & Grossman, in press; Kretchmar & Jacobvitz, 2002) has clearly shown that if there is a secure comfort base in attachment to mother, the bond and role of the father in enabling the characteristically human exploratory, adventuring drive is of immense significance to an adult ability to excel in the sphere of social relationships. John Bowlby used to talk about the imaginary elastic band that tethered a securely bonded and attached toddler to the mother sitting in a park. However, what he overlooked was the need for and role of the father in generating excitement in exploration and adventures and in enabling greater doses of excitement to come to be tolerated by a developing youngster.

John Bowlby was profoundly interested in and bonded "almost worshipfully" with Darwin. Richard thinks he wrote his last book about Darwin essentially for himself, to discover more about his hero. Dyslexia runs in the Bowlby family, and Richard thinks that his father, John, who read little outside his professional passions and interests, was—like Churchill and Darwin—somewhat dyslexic, as is Richard himself, as well as an uncle. But today brain imaging techniques show how widely the brain of a dyslexic lights up in response to a stimulus, how much richer a range of attention is involved in the processing of observable experience than in the narrower, more localized areas employed by those considered non-"handicapped" literate. He describes his father as passionately interested in everything.

John Bowlby involved me intellectually: Winnicott engaged and stimulated me in personal as well as professional ways. I had several unexpected—indeed, pivotal—personal encounters with him.

Encountering Winnicott

Personal contacts

In 1965, when I telephoned Winnicott about the possibility of having personal analysis with him, he graciously rejected me with "Thank you for asking me. I consider it a compliment. But, my dear, I am much too old to take on new candidates." Shortly thereafter I witnessed him blithely, uninhibitedly skipping down the corridors of the Rijksmuseum, hand-in-hand with Clare, while other sedate participants at the Amsterdam International Psycho-Analytic Congress seriously studied the paintings.

In 1967 Winnicott and I shared a journey from London's Cromwell Road bus station to Copenhagen airport that was of immense significance for me. During these hours he bewitched, bothered, and bewildered me and mischievously disabused me of any illusions about psychoanalysts and their world. I was entertained—indeed, enthralled and somewhat shocked. The many hours that followed did nothing to alter my level of delight, discovery, and inner series of opening awarenesses and growth.

Because we would have little opportunity to learn from Winnicott unless we approached him ourselves, I initiated and organized the series of seminars held every two weeks at his home from which grew his 1971 book of case studies, *Therapeutic Consultations in Child Psychiatry* (1971d). He supervised my first child analytic case—that of the precocious fatherless toddler mentioned earlier. I consulted him on important life decisions. When it was crucial to me that he did so, he told me he "had the capacity to dream about me" and had "watched me grow quieter" over the years I went to him for supervision. When, for reasons known only to the Training Committee, I had to leave Charles Rycroft and change analysts, I went to Winnicott to discuss the problem. He scrunched himself into a foetal position in his chair, head buried in his hands, and confided that he felt guilty about having referred a number of well-known professors of psychiatry to analysts with "headpieces" that did not match, so that their analyses had failed. He regretted that he had done "such damage both to psychiatry and to psychoanalysis" (in the United Kingdom) and indiscreetly rattled off a list of eminent names. Concerned that I should be in analysis with someone with a "matching headpiece", as he called it, and despite my reservations, he directed me to Masud Khan to complete my formal analytic training requirements and, with my permission, he supervised Khan (Cooper, 1993; Groarke, 2003; Hopkins, 2000, in press; Sandler, 2004; Willoughby, 2004). He helped Masud to enable me to experience "being"—and to minimize his "boundary violations" (Godley, 2001a, 2001b, 2004; see also Appendix A)—during the period I was in analysis with him while Winnicott was alive. Masud said that Winnicott had told him that I had learned more from him in five years than others had in twenty-five—but that may not be altogether true (Hopkins, in press; Issroff, 2002b). I wish I had been able to make my own all that Winnicott so generously offered me.

After Winnicott's death, his widow Clare (Kanter, 2004a) and I were friendly. I became her confidante for a while, and naturally she spoke about him freely. We enjoyed concerts, dined together, spoke frequently on the telephone, discussed what she needed to do as executor of his estate, and so on (Issroff, in preparation-a).

Vicarious encounters with Winnicott are presented in his writing and are unavoidable in all his case presentations. Many people describe personally memorable meetings with him (e.g. Clancier & Kalmanovitch, 1984; Hopkins, 2002; Milner, 2001; Pena, 2001a, 2001b; Roazen, 2002). Marion Milner discussed her own tangled relationship with Winnicott with me, providing me with unexpected glimpses of him in a different personal context. Through Marion Milner (1969, 1978, 2001) I met and have interviewed two women who lived for some years in the home of Donald and his first wife, Alice (Issroff, in press). Donald and Alice are described as having been "made for each other", but Alice appears never to have been as interested in or involved with his working life. My impression is that while they were affectionately most compatible in many ways, she was not as successful as Clare in sparking off with him playfully and intellectually in relation to his professional life and ideas. Joel Kanter (2004b) depicts Clare and Donald's professional and personal compatibility in his biographical introduction to Clare Winnicott's published works, and this is clear in memoirs such as her engaging interview with Michael Neve, which Rudnytsky discovered and transcribed (1991), and her spontaneous reminiscences in 1982, in which she recalls the impact of his "reality", integrity, and humour, along with much else. He was tough, caring, musical, and notorious for "hair-raisingly" dangerous driving. His sense of timing and capacity to listen were great. He kept a list of friends who had been killed in the War and for whom, he felt, he had to live every moment and make something of his life.

Clare and Donald's wartime work greatly impacted on the development of his ideas and on the ethos of various residential schools and therapeutic communities. Clare calculated that he had been involved with "60,000 cases" during his long life as a paediatrician, and he left copious, meticulously detailed records. Clare thought he identified with his mother's liveliness and that the whole family had a remarkable ability to communicate with children: he was confident of being loved, yet he needed to feel appreciated, liked, and loved (C. Winnicott, 1982, and her much re-printed "D.W.W.: A Reflection", 1978).

Winnicott's ability to trigger personal insights— "turning points"

From Winnicott I received a series of astonishing—not always comfortable, yet always insight-deepening and growth-promoting—self-revelations that changed me in relation to myself and others. Although I was never in analysis with him, I was, on several such occasions, profoundly affected and altered by the impact of one of his remarks or gestures: in retrospect, I am sure that he was totally cognizant of their effect.

One example of this is our encounter, early in 1967, during the one and only lecture that Winnicott was invited to give at the Tavistock School of Family Psychiatry and Community Mental Health during the five years preceding his death. What happened during that lecture had an impact on me that I can only liken to the kind of unexpected personal awakening described in Zen Buddhist literature. What I experienced was, while not exactly *satori*, akin to an awakening or opening of "gateless inner gates". It was not a pleasant experience, but one that exposed me to myself in a kind of private insight striptease that probably saved me months of analysis. This incident was so significant that I will elaborate below. The mutative quality of this personal experience is mentioned to illustrate a rare and special gift of Winnicott's—one that I attribute to a measure of genius.

What happened inside me has driven out the overt stated subject of that lecture. I remember feeling somewhat stunned with the revelation of paradox, with remarks like: "You see, if you ask a direct question, then you are liable to create a liar" (cf. conventional psychiatric history taking). In my language he was implying that a direct attempt to teach anyone something might well function like an antigen provoking an antibody response, creating a locked, closed, even potentially explosive and personally destructive situation rather than one in which the words might act as a lubricant to facilitate further movement and genuine personal growth.

Of course, some of these notions are familiar ones in terms of increasing resistance when interpretation is premature or rouses too much pain or traumatic memory re-experiences. The main thrust of the lecture was to emphasize that Winnicott was opposed to preaching and to teaching, and to too many impinging interpretations. His technique was in fact a total antithesis to that of the Kleinians, to whose influence and beliefs we trainees at the Tavistock at that time were exposed and subjected daily.

People integrate experience into liveable knowledge only when they discover what they are capable of comprehending to make it their own. What Winnicott was trying to convey to us, or enable us and his patients to discover, was that the optimal way of facilitating a professional's or patient's development and work with one is to follow the patient's way and enable the professional to develop hers/his.

Winnicott was astonishingly adept at capturing his audience: he would roam about or be very still, somehow building the subject in such a way that one's appetite was whetted, one's excitement grew, and he drew one with him to his climax—the main thrust of wherever he was inviting one to follow along his thinking with him, if one could. However, he did not express himself in ordinary linear language, and definitely not in an unwritten lecture about communication and interpretation. On this occasion, in a particularly tortuous, roundabout fashion, Winnicott had also been talking about the responsibility of knowledge. Trying to clarify, not sure, yet summarizing my understanding, I asked my question. It is no longer clear in my mind, but was something about *then how could one ever give an interpretation if one could never say anything directly to anyone because people could only discover things for themselves if they were to have genuine personal significance, and if making a premature interpretation was a spoiling kind of activity?*

His answer was: "Your question is a better answer than any I could give."

As is usual in such situations, many in the audience were not listening, preoccupied with their own thoughts, so immediately a hum of "What did she say?" broke out. A newcomer took it upon himself to explain what I had said, and out came something quite different. I started to correct him and to explain myself. Then I caught sight of Winnicott looking at me, frowning slightly, raising a finger to his lips, narrowing his eyes, and in a flash I experienced a welter of diverse feelings and awareness.

I realized that it really didn't matter whether anyone had understood correctly or exactly what it was that either Winnicott or I had said; and it certainly didn't matter if this chap was attempting to find his place and introduce himself to the group by trying to identify with me as the one at present temporarily apparently in favour because perhaps I had understood something and received a compliment. As if under a microscope suddenly the field of observation comes into focus, so I perceived myself in stark clarity and detail. Simultaneously, I was totally conscious of what I imagined Winnicott was signalling to me, myself, in the way of not yet having internalized and put my insight into practice: namely, that *however anyone is or understands at any particular moment is the best that that person can manage, given the circumstances, personal makeup, history, and experience.*

I have related this very personal incident in order to try to illustrate Winnicott's almost uncanny ability to communicate in non-verbal ways and to enable people to reveal themselves to themselves.

At that moment, after his inspiring talk, acceptance of that knowledge and the other complex levels of awareness raised in me assumed proportions almost of a moral responsibility.

Maturity and the ability to be childlike

Winnicott stressed that maturity was more or less even, age-adequate, age-appropriate behaviour in different developmental areas. He was very much his age—that is to say, every age was alive within him and available to him to meet the requirements of those who came to see him or had the good fortune to bump into him and experience a luminous moment somewhere or other in his life's adventuring-exploring-musing-amusings. He was far from childish, but the child in the adult was always presentable.

Over many years Winnicott lectured in various public settings, and these lectures/happenings were always most stimulating. I once sat up all night listing ideas about the question he had left with us: "When does play become work?" Clare Winnicott described students throwing away their notebooks and learning alongside Donald as he settled in to playing with some child in his outpatient clinic (1984, p. 4). Here was my illustrative learning-therapeutic experience of the method in action. It was easy for me to understand such an inspired and original educationalist as George Lyward asking: "So where does teaching begin and therapy end, and vice versa?" (Bridgeland, 1971, pp. 161–167; Lyward, 1958; see also Appendix B). Experientially, not merely cognitively, I could grasp such a Winnicottian axiom as: *"the locus of therapy lies in the area of overlap of the play of two subjective realities, that of the therapist no less than that of the child"* (Winnicott, 1971d).

Note that my therapy-learning occurred almost totally non-verbally, in a public place, yet was an exceptional, profound private experience. There were always meta-communications, signals, and messages at play during our multi-level encounters.

David Holbrook (2002) describes similar experiences:

> As he spoke, you had the feeling that something outrageous had been said, something quite shocking, in a positive way, to which you had to adjust. . . . It was rather like being hit on the back of the head, though it was not painful or shocking—indeed, it had been said in the gentlest of tones and the most simple and direct language. But it came from a perspective that cut through the ordinary defences and obscurities and threw light on some aspect of experience to show it in a startling and vivid new light. There were several remarks of this kind. At first they seemed mad things for anyone to say, but then, as one came to terms with them, they changed one's view of life altogether, being the truths of inwardness. [Holbrook, 2002, pp. 147–148]

Holbrook also does not remember what his "original question had been, but", he writes, "Winnicott's response was one of the most illuminating I have ever received" (2002, p. 149).

Joel Kanter (personal communication) relates how one of the women he interviewed who had attended his LSE (London School of Economics) course was observing Winnicott dealing with parents and children in the big room at one of his Saturday afternoon drop-in clinics. It transpired that an ordinary non-professional who had listened to his war-time broadcasts had used her son as an excuse to drop in to listen to and observe him at work. Winnicott spoke first for some 15 minutes with her little boy—he always preferred to test himself, he said, by getting the child's-eye viewpoint and then seeing how it might match the parent's. Then he chatted with the mother for about 15 minutes and told her that her little boy was perfectly healthy—which she already knew. So he did connect with his very different audiences, even the remote ones, while sometimes his words passed by a significant number of others. Of his ex-social work students at the LSE, while many were Winnicott enthusiasts, there were also some who were relatively untouched by him: his style could be mystifying to teachers, yet he enthralled some social workers. He changed his style and language according to his audience, so we find similar things stated in a variety of ways throughout his writings.

Winnicott's way of being in the world

In line with Freud's attitude to the parapraxes of everyday life, Winnicott visualized the meaning and significance of ordinary activities in diverse and unexpected ways. For instance, he drew our attention to the kinaesthetic motoric ways of communicating. Once during my supervision he crawled backwards to demonstrate a schizophrenic child's way of joining up his thoughts. His papers "String: A Technique of Communication" (Winnicott, 1960c), and the seminal "Observations of Infants in a Set Situation" (1941a; Davis, 1993; Jackson, 1996) are examples of how observant and insightful he was. It was in these clinical observations of a young paediatrician that many important ideas he developed later had their origin. He was the last person to overlook the crucial significance of fantasy, of play (1968e, 1971a, 1971b), of symbolism, of thinking and dreaming, of an individual's relationship to his inner self and inner world, no less than his "transitional" and real interactions with the outer world in all its complexities. These included levels of dependence, of need, of caring and of lack of care, and of play, and its gradation into work. His prodigious originality and diversity of approach is clear even in the limited sample of his ideas to which I allude here. He did not strive for simplicity and economy in formulations, as did Bowlby. He would never have been prepared to overlook the content of what was said by a child or the content of play, as Bowlby was prepared to do under the influence of primatologists. Both were men of common sense, but Winnicott said: "I absolutely believe in looking at things straight and doing things about them; but not in making it boring by forgetting the fantasy, the unconscious fantasy."

Playfulness

Winnicott rated the ability to play as a more significant indicator of a child's health than cognitive ability. The capacity to play is a component of health and a sign of the ability to engage in a therapeutic process. Michael Parsons (1999) spelled out how play is constantly at work in psychoanalysis, continuously sustaining paradoxical realities that allow things to be simultaneously both real and not real. Winnicott embodied this life approach. John Bowlby did not. One grew to expect some "peak" moment (Maslow, 1970) in any encounter with Winnicott—paradoxically along with a deep peaceful secure kind of rapport. Winnicott asked, "If play is neither inside nor outside, where is it?" True play transcends the opposites of serious and unserious (Milner, 1972, p. 5).

Bowlby could be most interesting. It was nice to see him, but never was the encounter exciting or "heady" or calming in the way that time with Winnicott invariably was. However challenging and exacting intellectually an hour with John Bowlby might be, time with Winnicott was always at least as demanding intellectually and was also in other ways "quality" time, demanding all manner of inner resonance capacities, so one would leave alerted, a-joying, remaining very much engaged until the next encounter. In what could be a kind of identification with, send-up, or parody of Winnicott at his most provocatively thought-provoking and idiosyncratic, I think Cox aptly describes this rich type of encounter as happening "through reciprocal projective identification, to being inside each other enough to trust the more threatening possibility of actually entering oneself, enough" (Cox, 2001, p. 113). Winnicott simply played with ideas, and the ideas abounded from all manner of angles without any pronouncements about what was happening.

Once during a supervision we discussed asthma. "Have you thought about breathing?" He drew a folded slip of paper from his breast pocket on which he had scribbled while in hospital in New York in 1967 and had carried around thereafter. He read out: *"Air breathed me in and life foretold: I breathed out and death beheld."* He said he had calculated how many breaths he had drawn in his lifetime—I forget the number.

Bowlby was not playful, although he could very occasionally allow himself to twinkle almost mischievously. However, as Cox pointed out, Winnicott sported in and out of the unconscious in the "the perpetual polarity of playfulness which is both predictably unpredictable, safely risky, and repeatedly novel". Winnicott was master of "the paradoxically successful invasiveness of the aesthetic imperative, which does not invade", of "the image" that "has touched the depths before it stirs the surface" (Cox, 2001, p. 120).

Milner pointed out that the surface of water is the place of submergence or emergence (1972, p. 60). She describes Winnicott:

> Often over the years when we had a gap of time and we had arranged to meet and discuss some theoretical problem, he would open the door, and then be all over the place, whistling, forgetting something, running upstairs, a general sort of clatter, so that I would be impatient for him to settle down. But, gradually, I came to see this as a necessary preliminary to the fiery flashes of intuition that would follow when he did eventually settle down. [Milner, 1972, p. 5]

Bowlby, Winnicott, and the training of a child, family, and social psychiatrist

Supervision with Bowlby

I looked forward to my hours with Bowlby. They were a great pleasure, very stimulating, and I would always go away having learnt something new or pointed to some important area I would read and explore. He was interested, head cocked, listening carefully, yet diffident, almost shy in recommending something like Ella Freeman Sharpe's book about dreams (1937). He liked clinical material and linking it to his traumatic separation or "minimal brain damage at birth" type of explanatory models. He concentrated on ensuring that language used was not loose, and on keeping speculation to a minimum. He made use of his encrypted notes to help one gain a transgenerational familial picture and to map probable major traumatic life events. He thought that I was over-involved emotionally with patients when I pointed out that there might be ethical problems involved in referring a client who had suffered multiple bereavements early in life and again recently to one of the Tavistock trainees who, we knew, would be leaving at the end of the year, rather than to a member of the non-transient staff. I do tend to express myself with some vehemence at times, but I could not understand how he seemed oblivious to this particular ethical problem, which occurred not infrequently.

The atmosphere was formal and distant when Bowlby supervised me. He was interested in ensuring that I understood the whole range of activities and interfaces with other organizations that are important in dealing with any child and family. He seemed not quite at ease with me, and I felt a bit the same way. I felt he would have preferred to be writing. The cases were used as starting points for various discussions, including about matters such as not leaving traces in notes of things that might follow someone for life. Occasionally we discussed dreams. Often he held forth about the importance of language used for conceptualizing. He might request that I review some book for him perhaps—usually one that would not have particularly interested him. I admit that I cannot recall leaving feeling inspired or enlightened. After a year I moved on to enjoy the dramatically different style of Derek Miller in the Adolescent Unit. Supervision with Winnicott was of a different, almost spell-binding order.

Seminars and training concerns

Bowlby believed that the ambition of all decent-minded men should be to improve society (van Dijken, 1997, p. 38). He ran a special seminar for those of us who were 1967/8/9 Registrars and Senior Registrars in the Tavistock Departments of Child Adolescent and Adult Psychiatry and distinguished international visitors, such as Ken Adams, Gert Morgenthal, Bruce Hauptman, and Edward Ziegler. Six of us attended. The seminar examined the issue of preventive psychiatry and, indeed, was prescient of the HAS Report that currently influences child psychiatry and primary care provisions in the United Kingdom, as did all of our training across what today are looked at as Tier 1–4 types of provision of help (Williams & White,

1996). As Hauptman describes in his chapter, Bowlby sent trainees out to acquire experience in children's homes and in ordinary schools and schools for "maladjusted children". Prior to medical school, Bowlby, himself, had been profoundly influenced by his experience working in Priory Gate, a progressive school for maladjusted and delinquent children (Coates,2004). We visited therapeutic community schools like Dockar-Drysdale's Mulberry Bush (1991; Reeves, 2001) and special communal schools like Summerhill (Shaw, 1969) and George Lyward's "place in Kent" for gifted misfits (Burn, 1953; Lyward, 1958). We observed nursing couples, baby-and-mother clinics, nursery schools. We were sent to work with police whom he saw—like hairdressers—as practical front-line workers in crisis-intervention and preventive psychiatry; in prisons; we worked with and learned from probation officers, social service agencies, educationalists, health visitors, and GPs, long before liaison work became recognized as part of the necessary field of engagement of any child, adolescent, and family psychiatrist. (As a medical student he had run Bogey's Bar, a sandwich shop.) I also attended neurology rounds at Queen's Square and weekly clinical meetings at the Anna Freud Clinic and the Kleinian child psychotherapy and infant observation seminars at the Tavistock. In addition, in the evening I went to adult group therapy training with Bob Gosling and Pierre Turquet and to adult psychotherapy training seminars with Jock Sutherland, Henry Ezriel, and David Malan's adult focussed brief psychotherapy sessions, as well as Enid Balint's marital therapy course. Family therapy was not yet officially started, but we did it and discussed it. Salvador Minuchin introduced his perspective on family therapy. We all attended the meetings of the Tavistock Institute sociologists and organizational management business consultants and group relations training people like Cyril Sofer (1961, 1973; Trist & Sofer, 1957), Pierre Turquet, Eric Miller, and Ken Rice; Ronnie Laing discussed community therapy, sanity, madness, LSD, meditation, cross-cultural work, and whatever he decided to discourse on that day, and Herbert Phillipson, originator of the Object Relations Technique—who devised the Thematic Apperception Test (TAT) and Child Apperception Test cards (CAT), exposed us to a variety of projective tests (Laing, Phillipson, & Lee, 1966) and Elsie Osborn, an educational psychologist, to cognitive psychological tests. It was tremendously exciting, enriching, and eye-opening being at the Tavistock, where visitors like Nikko Tinbergen (1951, 1958; Tinbergen & Tinbergen, 1972) might discuss autism and Alexander postural technique. Every day was an adventure, revealing new horizons.

Bowlby held that almost a quarter of our time should be spent on trying to disseminate professional knowledge to the wider public as well as to other workers. He recognized that there would never be a sufficient number of adequately trained professionals to deal with the need and amount of damage and disturbance in postwar society. My training with Bowlby occurred prior to the publication of deMause's disturbing, scholarly compilation of the recorded history of childhood (1975, 1982, 2001a, 2001b, 2002). We did not yet recognize quite how prevalent the incidence of actual abuse, neglect, torture, exploitation of children, and slavery was then; now, three and a half decades later, it remains difficult to accept, despite the evidence—including that of organized and ritualistic group abuse of children. Bowlby's and Winnicott's work during their lifetimes and beyond have contributed in no small measure to change from the dreadful universal prevalence of these ills to aspirations towards becoming a more child-caring society. In equal proportion to our time spent in actual clinical work with patients, Bowlby wanted us to be trained to run organizations, to train others, do research, and carry out interdisciplinary activities. We had to understand budgetary and managerial constraints and the nature of authority and groups. He in no way discouraged us from pursuing psychoanalysis and psychoanalytic training, including in child psychoanalysis and psychotherapy—quite the contrary. However, he was equally concerned that we be exposed to ethology (de Vore, 1965; Eibl-Eibesfeldt, 1969, 1971, 1989; Harlow, 1958; Harlow & Harlow, 1966; Hinde, 1966: Lorenz, Huxley, & Wilson, 1952; Tinbergen, 1951, 1958; von Frisch, 1967) and to social theory, philosophy of science, as well as cybernetics, information theory, and research methodology. Of course, we discussed ethics and public policy considerations; we learned how to prepare court reports, to try to think and write clearly, review books, and not to speak unless we had something pertinent to say. He planned that we learned to use our time well.

For many years John Bowlby ran a once-weekly group for well mothers and their children—babies and toddlers: I was privileged to sit in on this group for several months. He was very much at ease with and involved with these women, and they with him. Brave and Ferid (1990) have written about John Bowlby and feminism, showing how he and his views were misinterpreted by the movement. Winnicott (1954a) wrote to Bowlby, concerned that public misperceptions about his work be rectified, and because of the common misunderstandings, Winnicott himself wrote about "This Feminism" (1986c).

Other remembrances of John Bowlby

Unlike my reconstructions, John Southgate's remembrances of Bowlby (Southgate, 1990) are based on notes he made at the time they met in 1987 and after subsequent supervisions. With Southgate's kind permission I extract from what he published in *The Journal of the Institute for Self Analysis* special *On Attachment* issue commemorating the work of John Bowlby (Southgate, 1990).

Bowlby "explained that life had been difficult and that he had felt isolated in the 1950s and 1960s, though he had tried to keep on good personal relations with people. . . . He said that he originally took up work on infants separated from their parents and in care because there was no question that parents could be considered responsible for this situation"—because it was due to war, illness of parent or child, birth of a sibling, and so on. Bowlby said that at the age of 81 he could "count my close supporters on one hand, or maybe two". Some people "accepted 20%, 30%, 50% or 90%" of his ideas. In the last decade "many people in the psychoanalytic scene were questioning fundamentals and listening to others". This Bowlby saw as a change, albeit a slow one (p. 5). Bowlby admitted that he had "had a prejudice against considering the first year of life because of all the unlikely theories associated with Klein that were currency during his early work" (p. 6). When Southgate tried to sound him out about the theories of Ignacio Matte-Blanco and Jacques Lacan, tactfully dodging the question, Bowlby said that he "preferred to use findings that had some real practical value for his work" (p. 7). Southgate—who has been a jazz musician—considered his subsequent supervision sessions with John "without exception, the most stimulating, lively, creative hours that I have experienced with anyone at any time". They would have a brief chat about news and personal things. There was a liveliness about him, a twinkle in the eye and laughter. Sometimes he would scrunch up his eyes and lower his head looking like he was concentrating intensely; then he would look up and tell me what he had worked out. What is hard to put into words is that the experience was so profound and yet so simple. He could draw upon a rich experience and apply it to a field he had never been involved with [victims of sexual abuse who suffered from dissociative identity or multiple personality disorder].

John was interested in detail and would make notes of the age gap between siblings, parents, grandparents, year of birth, the culture at the time for example 1930s or War etc. . . . First he would listen patiently to all I had to say. Then he might speculate about what theory you could have about the person, what hypothesis could you make? . . . He had no trouble at all in our use of letters, drawings, or physical contact for holding very regressed clients. Also surprising was his encyclopaedic memory for facts, books, references or people on the widest range of topics, including other sciences like ethology, biology, etc. When we were discussing working with the Multiple Personality he proposed a book written in 1910 which was one of the first attempts to understand the phenomenon. We did talk about whether everyone is in some sense a multiple personality, and John said, "Well, two personalities is multiple."

John advised us not to bother with controversy by attacking other people's theories but to concentrate on producing a really good theory and practice of our own, on the grounds that this way, though slow, would produce the best results in the end. [p. 8]

What John Bowlby thought he had in common with Alice Miller, Karen Horney—and presumably also Donald Winnicott—is "the support for the innocent child or infant". He saw sexuality as a different behavioural system from attachment.

John Bowlby's personal history was of a remote and inaccessible father who, himself, had been deprived of fathering. Much of "Bowlby's personal and intellectual style was a response to the cumulative weight of the losses he had suffered". The tragic accidental death of his closest friend Evan Durbin (Durbin & Bowlby, 1939) and that of his nanny in childhood were severe. Through these losses Bowlby came "better to appreciate the personal sources of his passionate—at times even provocative—allegiance to attachment theory" (Coates, 2004, p. 593).

What is overlooked by many psychoanalysts is that John Bowlby selected out the attachment system to study as "the best bet", and, while not dismissing any of the actual findings of psychoanalysis, he wanted to reformulate the data in a different way. Bowlby required that his theories be consistent with the findings in allied disciplines. He formulated them under the constraints of evolutionary biology and ethology (Coates, 2004, p. 578), as reflected in our intensive training exposure to these disciplines. Certainly he did not agree with many of the inferences some psychoanalysts seemed to treat as facts on which to base their hypotheses and theories. He wanted psychoanalytic practice to be as "unmystified as possible". "With a wry and mischievous smile" he told John Southgate, "Ordinary blokes like you and me have to be able to do this work" (Southgate, 1990, p. 10). I did feel that John Bowlby aspired to be an "ordinary bloke". When he died, John Southgate took care to put on record "how he supported with his wisdom members of [the] Institute [for Self Analysis] in a field in which he did not have personal experience—the abused child within the adult". He was keen that his attachment theory be applied to this work.

Winnicott as supervisor

I do not now recall whether it was before or after a particularly poignant session with a little girl whose analysis Winnicott was supervising when he made the aforementioned comment to me wondering about what girls want of a father, but I would like to recall the material of that session. The child was about 3½ to 4 years old at the time. During the session she climbed up the back of the chair on which I was sitting, clambered over my head and down through the overall I used to wear when I saw her. She came out between my knees on to the floor and then proceeded to strip herself naked. With a little wiggle, she said to me: "Look I'm a 'ooman'!" I was moved not only by her re-birthing behaviour, but also the immediate recognition that in her new beginning to life she required the presence of a father to see herself accurately reflected. For she had no father. She had never known one and had spent a great deal of her analysis looking for one in every possible place, noise, conscious (*Cs*) fantasy, and—inferred—unconscious (*Ucs*) phantasy. She had to protect herself from an extremely inappropriate and impinging mother, who never could mirror her back to herself or respond in an appropriate way, as was evidenced in the very first session, when the child was 2½ years old. The mother came into the therapy-room. The child pointed to a doll's bottom and asked: "What's this?" Her mother replied, "That, my dear, is an indentation!" So it was no wonder that this child spent the first period of her analysis "unlearning" language, skilfully jumbling consonants and vowels in ways that left me feeling as linguistically confused as she herself was (in the evoked countertransference proper that being with her provoked). As a result of this incident, with Winnicott's support, it was deliberately decided that I would make as few interpretations as possible and not bombard the child with my own understanding. I spoke little. However, my understanding of transference/countertransference interplay and what was happening in the sessions was strictly psychoanalytic and important: I was always thinking about what might be related to conflict or defence against anxiety or drive or remembering by repeating some traumatic incident or what developmental level was manifest. In other words, I followed the material, and Winnicott and I understood it, but rather than a therapeutic aspiration towards a corrective emotional experience, the psychoanalysis was tailored towards attempting not to reproduce the traumatizing, confusing, disruptive situation in which she lived and that she continued to live within.

Winnicott's understanding of what went on in this analysis was in itself a "holding experience" for me in which his weekly comments were almost prescient and predictive of the material that emerged during the following week in what at times seemed to me quite an uncanny way.

For instance, at the start of one supervision I said no more than that when I went to get the child in the waiting-room, she dropped to her knees, pretended to be a lion, and crawled down the passage to the door of "our" session room. As she got inside, she stood up and continued with her previous day's play with Plasticine, which she fed to me, and with various little chicks and a mother hen that she loved to locate physically nestling in my rather wild and curly hair. However, I did not get to tell Winnicott about her play, for as soon as I had described her behaviour between the waiting-room and the consulting-room, Winnicott began talking. He said that she was clearly demonstrating that she could not be her real self with her mother, because it was too dangerous. Accordingly, she had to organize a false self as a lion in order courageously to protect herself from this impinging, demanding, inappropriate mother. He suggested that she could only become and be herself in the treatment room in which she had already re-birthed herself. He went on to discuss whether one might therefore consider that in some cases, such as with this child, the analysis itself may become the primary mothering experience for the birth of the true self. His exposition was fascinating, and I wish that I had been able to record it. Though I cannot conceive of any supervision with Bowlby taking this kind of course, I am convinced he would have been quite as fascinated as I was by Winnicott's speculative understanding of this very small piece of observation.

Winnicott was quite capable of getting down on his hands and knees during supervision. As previously mentioned, he once crawled backwards across the floor in order to demonstrate to me how a schizophrenic child might try to join his thoughts together in concrete operational, physical-exertion thinking. Without ever saying so explicitly, Winnicott was conveying to me that there were aspects of this child's behaviour that roused his suspicions about possible later manifest schizophrenic illness—which did, in fact, develop during her adolescence. Simultaneously, Winnicott was teasing me by glancing sideways at his anti-angina medication perched on a shelf, knowing full well that I was as worried as he was that he might have an angina attack, as, at the time of our journey together in 1967 from Cromwell Road Air Terminus in London to Copenhagen for the International Congress, Winnicott had packed his medication in his luggage, which got lost, and I had shared an extremely anxious time with him, because though he was not afraid of dying and hoped to be conscious at his death, he was very much concerned about suffering pain with nothing to relieve it. So he teased me to remind me that he remembered how we had become acquainted. He behaved like the small child whose analysis he was supervising might, to enable me to be free to contain the anxieties the analysis itself aroused. The child had no father, and Winnicott knew that I had lost my father as a child. He teased me to prepare me for his own death as he played with his personal preparation for another attack of angina and his end—better something one brings about actively by one's own volition than an act beyond one's imaginary psychic omnipotence. This idea is explicit in his thoughts about birth (Winnicott, 1949a; see also Christopher

Reeves's 1996 article, "Transition and Transience: Winnicott on Leaving and Dying"). I must emphasize that we both knew that there was no need for him to crawl around in this apprehension-provoking fashion—so I wonder whether perhaps he needed me to help contain his own anxiety about attacks he experienced not infrequently at that particular period.

I could never imagine John Bowlby crawling about to illustrate a point, although he was extremely affable, warm, intrepid, and delightfully interactive in a far more informal fashion during the well mother and baby group. However, I never saw him get down on the floor with a child, whereas I could well imagine Winnicott doing so in a similar situation. I suppose I am implying what I have also learned from others who knew them well: namely, that Winnicott was capable of behaving in outlandish and eccentric ways, while Bowlby perhaps was not, or at least did not give that impression. Clare Winnicott described very poignantly to Pearl King (2004) how she and Donald "played their way through problems and towards creative solutions". For them, playing "was an essential part of their enjoyment of life: it was an experience and always a creative one". She wrote: "We played with things . . . we played with ideas, tossing them about at random with the freedom of knowing that we need not agree, and we were strong enough not to be hurt by each other."

Winnicott seldom referred to Mrs Klein's work in my supervisions, but not infrequently he talked about different mechanisms of defence. However, he used the concept in a far more fluid way than those described by Anna Freud (1945). He was quite capable of saying: "I think this is an organized confusion against confusion."

How did they present themselves?

Bowlby was always spruce, ironed, Winnicott almost never, but rather crumpled and rumpled, glasses perched atop his head, hands and furrowed brow working as an integral part of his mobile embodiedness. In his Introduction to Winnicott's *Holding and Interpretation* (1986), Khan (1986) describes him as someone in constant motion. Yet I think of him as someone who could be immobile, body relaxed, languid, at ease, very still and centred.

Paediatrician Peter Tizard began his funeral oration:

It would be wrong to say that Donald Winnicott was a many-sided man: in reality he was a man of many depths and there is so much to be said about him at any level that it is difficult to know which aspects of his life and work and personality to select. [Quoting Ben Jonson about his friend, William Shakespeare] I loved the man, and do honour his memory, on this side idolatry, as much as any. . . . I shall remember him best as a conversationalist. He was the diametrical opposite of a bore. . . . One is profoundly blessed if in the course of a lifetime one can get to know well someone who seems to have the truth in him, that is to say profound wisdom with never a trace of pretence. Donald was such a man. It was an endearing aspect of his character that he could afford to acknowledge his own weaknesses, normal human attributes which most of us cannot admit possessing . . . he had a certain vanity in wanting to be loved and admired; he was easily hurt; . . . But it is of his enormous zest for life which I like to think . . . and his never ending curiosity and wish to learn.

Simone Decobert (quoted in Clancier & Kalmanovitch, 1984, p. 5) describes her first sight of Winnicott "sitting in the back row of a room like a disjointed marionette in an attitude that could not have been more different from that of the dignified chairman . . . a jack-in-the-box who unwound like a spring and brought back life to an audience". She was soon impressed by "his presence, evident depth of thought, humour and charm—the human quality of the man himself".

Winnicott had a penchant for clowning, being witty, pithy, poetical: "saying it slant" was one of his natural talents.

I always admired Bowlby's sartorially elegant red braces and the distinctive green ink he liked to use in his pen. Bowlby's writing was careful, legible, unlike Winnicott's bold creative and inventive scrawl that could be difficult to decipher and went everywhere on a page. More than once he amused himself by squiggling his signature into a kind of mouse. Both were self-authorized, determined men who vigorously pursued their interests, at times with passion, even when they faced opposition.

Approachability and openness

Neither Bowlby nor Winnicott was rigid or dogmatic—both were careful, courteous listeners, cautious, open-minded to any kind of idea and discussion. However—as confirmed by Colin Murray Parkes, George Allyn, Bruce Hauptman, and Dorothy Heard—there were occasions when Bowlby avoided argument. I suspect this was because he did not want to be deflected from his strategically focused course. Winnicott was much freer and playful in his ability to speculate and to invite speculation. Both were self-authorized, determined men who vigorously pursued their interests, at times with passion, even when they faced opposition.

Interviewing and note-taking

Winnicott paid no attention to what he termed his self-styled "schizophrenic" dissociated hand as he scribbled away, diligently noting as much as he could, apologetic about the way the most intense and significant moments are the ones when recording stops, so one has to reconstruct them afterward—if there is an immediate opportunity. Those who lived with him and Alice during the war years recall him always writing notes on his lap in the kitchen (Issroff, in preparation-a).

In complete contrast, Bowlby advised that as little as possible be kept in publicly accessible notes and records lest they follow patients around and be misused later. He had a small notebook in his breast pocket in which he kept detailed encoded notes of basic factual data in initials—especially, as Southgate (1990) and I noted above, as they related to separations, moves, traumas, and losses, which necessitated details about siblings, gaps between children, and the extended family. Particulars about pregnancy and birth, mother's circumstances during first year of life, and supportive network for parenting were carefully recorded about cases he supervised. He updated these notes and referred to them, always seeming on top of the important details in the material from his perspective.

In contrast to Bowlby, Winnicott always kept copious notes dictated immediately after sessions and consultations from his scribbled notes. But he recorded nothing during supervision. A great clinical store in New York and other archives awaits future scholars. Unfortunately it is unlikely that it will be available to anyone who worked with Winnicott himself. But hopefully he has left enough indication of the way he thought for someone to study and then to build on. The publications of people like Patrick Casement (1991, 2002a, 2002b), Didi Goldman (1993a, 1993b), Bonaminio (2001), Ogden (1985, 1986, 1989, 1994), Schacht (1972, 1988, 2001), Eigen (1985, 1986, 1989, 1991, 1993, 1995, 1996, 1998, 2004), Fromm and Smith (1989), sampled from numerous others, show how internalized and useful Winnicott's work can be clinically.

My own approach to note-taking combines elements from both Winnicott's and Bowlby's practices.[3]

Winnicott's spontaneity and playfulness vs. Bowlby's restraint and penchant for "objectivity"

Winnicott drew attention to "the stultifying effect on the creative spirit of too great insistence not just on propriety, but on objectivity. This insistence on objectivity concerns not only perception but also action, and creativity can be destroyed by too great insistence that in acting one must know beforehand what one is doing." Winnicott advocated and embodied "the spontaneous gesture". Bowlby was much more cautious and restrained—he seems to have thought carefully before committing himself to action, and, once underway, he was loath to doubt his decisions or opinions.

Winnicott had an insistence on being himself. He was serious yet full of humour, irony, parody, even caricature. He was hard-working and yet milked as much fun out of life as he could. He described life as "a comic opera". He was a gentleman who could behave quite rudely. But in his obituary of James Strachey (1969c), to my surprise, he describes himself as essentially a shy man—a shy entertainer–performer? Interestingly, in a short personal memoir, Marion Milner (2001) wrote that she always thought of him as an acrobatic clown, twirling and spinning like a giant Catherine wheel throwing out sparks as it spun against a dark sky (Milner, 2001)—so she, too, saw him as a performer.

Donald Winnicott was certainly among the most charming, witty, tactful, beguiling, fun-full, and wise human beings I have ever met. He was a delight to be with—natural and totally engaging. He tossed out ideas and questions to play with in a way that reminded me of childhood ballgames. There was nothing mundane or forced about him. One felt accepted, appreciated, and listened to; one was enjoyed and knew that one was privileged. Yet once when he was ridding himself of someone with whom he did not want to be in further conversation—perhaps he was tired or in pain—I remember him masked, fey, and phoney—I was almost shocked at this "false" self that suddenly appeared.

I think Winnicott was aware in himself of inherently contrary pulls and apparent contradictions. Interestingly, Bowlby commented on this to John Southgate, saying that "Winnicott was an artist and could be read for inspiration. They never disagreed about practical matters connected with children and their caregivers. But Winnicott could hold incompatible notions in his head without, apparently, worrying about it" (Southgate, 1990, p. 10). I wonder: did Bowlby mean that he could not? After all, Bowlby developed the model of an inner world in which there co-existed separate and uncoupled inner representational working models that could develop different, not necessarily compatible plans. Can one infer from this an implication that sometimes they did come to similar conceptualizations without realizing this? Winnicott always spoke of paradoxes that have to be seen and confronted, contained, not resolved, because irresolvable. So he could demonstrate both concern and lack of concern. Sometimes his comments were ironical, yet he was careful to try not to reject or offend or dismay. He was mistrustful of sentiment yet capable of it.

With both of them, one always felt one had his full attention. Bowlby would watch one quizzically with his head tilted slightly to one side, looking at the floor before saying anything. Winnicott might have his eyes shut, be slumped in his chair, or angled across the pouffe, or on the floor. Winnicott's face would sink into his hands and crinkle into a myriad wrinkles, almost as if he were tormented by the effort of articulating whatever it was he was trying to say: a large part of the communication was simultaneously non-verbal, part of *The Silent Language* described by Earl Stanley Hall (1959).

Bowlby's attitude to our training in observation and research

The widely acknowledged central significance of attachment and separation theory in child development research and clinical formulations is tribute to Bowlby's immense contribution. As part of our

Tavistock training we were expected to observe children in all manner of settings and stages of development, as previously outlined. John Bowlby adopted an ethological observation approach to research conducted at that time. What we were expected to note about the young children we observed in a children's home were crude patterns of behaviour in strict primatologists' fashion. Observations were conducted over a period of time that was, in my opinion, not appropriate to children of that age group, perhaps because human primates have a different time rhythm for concentration and change of activity. From what I had observed, I thought we should alter the time parameters of the observations. Moreover, however appropriate and correct in ethological attitude, the observations did not include anything the children said or a detailed description of play content. Until 1989, when I read Winnicott's criticism of Bowlby (Winnicott, 1989a, pp. 423–432), I did not know that I shared common ground with him when I protested to Bowlby that we were observing the interactions and behaviour of young human beings, not of some other animal or primate. I thought the nature of their play, the content of verbalizations, and even the number of times they might glance at the observer were just as important as the selected defined patterns of behaviour we were looking at and quantifying. I argued that that which makes human beings distinctly human is the communicable aspect of inner world experience—not necessarily only what is verbal but including affect—and the actual nature of what is vocalized or can be inferred from what is said is most important, as are the observations and inferences we draw from them in play therapy and in ordinary life. I objected to leaving aside this dimension of what we were observing outside the area of what we were recording. Unfortunately we were unable to discuss this problem adequately, as happened with many other problems. Was this because of Bowlby's strong tendency to remain focused and get on with what was being done? Or was it his reluctance to engage in an argument or challenge to his authority? I was surprised and disappointed. However, at that time I was promoted to Senior Registrar in the Adolescent Unit under Derek Miller and could not continue with this work.

Reactions to criticism and rejection

> Attachment theory initially met with a hostile reception from psychoanalysis—despite the fact Bowlby framed his arguments non-contentiously. [Mary Ainsworth] always admired the way in which he reacted to these hostile criticisms. He persisted in expositions of his new approach without feeling it necessary to be defensive and with no sign of reactive hostility, although undoubtedly feeling quite confident that he was on the right track and recognising the difficulty encountered by those thoroughly dedicated to one theoretical paradigm in accommodating themselves to a new one. [Ainsworth, 1990, p. 13]

In contrast, Winnicott seems to have taken criticism to heart. In "Reminiscences of a Survivor of Psychoanalysis 1937–1993" (Pearson, 2004, p. 206) Charles Rycroft spoke of Winnicott and Klein at Psychoanalytic Society meetings:

> In the latter exercise mutual miscomprehension had a most peculiar flavour about it. It was not just that they had different ideas about infancy, mothering, early age development and object relating, but that Winnicott always seemed to be pleading to be understood and appreciated by Klein. [Pearson, 2004, p. 206]

There is evidence of this in several of his letters (Winnicott, 1987b). His second—or third—heart attack, complicated by pneumonia, was precipitated when the American psychoanalysts failed to appreciate his "Use of an Object" paper when it was presented in New York in 1967 (1968h). In this paper Winnicott equated object relating with attachment behaviour without mentioning Bowlby, but I think with Bowlby's work somewhere in mind.

Why did Winnicott react so profoundly to poor reception of one of his most important contributions? This paper mattered deeply to Winnicott. It was generated in a dream (1963a; see also Appendix C) in which:

a. He realized he had mended a split in himself. Without that dream, Winnicott concluded, he would have remained split. Then he "would have resorted to solving the problem of integration of his selves in lived behaviour as so many individuals do, alternately in sadism and in masochism, using object-relating, that is in lived out relationships to objectively perceived objects, other people" (Winnicott, 1963a/1989, p. 229).

b. He answered to his satisfaction his own lifelong question about how the inner and outer worlds become differentiated, and also how significant attachment figures and others who exist reliably in the outer world, and who were imaginatively indestructible, become usable—an "enlightenment"—to use his own term—that led to his major late contributions.

c. He had an acute awareness in the third part of the dream that "destructiveness belongs to relating to objects that are outside the subjective world or the area of omnipotence"—essentially the world of imagination and of dreaming.

Winnicott's "new enlightenment" from this dream was: "In other words, first there is the creativeness that belongs to being alive, and the world is only a subjective world. Then there is the objectively perceived world and absolute destruction of it and all its details" (1963a/1989, p. 229).

This realization led Winnicott to profound ideas about the nature of the way in which developmentally we build up a picture of external reality, and how we come to differentiate between inner and outer worlds. He did not live to expound on these ideas, but I am certain they are fertile ground for us to dig in our attempts to understand many aspects of human behaviour, including our propensity to violence (Issroff, 2004, in preparation-b).

His paper about object relating and object use well demonstrates his cognitive complexity. His heartbroken reaction to its cool initial reception indicates the depth of his responsiveness (Davis, 1992).

I think he questioned himself more, was more emotional and more vulnerable to the opinions of others, and he lacked Bowlby's self-confidence.

Winnicott's scientific attitude to clinical work

In his way Winnicott was also every bit the scientist in his approach. He said, "In poetry, something true crystallises out; to plan our lives we need science" (1965e/1986, p. 173).

In November 13, 1946 Winnicott wrote to Ella Freeman Sharpe: "I enjoy my true psycho-analytic work more than the other kinds, and the reason is to some extent bound up with the fact that in psycho-analysis the art is less and the technique based on scientific considerations more" (Rodman, 2003, p. 147). I think this quotation well demonstrates how Winnicott's attitude towards his analytic work was essentially "scientific", while the way in which he engaged in it was often poetically nuanced (see Winnicott, 1961a).

There is a consistency in Winnicott's books. "The theory, the technique itself, and its field of application meet the scientific requirements of simplicity, parsimony, and of reasonable internal consistency" (Hamilton, 1982). Crystallizing out of Winnicott's work and imaginative life were theories, his scientific attitude no less his daily life's accompaniment and expression than dreams, play, poetry and music "As yeast is to dough, and egg white to meringue, so were his élan and eagerness to heavy theorizing" (Martin James once remarked). For Winnicott there was no differentiation between scientific or poetic truth (Isaacs, 1972, p. 29).

Did Bowlby appreciate that Winnicott's clinical work was based on a scientific attitude? Or was "science" for Bowlby a matter only of statistically significant samples? I wish I had discussed this point with him. Bonaminio's discerning and enthusiastic examination of reported fragments of case material well appreciates Winnicott's mastery of the synthesis of scientific attitude and virtuosity in the subtle artistry of communication (Bonaminio, 2001). "Winnicott's originality of thought and originality of person were inseparable" (Clancier & Kalmanovitch, 1984, p. 139).

*Playing with possible meaning
envisaged at many levels in ordinary activities*

Winnicott was always asking questions. He loved to watch football, *Match of the Day*. But TV-viewing was accompanied by thinking, such as: "I wonder what kicking a ball about means?" Winnicott answered the question to his own satisfaction by saying that, of course, it meant many things, for every act, like every part of the symbolism of any dream, draws on many sources and is saturated with deep personal meaning. To Winnicott the ball represented some kind of not always predictable impingement: accordingly, kicking it could be understood as representing a motor attempt actively to master the numerous maternal impingements or intrusions that beset us during childhood and daily life. In "maternal", of course he also included "paternal" and other "authority" figures. I give this example to illustrate another aspect of Winnicott's way of being in the world. This type of almost flip "fun" comment might accompany almost anything and appear as if without discernible stimulus, but I always thought it was aimed to jolt me back into multi-layered thinking, away from my own Bowlby-like tendency to scrutinize data for reliable "facts".

Prominently on Winnicott's bookshelf was Gillespie's (1960) *The Edge of Objectivity*—unsurprising in view of his preoccupation with transitional areas of overlap of subjectivity and objectivity, of inner and outer worlds, his distinctions of what he experientially found within the realm of subjectivity. An example in his own dream world was his discovery of his ongoing "club dream" (1967a), which he distinguished from "deeper" dreams. He described this as a recurrent dream occurring during light sleep in which he revisited a familiar club-like place, meeting people in apparently convivial, inconsequential ways. For him it was another example of maintaining an inner continuity of experience in some layer nearer to consciousness than that occupied by the deepest uncensored over-determined dreams. It was never a dream he tried to interpret; rather, it seemed to be an inner conflict-free area—perhaps a potential inner place where he might "touch base" with the lost world of school, university, and naval service acquaintances and of friends who were killed in the war. We only learned about these dreams, which occupy a place in his implicit structural metapsychology, almost two decades after his death, with the important publication in 1989 of *Psychoanalytic Explorations*. I wonder what additional use he might have made of such fragments, had he lived longer.

Dreams were of the greatest significance both to Bowlby and to Winnicott. It was losing touch with his own dreams that brought him to discover psychoanalysis (C. Winnicott, 1982). If Winnicott was adamant about anything, it was that if a dream was brought to a session, it should be interpreted. He asserted that the most profound work could occur at the level of dreams, particularly the deepest uncensored dreams; dreams such as his "club" dreams (1967a) were postulated to occur at a different, wish-fulfilling, less symbolically saturated and interpretation-imperative level.

I am indebted to Bowlby for recommending that I read Ella Freeman Sharpe's *Dream Analysis* (1937)—another indication of how Bowlby actually never lost sight of the inner world, or of what an analyst such as Sharpe had contributed to psychoanalytic discourse and the understanding of symbolism, even though he was engaged determinedly in a radical reformulation of psychoanalytic theory and discourse in an attempt to bring it into line with what enthused him about changes in what he considered to be more acceptable scientific formulations.

However, I felt that his recommendation was made almost shyly, as if against his better judgement, rather than with the deep enthusiasm he expressed for the work of ethologists. Through his influence I read a great deal in that area with interest, but, except occasionally anecdotally, I found little of help in my clinical work, as compared with papers of Winnicott's such as "Fear of Breakdown" (1963b) and "Primary Maternal Preoccupation" (1956b)—that, in turn, stimulated papers like Joan Raphael-Leff's "Primary Maternal Persecution" (2001)—among all the rest of his exceptionally prolific output.

Intellectual interests in the philosophy of science

Part of our Tavistock training in the 1960s was in the history and philosophy of science. Profoundly influenced by Popper (1965), Bowlby strove to formulate his psychoanalytic ideas in terms of the science of the day—careful hypotheses testable in refutable ways. We are still more influenced by a science dominated by probabilities and a desire for predictability. Winnicott was a natural thinker in terms of contemporary science's fuzzy logic (Kosko, 1993), quantum (Zohar & Marshall, 1994, 2000), chaos (Gleick, 1987), and complexity (Nicolis & Prigogine, 1989) theories; but the latter were not yet widely accepted in those days. Bowlby strove for objectivity—he did not concern himself with the complex implications of the physics of Schrödinger's cat, who is both alive and dead in a box until the observer opens that box and finds him either alive or dead, thus demonstrating the influence of the so-called "objective" observer on the subject observed in an experiment (Gribben, 1984). Whether or not he was familiar with the physics, Winnicott was intensely concerned with the nature of "reality" and worked within the edges of the overlap of "objectivity" with subjectivity (Gillespie, 1960). As a result of his important dream partly discussed above, to which I return, one of his major contributions was his attention to the way subjectivity discovers what survives the conscious and unconscious fantasy that accompanies all bodily activity to become discerned as reliably objectively there, and thus, eventually, usable (Winnicott, 1941a, 1968a, 1968h). In drawing attention to the way subjective and objective realities overlap, Winnicott drew attention to what he called the "potential space" of transitional reality and transitional space (Winnicott, 1951), the locus of play, culture, and our non-genetic, accumulating rich storehouse of human knowledge (Winnicott, 1967a, 1968f, 1988b), which Teilhard de Chardin (1964) designated "the noosphere". This is our accessible realm in common of the imagination and of "public and reliable"—scientific—knowledge (Ziman, 1968, 1978, 2000).

Reading interests

Shakespeare fascinated Winnicott: he was an avid reader of Rabindranath Tagore, Coleridge, and T. S. Eliot (personal communication), and of Henry James and Virginia Woolf (Clare Winnicott, 1992, interviewed by Michael Neve). He advised me to read John Stuart Mill's autobiography (c. 1840), particularly about his precocious and pressurized childhood. He was delighted to discover Virginia Woolf's depiction of "one rose: seven" viewpoints in *To the Lighthouse* (1927). In his latter years he made Freud his constant bedside reading companion, overcoming his early reluctance to re-read his work.

Bowlby, in addition to his interest in von Frisch (1967), ethology (Eibl-Eibesfeldt, 1971; Harlow, 1958; Harlow & Harlow, 1966; Hinde, 1966; Lorenz, Huxley, & Wilson, 1952; Tinbergen, 1951, 1958; Tinbergen & Tinbergen, 1972), and Popper (1963, 1965, 1972), was clearly also influenced by his Oxford exposure to William McDougall (1923) and steered us to Jean Piaget (recommending Flavell, 1963), Karl Pribram (1971), and neurology readings. We were introduced to research in what was then described as minimal brain damage, as well as to literature about mother–infant interactions like Merrell Middlemore's *The Nursing Couple* (1941). Naturalism loomed large, but literature was never mentioned.

Bowlby on science

It is interesting that Bowlby (1988b, p. 81) criticized a paper "where as a way of understanding human beings, empathy is described as "a subjective and totally unscientific method" (Maratos, 1986, p. 305). There Bowlby made explicit his own scientific approach:

> There are two main phases of science. The first is to frame an hypothesis. In order to produce a reasonably promising one, both detailed and first-hand knowledge of the problem is required, together with a dose of intuition and imagination. This means that it is thoroughly sensible to use empathy in any attempt to understand human psychological problems, and I would certainly claim to have done so. One of the reasons behaviourism has been so barren is that it has failed in this respect.
>
> The second phase of science is to examine the idea, consider its implications, match it against other observations, use a variety of other methods of observation to view it from other perspectives, compare its explanatory powers with those of other hypotheses, and so on. My criticism of so much work in our field is not the way it starts (also the way I started) but the absence of a follow-through. [Bowlby, 1988b, p. 81]

Bowlby would put some hypothesis of his to a practical test. For instance, he surmised that we carried around as "instinctual innate patterns of behaviour" ways of reacting appropriate to the hunter–gatherer nomadic troops of primates in Africa from whom we had evolved. Accordingly, he argued that a helpless and dependent crying infant primarily cried to maintain proximity to protective caretakers. This would minimize chances of the infant being left behind and vulnerable to a predator when the troop moved on. He thought, therefore, that it would be likely that if a cradle were made to rock at roughly 72 times per minute—which, he calculated, was the movement of human walking—then the infant would stop crying. He told us he had his son Richard build such a device, and it worked with his grandchild.

Examples of Winnicott's good practice

It is Winnicott—a community paediatrician who ran a community paediatric outpatient drop-in clinic for sick children in Paddington Green Hospital—who repeatedly told us that: "Good psychiatry begins with a responsible Doctor undressing the patient and carrying out a proper physical examination." He was referring to the common presentation of physically remediable ailments that are often overlooked or neglected, and that can present as "psychiatric" and psychosocial problems. But to him good practice also implied communicating in the kind of way the person he was attempting to reach might understand, and by responding to someone in as appropriate a manner as possible. I reiterate that it meant also putting into practice what one had understood and a tolerant respect for not demanding more of someone than that person is capable of.

Some illustrative examples of Winnicott's responses in different contexts are given in the following:

a. *To a stranger in need*

Once it was Winnicott who took the trouble to respond to a desperate plea for help in a letter to *The Times* by some unfortunate woman who was being attended to bit by bit, each parcelled off to be dealt with by some different Service or Agency or Hospital department. Winnicott took on the challenge: he invited and organized all the different agencies and medical specialists who were involved with her to meet together with her and him, giving them a chance to integrate at the larger level. His house provided an external and objective "container" to allow for the integration of all of these services and to facilitate their intercommunication.

This unpaid gesture Winnicott took on himself: part of what Clare termed his "delusions of munificence". He saw many patients without pay—some from his hospital practice at his private consulting-rooms in the immediate post War period in Harley Street, and later in Chester Terrace. He used to keep in touch for years with both private and hospital patients. George Allyn told me about his sending authentic Buddhist "wisdom" texts to a youngster who was imprisoned, who phoned while George was present. He acted like this quite naturally, in addition to running his drop-in outpatient clinic, conducting his analyses and supervisions, attending meetings, writing, giving and responding to papers and to letters. Clare would tease him also about his "delusions of benignity" (C. Winnicott, 1978, 1982 and in personal discussions).

b. *To colleagues*

If Winnicott was not in the chair (as President of the Society) and personally able to respond to someone's paper, he would take care to write to apologize for not having been present at a meeting, or to take up a point and to meet what he perceived as someone else's "gesture" in attempting an open communication. This is amply evident in the letters Clare Winnicott selected and Rodman edited as *Spontaneous Gestures* (1987b).

He moved towards what he perceived as *the important real business* of the British Psychoanalytical Society membership—namely, sharing observations and inferences in a scientific and creative fashion. For him warfare around personalities precluded real discussion. He wanted his own papers taken seriously, and a response to them when he presented an idea. He took everyone else's work equally seriously and responded to it—and at times this was misunderstood. In his spoken and written responses he usually was gentle, though he could powerfully bring about "self-awareness", a "turning-point" encounter, even in a lecture situation, as I have described (Issroff, 1995a). This is particularly clear when his discussion was reluctant and rephrased in words he hoped might reach the analyst concerned because, without any condescension, he realized the problem might not lie in intellectual ability. This happened, for instance, when he thought someone's psychic makeup, such as a defensive split-off manic flight to intellectuality, would preclude that person's fully grasping something beyond his experiential capacity, or comprehending some point too threatening to his personal defensive manoeuvres. Winnicott appreciated these as necessary to defend against "primitive agonies"—"unthinkable anxieties", as he called them. It is amazing to see how his language changes, and how he can respond, say, to Fairbairn, in Fairbairn's language (Winnicott, 1953a), or to Sandler (Winnicott, 1960a) in Sandler's mechanistic conceptualizing. For example, when Sandler introduced what Winnicott saw as unnecessary concepts in understanding superego development, Winnicott hinted that Sandler was perhaps personally unable to give full weight to the primitive instinctual experiences and the kinds of fantasy that accompany such primitive bodily excitements, whether discussed and conceptualized in Freud, or Klein, or by Winnicott himself (1960a).

"A quality that underlay his ability to be original was courage, which was combined with a certain ruthlessness—a strange thing to say about such a gentle person as Donald Winnicott." As an example, Gillespie relates overhearing Winnicott say that "children would have been better off bombed than evacuated" (Gillespie, 1972, p. 2).

The many case reports Winnicott documented illustrate his clinical responsive sensitivity (1960a, 1971d).

*Winnicott's eccentricity
and critical attitude to statistical research*

Winnicott showed us what he thought when the following took place: I—and others—remember a meeting at the Tavistock Clinic in which one of Bowlby's followers was presenting a classical evidence-based, statistically analysed, valid study of some aspect of attachment theory put to the test.

Winnicott had been sitting in the middle of a row near the back of the crowded room. He grew increasingly restless, wriggled in his chair, looked around, and rolled his eyes in a parody of increasing desperation. Then he could bear it no longer: finger ostentatiously raised to his pursed lips, eyes rolling, clowning unabashedly, in high burlesque he clambered across the knees and toes of several people. With his finger still to his mouth he tiptoed out of the room: maximal disturbance, maximally devastating comment, nothing said. Many were surprised; some were appalled and scandalized. Winnicott could not have made a more deliberate or disparaging, albeit comical, comment on what he personally felt about such a formal lecture demonstrating the selective, evidence-based approach to the work of science. John Bowlby was in the chair, his face stern and impassive. Bowlby would never have behaved in such a fashion.

Later I encountered Winnicott loitering near the front door in the upper parking lot, rather forlorn, waiting to be fetched. He perked up when he saw me, beamed happily, and indicated the stairs going down to the lower parking lot. "What's there, I wonder?" he asked. "The lower parking lot", I answered matter-of-factly. His face crinkled in disappointment and with a dismissive wave of his hand at my mundane, reality-oriented, correct, and courteous reply, he turned away with pantomimed disappointment, "Oh dear, that's all?" . . . meaning, "Nowhere to play?" or "Where's your imagination, woman?" With a flutter of his hand and a backward glance of exasperated music-hall disparagement and irony, he drifted off, leaving me feeling abashed but somehow awakened to more of the world's possibilities.

At once I realized that Winnicott was continuing his "comment" on the paper that we had both just heard and was bringing me back to the significance of imagination, the underground unconscious, and play. He awakened me to what Ogden (1999) has described as listening to "the music of what happens" during psychoanalysis, and life outside. Winnicott knew very well that I would understand this, would within myself be reminded of the other aspect of the nature of the work that we do, the duality or multiple layers of the non-surface lives that we live, the interaction between the inner and outer worlds at all their many levels. In his inimitable way, he was reminding me not to remain fixated on a search to reformulate psychoanalysis in ways that can be put to the test of refutability. On the other hand, coming from a rigorous biochemical medical research background, another part of me saw it, and well understood and valued that John Bowlby strove to achieve this "evidence-based" goal.

These incidents exemplify Winnicott's exhibitionistic, incident-action talent to communicate powerful non-verbal "lessons" of the "unsaid known", as Bollas (1985) has termed it. I record them to illustrate how very different these men were. Winnicott was undoubtedly an outrageous eccentric. I could enjoy that side of him immensely while a conventional part of me certainly did not always approve of his behaviour. However, I could also see an admirable freedom from convention and was grateful for the insights and directions offered me so obliquely, personally, and spontaneously, while at the same time in part I felt quite abashed. Winnicott always had the capacity to provoke a welter of feelings and thoughts. I consider myself "cloud-minded" so was never confused by the multiplicity of levels and complexities of strands of thoughts and feelings he could set going in me. Never were my personal encounters with Bowlby so confounding or complicated.

Winnicott's constant creative output

Winnicott was an acute clinical scientist who noted down and reflected on everything he observed as he went along, constantly generating, testing, and discarding or elaborating working hypotheses. He was a prolific producer of clinical notes, fragments of ideas, and papers—I once listed what I thought were original or additive ideas of his in psychoanalysis and stopped at 100. He produced some witty poems and doggerel—notably yet to be published. Clare gave me a copy of this example, which he sent in a letter to paediatrician Tizard after Enoch Powell's rabble-rousing, racist so-called "Speech of Blood":

> If I could make Enoch
> 's knees knock
> or set off a howl
> in the Powell bowel
> I'd feel cleaner.

He would sit down at the piano whenever possible. He composed witty songs that he performed with aplomb. He amused us with "The Boston Analysts' Tea Party", exuberantly performed during a strawberry high tea produced to celebrate the conclusion of the private fortnightly "Squiggle" case-presentation-based seminars. He daily scribbled innumerable doodles, sketches, and paintings. Copious amounts of yet unpublished correspondence exist. There are "thousands" of case studies in the Cornell Medical School archives in New York—according to Clare—that surely contain important material for additional Winnicott publications at a later date. In his open clinics at Paddington Green, he did see thousands of cases in his long practice as a community outpatient paediatrician who deliberately did not want beds as he did not want his sensitivity to become defensively—and self-preservatively—blunted.

He loved quoting Rabindranath Tagore's (1931) lines about the endless shoreline where children play their—innumerable—games: "*On the seashore of endless worlds children meet.* . . . On the seashore of endless worlds is the great meeting of children. I always felt we were absorbed in some similar "potential space" imaginatively and intellectually with just the kind of enjoyable intensity that marks early childhood experiences like exploring tidal pools, never tiring of ad-

FIGURE 1

venturing along the wave-lapped shore, its discoveries, and the possibilities arising from this.

The painting of the stairs DWW negotiated daily in Chester Square—the staircase on which he died (Figure 1)—is a typical hand-painted card such as Winnicott enjoyed sketching and sending. Note his study of stairs: I speculate whether this was painted at around the time when he asked me: "What's down there, I wonder?" about the stairs down to the Tavistock underground parking lot. In this little Xmas card I am confident he was also wondering about "What's up there?" and about staircases as physical transitional spaces. Two women I interviewed who had lived with him and his wife, Alice Winnicott, in Pilgrim's Lane, Hampstead, recalled with delight how he loved to slide down the banisters, or come down the steep stairs, clucking like the chickens they kept in the garden during the War (Issroff, in preparation-a). He may have been playing with ideas about stairs as a symbol, as he often thought about notions such as "black and white" or what a snake might symbolize—such as motion, healing, movement, vitality, and/or removal of blockage to a growth process, not only or necessarily a phallic symbol—as he once suggested to me during a supervision.

Joyce McDougall thinks "of the internal universe of the creative personality as something resembling a volcano, a mountain churning with energy that sends out sparks, rocks, and flames when it is ready to do so: if this showering were to be blocked for any considerable time, it would cause an immense explosion" (McDougall, 2003, p. 31). Winnicott's professional and personal output was prodigious, unblocked, a constant expression of his vitality, as natural to him as was breathing. It worked for him even when he was sleeping.

Apropos of Winnicott's creativity and thinking, Renata de Gaddini recalls Phyllis Greenacre saying that "a 'minuet' was taking place between the clinician and the theoretician" (Gaddini, 2004, p. 226).

Winnicott recorded that his self-styled "new enlightenment" derived from an important 1963 "creative" dream about an immense—atomic cloud—explosion of total destructiveness that he had when he was reading Jung's autobiography (Winnicott, 1963a, posthumously published in 1989). One of the personal illuminations he derived from his dream was that "first there is *the creativeness that belongs to being alive*, and the world is only a subjective world. Then there is the objectively perceived world and absolute destruction of it and all its details" (p. 229; emphasis added). I will continue to discuss this dream, to which I refer in several different contexts, because it was of deepest personal significance and, as already mentioned, also led to most important theoretical contributions—particularly because Winnicott attributed his answer to the question of how the world becomes real and external and distinguished from subjective reality to this dream, which was his personal precursor to his "Use of an Object" paper (1968h). (I reproduce the dream in Appendix C.) Winnicott said: "If we (psychoanalysts) fail to come to terms with Jung we are self-proclaimed partisans, partisans in a false cause" (Fordham, 1972, p. 23).

As lecturers and writers

Because Winnicott was frequently busy trying to answer a private question that he did not always make explicit and thinking through his answer with or without his audience in mind, at times what he was thinking or saying was ambiguous and not clear. But Bowlby always asked himself whom he was addressing and why, and he tried to make everything as clear as possible. In contrast, although the language Winnicott used changed according to his audience, which is why he discussed similar things in the many different ways one can see if one looks at the themes running through his complete writings, he was all too acutely aware of the need to enable his audience to "discover" what it was he already had, and/or wanted to convey, so that they might "make it their own"—to this end he strove to communicate, but did not always succeed—akin, in my view, to his refined analytic technique. This was about as far removed from Kleinian theory and practice as any could be, except for Bowlby's approach, which occupied a different landscape.

Tizard (1987) described Winnicott as "sometimes a great writer, sometimes not, but always a marvelous lecturer with rapport with his diverse audiences, and a truly brilliant, dazzling conversationalist", adding that it is all our loss that there was no Boswell following him around recording all his conversations. He was a theatrical lecturer–performer. Sometimes he would entice his audience into a state of high expectancy, taking everyone with him to the delayed climax. But at times, both because of his idiosyncratic language and novelty of exposition that broke new ground, his audience did not "get it". When Winnicott addressed an American psychoanalytic audience in New York, he failed to communicate his most important distinction between use of an object and object relating (1967a, 1968f, 1968h, 1969f), perhaps as much because of the unpreparedness of his listeners for what he said as in the non-linear and non-jargon—to them unusual—style of presentation, with the result, as previously mentioned, that he suffered a serious heart attack.

Bowlby was a more formal lecturer, always dignified, always choosing his words extremely carefully. He did not think a point through with his listener; rather, he tried to communicate it didactically in straightforward, elegantly clean, precise prose. He did not leave room for misunderstanding. One never becomes confused when reading Bowlby's terse, informative summaries of the literature, as in his masterly lecture-essays *The Making and Breaking of Affectional Bonds* (1979) and *A Secure Base: Clinical Applications of Attachment Theory* (1981).

Winnicott was deeply concerned about the education of medical students and nurses (Winnicott, 1988, 2003). He noted that "the community relies on the objectivity or scientific attitude of the medical profession in its constant battle with superstition… the most important psychological contribution that society receives from doctors will always be the almost arrogant objectivity of scientifically based medicine. The arrogance belongs to the threat of superstition." He was adamant that the job of doctors "is to be watertight in their alliance to science" (2003, p. 52) He stated his credo- one increasingly validated as discussed—"we believe that the science underlying dynamic psychology is a science, and is, in fact, as real and as well based (even if young) as are the physical sciences" Winnicott, 2003, p. 52).

Choice of words

Both were very careful in their use of words and choice of words. In supervision Winnicott was always turning to the *Oxford Dictionary of Etymology* to look up the origin of some word. Bowlby disliked what he called sometimes "portmanteau" and sometimes "umbrella" or "omnibus" words like "aggression", which covered too many different broad possibilities and created confusion in the way they were used. He also "parked" the term "fantasy" in what I always imagine to be quite a capacious parking lot in his mind (cf. Winnicott's important work on that theme, which I discuss in some detail in chapter 2). Once in 1966, when Bowlby was discussing internal maps and plans, I challenged him at a seminar by citing a case I had seen that very morning of a—probably schizophrenic and deluded or hallucinating, substance-abusing—youngster who imagined he had green snakes growing out of his head. I asked Bowlby what kind of a plan this could be? His answer was to say that he would "prefer to park that question". Unfortunately we never returned to it. However, I always had an uneasy feeling that he thought I had made up the question in order to tease him or, worse, to ridicule his careful pedantry.

Winnicott was more open to any kind of discussion and idea. While Winnicott's idiosyncratic, witty use of language was constant and part of his charm, Bowlby, who was generally more formal and serious in his demeanour, could also occasionally be adept with words. When he came back from a year's sabbatical at Stanford University, we asked Bowlby how it had been, and how he had experienced his students there. He gave his characteristic throat-clearing little grunt and apologetically but firmly declared, "high on words, low on wisdom". His verdict on Melanie Klein was, "a frightfully vain old woman who manipulated people" (Karen, 1994, p. 44 from interview with Bowlby 14–15 January 1989). "Anna Freud" he said, "worshipped at the shrine of St. Sigmund, Klein at the shrine of St. Melanie" (Grosskurth, 1986, p. 325).

While Bowlby seldom used them, Winnicott was a master of metaphors that change things, mutative metaphors, and the "aesthetic imperative" (Cox & Thielgaard, 1987). Ogden's attention to the subtleties and nuances of language, the mode of discourse-experience that enlivens psychoanalytic encounters (1985, 1986, 1989, 1999) is greatly influenced by Winnicott. Ogden (2001) drew attention to the extreme compactness of Winnicott's language. "Winnicott, for the most part, does not use language to arrive at conclusions; rather; he uses language to create experiences in reading that are inseparable from the ideas he is presenting, or more accurately, the ideas he is playing with" (Ogden, 2001). Like Pontalis (1981), Ogden also notes how at times this occurs in part because Winnicott has not yet fully worked out the ideas he was presenting at this point. Moreover, the ideas under development sometimes involve irresolvable emotional contradictions and paradoxes, as when he was discussing depression. In his writing Bowlby never allowed himself to be revealed or entangled in such complexities.

"Winnicott is ... an original who wished to be true to his own experience so that he could 'tell it as it is' not as it 'might be'. This meant that his language was individual and so was his understanding of Freud" (James, 1982, p. 493). (For an excellent example of Winnicott's elaborations and extensions of Freud, see Appendix D). James continued: "... he eschewed the grand words and so, ... his way of writing ... set him further apart and ... this, together with a very English sense of humour, which included lightness on serious occasions, made him hard for some colleagues, writing in another style, to follow, and impossible until fairly recently, it seemed, for any overseas colleagues but the French. . . . Winnicott says it obliquely out of his determination, like Freud, not to be contentious, not to enter controversy" (James, 1982, p. 493).

Re citations

Both were men of integrity who strove to put into action what they believed. Nonetheless, both made use of the work of others without always citing them or acknowledging their sources. Winnicott did so, apologized (1967c), and hoped others would "join him up", I was told by the indignant scholar who claims that Bowlby, his supervisor, used his PhD bibliography without due acknowledgement. And Brett Kahr told me that he had seen in the New York archive Winnicott's copy of Bowlby's book that he had reviewed in 1953 (Winnicott, 1953b), and Winnicott had noted in several places that Bowlby had not cited his work.

Loose speculation was frowned on by Bowlby: we learnt not to spout off unless we thought we had something worth communicating or enquiring about. Although part of play with Winnicott was freeing up associatively, he did not approve of using such personal freedom of thought in a clinical situation, and he was most careful with what he said: he encouraged caution and reticence in interpretation. Indeed, the first book Winnicott referred me to when I started the supervision of my first child case with him was Virginia Axline's *Dibs: In Search of Self* (1967) and her *Play Therapy* (1955) rather than anything by psychoanalysts, other than recommending Bettelheim's *The Empty Fortress* (1967).

Melanie Klein and Anna Freud

As I mentioned earlier, never once did Winnicott refer to Melanie Klein's work in my supervisions. He did, however, at times talk of different mechanisms of defence, but he used the concept in a far more fluid way than Anna Freud (1945) has described it. He was quite capable of saying: "I think this is an organized confusion against confusion".

Bowlby was alienated both from Klein's style of theorizing and her emphasis on the inner processes of fantasy. When the mother of a child he had been analysing under her supervision suffered a breakdown and hospitalization, he was appalled at her clinical indifference. He made it clear that he was not comfortable with the Kleinian domination of child analytic training at the Tavistock. Yet he encouraged me to attend all these seminars and also my forays whenever possible to the Anna Freud Clinic meetings

Personal histories

Speculations about how personal histories may have affected individuals' styles and preoccupations are always interesting. In his remarkable review of Jung's autobiographical *Memories, Dream, Reflections*, Winnicott (1964d) called this "games of Jung analysis", using cricket imagery in his idiosyncratic, idiomatic, educated English way to hint at his own hesitations as to whether this kind of activity is exactly "playing the game" or "cricket". He asserted: "We ourselves undergo analysis, and we must be able to analyse our masters too" (1964d/1989, p. 492). The aim of an analyst's personal training analysis ought to be to rid him/her, insofar as possible, of unresolved personal issues that might stand in the way of analysing others, which is part of the ongoing personal process of self and dream analysis that accompanied Winnicott's life, as he noted in his obituary of his first analyst, James Strachey (1969c).

Winnicott considered the "game" valid only in analysis of what Jung himself chose to reveal about himself and his dreams in the first three chapters of the book that he wrote himself. To date we have little of this kind of personal, self-revealing material directly from Winnicott or Bowlby. However, on a couple of occasions Winnicott himself has analysed what we do have access to: he used his personal dream analyses—"the orchestral accompaniment to his life", as Clare put it—to build on theoretically (1963a/1989, pp. 228–229).

Moshe Halevi Spero (personal communication), having read Clare Winnicott's selected parts from Winnicott's autobiographical manuscript, suggests that Winnicott gives an over-rosy picture of his childhood. Perhaps. Perhaps Clare did. I know she enjoyed visiting his sisters in the family home in Plymouth where he had spent his childhood prior to going away to boarding-school. That separation and experience distressed him. Once he told me that he had restrained his impulse to throw himself into "the dirty, cold river Cam"—although when Clare spoke with Michael Neve (C. Winnicott & Neve, 1991) she emphasized how he had loved boarding school and how important it had been to him that he had managed to get away from the—for practical purposes—all-female, indulgent home of his early years.

Mothers

Richard Bowlby's Squiggle Association Winnicott Memorial Lecture (2004) described his grandmother's—John Bowlby's mother's—cold, remote, formal and distant, essentially absent style of mothering, and he suggested that it was the loss of his nanny that was a major motivating factor in John Bowlby's professional life. Bowlby's avoidant attachment style was not surprising—he saw his parents for an hour a day, rather formally, when not at a boarding school (Marrone, 1998; van Dijken, 1998).

Clare Winnicott (1982) thought Winnicott identified with his mother's liveliness. But evidently he was deeply affected when she was depressed and weeping at some stage, as can be inferred both in a poem about the topic (Milner, 2001, p. 266) and in his paper about the development of the manic defence of overuse of innate intellectual abilities as a defence against maternal depression (Winnicott, 1935). Marion Milner spoke to me at passionate length about the way Winnicott had failed her in her analysis with him because he had not adequately dealt with the impact on her of her mother's depression as it affected her difficulty in expressing anger and being "too nice". (She told me that there is something about this in her last book manuscript, which deals mainly with drawings of her son and has yet to be published.) Linda Hopkins (2000) suggests that this is an area in which Winnicott's own difficulties handicapped him so that he dealt inadequately with Masud Khan's destructiveness. Winnicott observed (confessed?): "It is precisely this primitive destructiveness (aggression) that is difficult to get at when an infant is cared for by a mother who is clinically depressed" (1989a, p. 490).

From incidents related to me by Marion Milner's patient "Susan" (Issroff, in preparation-a; Milner, 1969) who lived with the Winnicotts during the first years of her analysis, and from Margaret Little's record of her breaking a vase of Winnicott's during a difficult phase of her analysis with him (Little, 1990), Winnicott was certainly tolerant to an unusual degree of generally unacceptable behaviour. Susan told me about a very disturbed boy, Rick, who had lived with them before she did and loved them. He ran away from school and arrived by, literally, crashing through the glass of the sky-light. She described how he "sat on Donald's knee and punched his face as hard as he could. Donald was absolutely bruised—brave—he really had a streak of saintliness. He said, 'Poor boy—he has to get it out of him and I have to get him out of it'" (Issroff, 2004, in preparation-a).

Examples of sage advice and pragmatic activities

Winnicott and Bowlby were not mere armchair theorists. They put what they believed into practice. For instance, pragmatically, building on his wartime experience, Bowlby advised us never to knock on a closed door or attempt to work where one was unwanted or not appreciated. He was confident that there would always be somewhere where one could work effectively without compromising one's integrity.

In several cases Alice and Donald Winnicott had people in need live with them (Issroff, in preparation-a). Winnicott saw many cases for nominal fees and hospital cases in his private rooms.

Winnicott really did believe in the value of democracy. In early November 1938 he wrote to Neville Chamberlain's wife (Winnicott, 1987b, p. 4, Letter 2):

> I feel the prime minister is too busy to answer questions, but I do want to know two things. Would you try to answer this as many of us are urgently in need of answers that we cannot get.
>
> In fact, does the Prime Minister really believe that less good management by someone representing the majority vote of

citizens is preferable to better management by someone who keeps power by suppression of thought?

The second is, why does the Prime Minister never mention the Jews. Does he secretly despise them? When in England we say WE, we include Jews who are people like ourselves. I am not asking him to be pro-Jew, but I want to know definitely whether he is or is not secretly anti-Jew ... at present we seem to be secretly sharing Germany's anti-Jew insanity, and this is not where we want our leaders to lead us.

Unfortunately what we have of his correspondence is very one-sided: we do not know the effect of this or other letters.

Rodman (1990) draws attention to the fact that Winnicott could be "ruthless" and, in some of his letters, "could be unflinchingly frontal and confrontational". He wrote letters to medical journals and newspapers on matters of principle—matters about which he thought a statement ought to be made. For instance, he waged war against electroconvulsive therapy and leucotomy (1943, 1949b, 1951b). This is understandable in view of its effects on "Susan", who lived with him and his wife Alice before they separated while Susan was being analysed by Marion Milner (1969; Issroff, in preparation-a); the effects continue to "ruin" her "whole life" she said 65 years later, aged 84.

Preventive psychiatry?

John Bowlby asked the important question: "Where do politics and preventive psychiatry begin, end, and overlap?" He was sufficiently concerned to conduct a seminar for a group of trainee psychiatrists, including distinguished overseas Fellows on a sabbatical year, to discuss over several weeks the difficult issue of at what point preventive psychiatry ended and political action began. Clearly the boundaries are blurred. Any psychiatrist devoted to preventive action cannot avoid engaging with policy-makers. The question that follows is to what extent political engagement is useful, appropriate, or even able to have a significant impact on public policy-makers. Regrettably we did not record these wide-ranging and extremely interesting conversations. The questions remained unanswered as to whether it is part of a child psychiatrist's brief to try to reach and influence the knowledge base of politicians and legislators, although many in related fields have tried to do so. (See Goldstein, Freud, & Solnit, 1973, 1979; King & Trowell, 1992. Issroff, in preparation-b, includes further references.)

In 1939 Bowlby wrote a fascinating book with his friend Evan Durbin about *Personal Aggressiveness and War* (Durbin & Bowlby, 1939). They argue that war is due to the expression in and through group life of the transformed aggressiveness of individuals (p. 41). They say that "anthropology and psycho-analysis suggest a number of ways in which the powers of the human mind change and add to the causes of aggression". (Clearly at that stage Bowlby had no objection to using the word "aggression", and although he used and defined "projection", he was already beginning to prefer to use the term "mis-attribution".) They drew on psychoanalytic ideas, Susan Isaacs' (1930, 1933) observations at the Maltings School, and anthropology. Many of the themes touched on in our seminars with him about politics and preventive psychiatry are discussed in this still relevant book. One-sixth of the book—the concluding section (pp. 126–150)—is a semantic analysis of Hitler's speeches, highlighting the rhetorical extravaganza of racism and destructiveness of Nazi propaganda, comparing it to primitive Melanesian animism and Queensland aboriginal beliefs in "the noxious Mononga spirit". At great and detailed length they demonstrate the primitive irrationality of Nazi beliefs and conclude:

> These examples make it clear that in at least one Western power the tendency to find a scapegoat to blame and persecute for all the national troubles is no whit less powerful than it is in the so-called primitive peoples. Many other examples of a war-like attitude engendered by the scapegoat motive could be given but perhaps none so naked and unashamed. [p. 146]

Pertinent today, they write:

> It would seem probable that the main driving force in some European wars, as in Melanesian, is the desire to destroy a scapegoat, and that this is disguised as a necessity for economic expansion. In other words, we suggest that economic motives are as often used to justify scape-goat hunting as is moral condemnation of the enemy to justify greed. [p. 147]

They are quite clear that "Men do not die for business but for ideals" (p. 148). "Hitlerian propaganda is successful only in so far as there is a potential need for a scapegoat in the populace . . . there is a need latent in everyone" (p. 150).

Certainly I was influenced by John Bowlby and have spent years working at this kind of endeavour (see Appendix E concerning recommendations that I drew up and implemented in establishing and for a decade running a non-governmental professional organization). Bowlby's work with the World Health Organization is an example of his putting belief into action and inspiring all of us who attended this seminar to consider the topic, and for me, preventive psychiatry continues to be important.

It is preventive psychiatry that is embedded in all of Winnicott's broadcasts to the nation during the wartime years (1964b, 1986, 1987a, 1993) as well as in Bowlby's shorter earlier broadcasts. Christopher Reeves details their immensely useful, pertinent comments in his study of the evidence they both gave to the post-war Curtis Commission in terms of their common and divergent views and considers its current relevance in his Afterword.

Ambition and attitudes to authority

Through their outstanding ability both men were thrust into positions of high office and responsibility. Neither had a stomach for a political fight: Bowlby did not like the devotedly and decidedly politico-religious Kleinian direction that the Tavistock psychotherapeutic approach increasingly assumed. He made that quite clear to me. He said that all organizations had their day and that once they had established their reputations, very often there would be a period of relative mediocrity. He was extremely proud of the fact that for the first time in the entire world, in the Tavistock every aspect of work that dealt with human life and behaviour in health and in illness was covered "under one roof" (Dicks, 1969; Trist & Murray, 1999). He told me about the great mutual enrichment gained by multi-disciplinary colleagues, from clinicians and behavioural scientists to industrial and organizational consultants who had worked together in wartime Britain. They had been faced with problems such as how best to allocate army conscripts to the most suitable positions for them and, for example, to try to prevent claustrophobic men being assigned to the tank corps. He was therefore most interested in how organizations worked in theory and practice (Sofer, 1973). His working philosophy was clear and clearly communicated. For example, there will always be more tasks than it will be possible to undertake in a lifetime. If you encounter strong resistance or a brick wall, do not fight: move, and find a place where you will be able to function effectively. So, having been Winnicott's Vice-President of the Society and Training Secretary, he moved from the training establishment and the politics of the British Psychoanalytical Society—I think to the detriment of the Society. Had I not worked at the Tavistock Clinic initially as his Registrar, I would never have had the privilege of contact with John Bowlby, whose adages still ring within me not infrequently.

Relationship to academia

Although both lectured in universities, Bowlby had a respect for academia to which Winnicott appeared to be oblivious. Bowlby was honoured and very pleased to be invited to Stanford University as a scholar. Winnicott was indifferent to honours and, as "Susan" described to me, simply scrunched up notification of one and threw it into the waste-paper basket (Issroff, in preparation-a). To Winnicott, any kind of doctrinaire authoritarian approach was anathema: he loathed "teaching and preaching", any propaganda. The wording of his wartime radio broadcasts is very careful (see *The Child, The Family and the Outside World*, 1964a). When I met them in 1965, though Bowlby was eager to keep in touch with clinical practice by working with one psychotherapy case, he spent most of his time in teaching, research, writing, and organizational activities. However much he evidently enjoyed educating, supervising, and lecturing without "teaching" and, presumably, writing, I am certain Winnicott would have been loath to give up his clinical practice, which was his painstakingly recorded method of observation and research into the inner subjective purely human world of symbolization, thought, feeling, and behaviour in all its experiential complexity.

Bowlby was very conscious of the life course choices of his students. He was ambitious on behalf of his trainees, in particular with his eye on academia. The breadth of vision in his training programme has been outlined. He said to us one day that all of us would be professors and/or running departments or organizations at some stage or another. (I think we all have been.) Accordingly, he thought it appropriate that we should be trained in management and leadership. He ensured that I attended at least two of the two-week-long Tavistock Institute–Leicester University Group Relations Training live-in courses. We received training in organizational structure and function, delegation of authority, and budget management. He was very clear in underlining that the financial constraints are the bottom line to actualization of all projects. How might one address problems pragmatically? How can and how should one order them and determine priorities? Bowlby almost overdosed one with the external reality principle. My own tendency in this direction was tempered with Winnicott's repeatedly drawing me firmly into a relationship with the fullness of the inner world. We took for granted the fun of spontaneity, the imaginative and playful freedom of investigation into speculative linkages. He always addressed the interface of fantasy and dream with the outer world in its full practical, poetic, and emotional intensity.

However, Winnicott shied away from the exercise of power. I shared quite a painful moment with him when he "confessed" to me that he felt he had greatly failed both psychoanalysis and psychiatry in the United Kingdom in not exercising the power that goes with the authority of position-holding when he had had the opportunity to do so. As I mentioned above, he was curled up sideways in his armchair, unusually agitated, with his head buried, pulling at his ruffled hair, gaze-avoidant. He said he had been mistaken in underestimating the importance of what he called "a good head piece"—namely, high intellectual ability. This was because he now thought differently about innate intelligence. He had written a paper about "the manic defence" (1935) in which he described hypertrophic—my word, not his—development of intellect that can split off into a "false self" to protect the "real self" (Winnicott, 1971c, 1989a, pp. 43, 54, 467, 488), as a defence against failure of good-enough maternal attunement and appropriate care during early infancy (Winnicott, 1935). He considered this a special form of what he termed "false self development" (Winnicott, 1959a, 1960b) into the "split-off intellect" (Winnicott, 1960b, 1989c). Indiscreetly, he reeled off a list of names of several distinguished professors of psychiatry who had consulted him and whom he had referred—with hindsight, he felt in error and with regret—to what he had thought were "good motherly" female analysts. (Implicitly, "corrective emotional experience" appeared to be taken for granted as a desirable therapeutic manipulation.) Their analyses had "failed because of lack of matching head pieces".[4] I recognized some of the names as vocal and outspoken opponents of psychoanalysis and psychodynamic psychiatry, while others were less hostile. Winnicott's discomfiture, amounting to distress, his self-accusation, and his apprehension about the future were well founded, given prevalent attitudes at The Royal College of Psychiatrists and the euphoric spree of confidence in the clinical effectiveness of uncontrolled trials of cognitive behavioural psychotherapies. None of the trials reported is controlled in that they are not compared to the possible effectiveness of psychodynamic work with adequately trained psychoanalytic practitioners, probably because the latter are so relatively few and the training so comparatively rigorous, prolonged, and expensive.

Mutual provocations and influences? Did they appreciate each other?

Richard Bowlby tells how his father was always warmly appreciative of Winnicott and that while Winnicott seemed always intuitively to know it, John Bowlby had to find the data to allow him to be convinced that he could finally build with and integrate into the theory. Social workers who studied at the LSE in the social work programme that was entirely the territory of Donald and Clare Winnicott spoke of learning about Bowlby's work in a straightforward way and appreciatively from them. So whatever differences they may have had—at least in their roles as educators—it is clear that without ambivalence they recognized with appreciative understanding that their respective ways of addressing the same problems were directed towards the same ends.

My last encounter with John Bowlby took place at the Tavistock Institute in his honorary retirement office near the library, the day before he went into hospital for his final operation. One of the things he volunteered as we were taking leave of each other was, "You know, Winnicott was always of the greatest importance to me." I do not know whether or not Winnicott himself knew that, or whether he reciprocated this respectful attitude.

At times one can only guess how much of the other's opinions is not cited but "parked" in the background of what was written—perhaps with engines revving. My view is that their respective roles as irritants to each other's conceptual evolution were neither slight nor inconsequential. They undoubtedly heard each other speak. I do wonder, however, how much each actually read of the other's work. I have not been able to read the always congenial and collegial correspondence between them that Brett Kahr has told me is convivial (Kahr, 2004; Winnicott, 1954a), but they were both quintessentially courteous gentlemen. However, Bowlby roused Winnicott to react explicitly (1953b, 1959b), and, according to Kahr, who read the annotations marked in Winnicott's copy of Bowlby's book (1951), apparently Winnicott thought Bowlby had derived ideas from his work without acknowledging that he had done so, as I have noted elsewhere. This habit Winnicott rued in himself as characteristic (Winnicott, 1967c). However, I think Winnicott's public criticism of Bowlby's papers to the British Psychoanalytical Society that I discuss in chapter 2 (Winnicott, 1953b, 1959b) must have affected Bowlby profoundly because he did hold Winnicott in high esteem.

Drawing these personal reminiscences to a close, it is clear that I gained a great deal in very different ways from both John Bowlby and Donald Winnicott. They were highly distinctive individuals who at one time shared a common analyst in Joan Riviere, a common supervisor in Mrs Klein, a common inspiration in Darwin and Freud. Both found much in then accepted psychoanalytic theory to diverge from. Both remained psychoanalysts—Bowlby (1988b) wrote about himself a couple of years before his death that his starting point was psychoanalytic: he was striving to reformulate theory making use of accepted theory not available to Freud. But Winnicott added to and transformed it from a position of basic acceptance and a diligent scientific attitude to clinical practice—with a tendency to "self-ablation" noted by Rycroft (1985)—while Bowlby distanced himself from it in the way he tried to reformulate. I think it fair to suggest that their personalities are reflected in the way they approached their ambitious aspirations. They both helped to change the way children are treated in Britain and internationally. However, I wonder whether I would have thought of the two of them or tried to compare and contrast them had I not been invited to do so because I had studied with both simultaneously? In thought, work, and life they were so very different that there was never any possibility of becoming confused or confusing what one learnt from Bowlby with what knitted into one's very being from encountering Winnicott in person or in his writings.

Notes

1. See the adult attachment rating and classification systems re styles of attachment (Ainsworth, 1969, 1985a, 1985b; Ainsworth, Blehar, Waters, & Wall, 1978; Main, 1999; Main & Hesse, 1990; Main & Weston, 1981; Steele, 2002; Steele & Steele, 1998).

2. 63 New Cavendish Street, London WC1, then the home of the British Psychoanalytical Society.

3. I usually try to record verbatim, scribbling away using my private ciphers and initials, hoping the notes are difficult for others to read, as what is relevant for "good practice" and ordinary professional purposes goes into my letter to the referring agency and GP. Among the details I try to record during my otherwise deeply Winnicott-influenced diagnostic initial interviews are those Bowlby noted in his little book, along with something about dreams, ability to engage, to play, and to make use of symbols. I attempt to avoid asking direct questions: I take time and generally manage to acquire most of the data usually acquired in conventional psychiatric assessments. However, because from the patients' expectations point of view there is no such thing as a purely diagnostic or assessment interview, operating along the lines of Winnicott's *Therapeutic Consultations in Child Psychiatry* (1971d) model, I try to "cash in" on the patient's desire to be helped—and consider this an ethical approach. If I am seeing a child, I try first to get the "child's eye view" of the predicament and then see the parents. I always note the attachment styles of children and parents, and ensure I know details about pregnancy, birth, perinatal period as well as infancy, the child's special "transitional object", and a detailed developmental history. Diagnostic appraisals are conceptualized aetiologically, using a combination of both Bowlby and Winnicott, while I also use the DSM–IV and ICD–10 (with reservations and appreciation) as necessary.

4. I am confident that this was the basis of Winnicott's referral of Wynne Godley and me to Masud Khan for analysis, despite his agreement with my explicit reservations about Masud's trustworthiness.

CHAPTER TWO

Singing the same tune? Bowlby and Winnicott on deprivation and delinquency

Christopher Reeves

Winnicott and Bowlby: allies or adversaries?

Delinquency has never been a central concern for psychoanalysts in Britain, despite the involvement, during the 1930s, of Klein's daughter Melitta Schmideberg and the once eminent analyst Edward Glover with the pioneering work of the Institute for the Scientific Treatment of Delinquency. Since both of these individuals subsequently fell out with the British psychoanalytic establishment, an interest in delinquency seemed for many years almost to suggest a hint of deviancy. When therefore Winnicott broached the subject in a paper presented to the British Psychoanalytical Society (of which he was then President) in 1956, he sounded, for him, unusually circumspect—almost apologetic. He chose to talk about the "antisocial tendency" in preference to delinquency and suggested that the topic posed "awkward problems" for psychoanalysis (Winnicott, 1956a). One of these problems, he suggested, was that conventional psychoanalytic treatment does not work with delinquents, even though psychoanalysis itself has something to say, and much to learn, about delinquency. However, he acknowledged that there was one British psychoanalyst who had already made a major contribution in this field (while incidentally—though he did not say so—remaining in fairly good standing with the majority of his psychoanalytic colleagues). He was referring, of course, to John Bowlby, who in 1944 had provided Ernest Jones, then Editor of the *International Journal of Psycho-Analysis* and currently short of copy, with a long research paper, indicating as he did so that the paper had previously been rejected by the *British Journal of Medical Psychology* as being deficient in the discussion of theory. But Ernest Jones apparently entertained no such qualms about its suitability for the *Journal*, and Bowlby's famous paper, "Forty-Four Juvenile Thieves: Their Characters and Home Life" (1944), duly appeared. So well received was it that two years later it was printed as a separate monograph destined for a wider lay public. From then on, Bowlby became a household name. Among his fellow analysts he was dubbed "Ali Bowlby and his 40 Thieves" (Holmes, 1993, p. 21). Even Winnicott, with his habit of not acknowledging his indebtedness to others' work while engaged in giving personal shape to his ideas and insights (Winnicott, 1945c/1958, p. 145), could not afford to ignore the impact on him of Bowlby's contribution.

The message of Bowlby's 1944 paper had been simple: namely, that there was a demonstrable correlation between separation from or rejection by the mother in early childhood and that child's later antisocial behaviour. Extreme cases of prolonged separation or outright rejection could lead to the later formation of "the affectionless character", exemplified in the young persistent thief who strikingly lacked the capacity to show or receive affection and appeared utterly devoid of shame, guilt, or a sense of responsibility for his—or her—delinquent behaviour. The 44 cases cited in the paper, all based on his Child Guidance Consultations, provided, Bowlby argued, compelling evidence of the correspondence between the severity of early deprivation and the degree of subsequent delinquent tendencies.

It has become commonplace to regard Bowlby and Winnicott as having essentially the same view about early separation from the mother as a key contributory factor in a variety of disturbances of childhood social and psychological development, including notably juvenile delinquency. This near-identity of standpoint seems confirmed by a remark made by Bowlby himself in an interview given near the end of his life, in which he declared: "I always held the view that Winnicott and I were singing the same tune. We were essentially giving the same message, but again he didn't like my theoretical ideas" (Hunter, 1991, p. 170).

In this chapter I want to examine to what extent this properly describes their respective positions. In particular, what was the nature and extent of their differences in regard to the phenomenon of juvenile delinquency, its causes, assessment, and treatment? Was it simply a matter, as Bowlby seems to suggest, of Winnicott not liking his theoretical ideas? And if so, what theoretical ideas did Winnicott not agree with, and why? And what about Bowlby's own disagreements with Winnicott?

What is clear is that from the outset Winnicott and Bowlby were bracketed to a large extent in the eyes of psychoanalytical colleagues who disagreed with them over the role they ascribed to "environment", as well as by a later generation of psychologists and social theorists who took issue with what was perceived as their shared "message": namely, that mothers should stay at home to look after their children in preference to pursuing a job or a professional career. However, the danger of taking one's cue too readily from these critics within the psychoanalytic confraternity and beyond is that it may lead one to ignore the actual differences, not just of nuance but of substance, that to some extent kept them apart. This matters, not only because these differences are relevant if one is to form an accurate picture of where each stood on the issue of the relationship between actual upbringing and later pathology—what was often loosely termed "the environmental factor". They also have an impact on their respective attitudes to the function of social welfare provision at a national level in ensuring the healthy development of society's children and the advocacy of state-sponsored initiatives in order to bring this about. Exploring the first leads us to reflect on the nature of at least some of the crucial ideological disputes that divided the British psychoanalytic establishment during the middle years of the twentieth century; a parochial matter on the surface, no doubt, but one with wider current resonances. An examination of the second enables us to glimpse at how psychoanalytically informed insights and objectives, deriving mostly from the writings and broadcasts of Winnicott and Bowlby,[1] significantly influenced the formation of social policy and public attitudes in Britain during a particular period in the middle of the twentieth century lasting about a decade and a half, in a way that has not happened before or since. Nowadays, when psychoanalytic influence within the professions of psychology, psychiatry, and social work is on the wane and when many government social policy initiatives directed at young people give rise to concern within the psychoanalytic community, it is worth reflecting on the political and social context in Britain and elsewhere in Europe that proved to be so uniquely receptive to what these two psychoanalysts had to say.

Since I propose in this chapter to concentrate mainly on examining their differences, it seems only right that I begin by registering their several remarkable resemblances of background and experience. Both were born into comfortable and successful middle-class British families; both were sent away to be educated at boarding school, studied Natural Sciences as a preliminary to medicine at Cambridge, and spent time serving in the navy. In Winnicott's case this latter service was brief and took place in wartime. For Bowlby, born a decade after Winnicott, it was longer, more systematic, and undertaken initially with a navy career in view before a change of direction led him, after a short but significant detour, to university studies and eventual medical qualification. Both owned to a deep boyhood admiration of Darwin, rivalled but never quite eclipsed by their later admiration of Freud. Inspired by the latter, both men underwent analysis before completing their medical studies. Each decided on becoming a child analyst at a time when these were few in number, particularly in the case of men. They also shared the same analyst, Joan Riviere (though in Winnicott's case, this was only after a previous analysis of several years' duration with James Strachey). Each subsequently expressed reservations about Riviere's ability to understand, and her readiness to encourage, their interest in viewing the child patient within the context of his family relationships and lived environment, rather than treating him as a self-standing individual or, as Bowlby put it, a "closed system" (Senn, 1977 quoted in van Dijken, 1998, p. 98). Both, moreover, had Riviere's mentor, Melanie Klein, as a supervisor of their respective training cases. From the latter they subsequently acknowledged learning much about the theory of intrapsychic development and organization, while in differing degrees distancing themselves from her in matters of technique, in particular concerning the relative weight to be placed on inner processes as compared with outer reality in assessing the genesis of childhood disturbance. Neither ever became included in the Klein circle, though in Winnicott's case, unlike that of Bowlby, this separateness was the result of a long and personally painful process of detachment. Bowlby, it seems, never harboured ambitions of becoming Klein's acolyte, so he never resented his exclusion from the group—though he did, later on, feel pained at the relative lack of recognition by psychoanalysts of his scientific contribution to the study of attachment, rather as Winnicott did at their indifference to his work on transitional objects and phenomena.

Taken together, there is enough common ground here between the two men, as well as enough to differentiate them from the rest of their psychoanalytic colleagues, to lead the casual observer to presume a congruence of outlook over the priority issues within child psychiatry and psychoanalysis in the years leading up to, during, and immediately following the Second World War. In particular it would be natural to conclude that what marked them out was their joint preparedness to take into account the maternal and family dimension of the presented child, both as regards understanding his psychopathology and planning treatment. Hence it may come as a surprise to learn that in 1939, when Bowlby presented his membership paper before the Institute of Psychoanalysis in the expectation of gaining acceptance as a qualified child psychoanalyst, choosing for his subject "The Influence of Early Environment in the Development of Neurosis", the already qualified Donald Winnicott was among his foremost critics—so much so, indeed, that, along with John Rickman and Joan Riviere, he attempted—unsuccessfully—to oppose Bowlby's membership at the subsequent meeting of the Training Council (King & Steiner, 1991, p. 149).

Was it that at this stage Winnicott was, unlike Bowlby, still so in thrall to Melanie Klein and Riviere as not yet to be alive to the importance of the early maternal environment? Later Winnicott, as if acknowledging his earlier inattentiveness to the environmental factor, wrote that it was mainly through the effect of his wartime experiences of evacuation, and specifically of his acquaintance with evacuated children and their carers, that he first became alerted to its importance (Winnicott, letter to Robert Tod, 6 November 1969, in Rodman, 1987, p. 197). This being so, one might ascribe Winnicott's initial opposition to Bowlby as being due to ignorance or inexperience about its possible effects. However, this cannot be a complete explanation. Only a matter of six months later, Bowlby and Winnicott, along with their more senior child psychiatry colleague, Emmanuel Miller, were jointly writing to the *British Medical Journal*—Bowlby's initial attempt to get a letter on the same subject published in *The Times* having failed—and declaring that "the evacuation of small children without their mothers can lead to very serious and widespread psychological disorder. For instance, it can lead to a big increase in juvenile delinquency in the next decade" (Bowlby, Miller, & Winnicott, 1939; Winnicott, 1984, p. 14).

So here we see Winnicott apparently prepared to underwrite the very thesis that Bowlby had propounded in his membership paper, and this before his direct exposure to the evacuation programme and its effects had even begun—too soon, in other words, for him to have undergone the Damascene conversion to which he later alluded. Clearly, therefore, it cannot have been the proposition itself—that premature separation of the child from the mother is psychologically injurious—that Winnicott was as yet unprepared to countenance and that was responsible for his opposition to Bowlby. The real point of difference must have lain elsewhere. To see where, we need to establish what exactly was being proposed that was truly novel in this, Bowlby's first major paper concerning the importance of the child's early environment—at this stage the term "attachment" had not been coined—and what was the particular issue over which Winnicott had such serious reservations. As we shall see, although their views were later to converge, they were never quite identical—and the problem lay in large part with the slippery term "environment".

The environmental factor

Already as a student Bowlby had earned a reputation among his colleagues as a man of firm opinions, little given to self-doubt. His convictions once formed, he wished to share them. Moreover, in disseminating his views, he was never afraid of ruffling a few feathers. These characteristics he displayed in full measure when presenting his membership paper. Rather than first launching into a clinical description of a single analytic case complete with detailed case material followed by a theoretical excursus, the usual practice on such occasions, he announced at the outset his intention of putting forward nothing less than "a general theory of the genesis of neurosis" in which environmental factors would be emphasized at the expense of the genetic factors usually accorded prominence. As if this *démarche* were insufficiently bold, he went on to announce that his contribution would be based on material concerning the personal backgrounds of several children whom he had assessed during the previous three years at the London Child Guidance Clinic, declaring that "This type of research is of much more value in solving certain analytic problems than is research limited to analytic sessions" (Bowlby, 1940, p. 154).

Bowlby's third gesture of independence was to utilize clinical material, insofar as he used it at all, deriving from cases seen in once-weekly therapy sessions, not from the full-scale individual analyses of children such as he had undertaken as part of his training towards membership. He went out of his way to emphasize the scientific value of these once-weekly clinic cases, by implication challenging the introvertedness and exclusivity of much classical child analytic therapy as practised within the Institute.[2]

Basing himself on the findings from several of these cases, he put forward a number of important propositions: first, that the circumstances, character, and dispositions of the parents towards the infant were more formative of a child's own character than were processes of unconscious introjection and projection having their source in the interplay of instinctual forces within the child; second, that adverse events, particularly separations of the child from the mother in the early stages, could do lasting psychological damage and could, in particular, affect the child's capacity to form "libidinal ties". He concluded:

> If it became a tradition that small children were never subjected to complete or prolonged separation from their parents in the same way that regular sleep and orange juice have become nursery traditions, I believe that many cases of neurotic character development would be avoided. [Bowlby, 1940, p. 175]

We have no record of the discussion that took place following the paper, nor of the nature of the specific objections raised, so we must to some extent rely on conjecture and extrapolation from subsequent events to determine what these probably were. However, over the issue of the frequency of sessions, at least, we have documentary evidence to show that Winnicott took a view different from that of his younger and, at the time, more outspoken colleague, even if he was to shift towards Bowlby's opinion later on. For him, five-times-a-week child analysis was sacrosanct. Writing at the end of his life, he disarmingly confessed:

In the decade called the thirties I was learning to be a psychoanalyst, and I could feel that, with a little more training, a little more skill, and a little more luck, I could move mountains by making the right interpretations at the right time. . . . At one time I could have been heard saying that there is no therapy except on the basis of fifty minutes five times a week, going on for as many years as necessary, done by a trained psychoanalyst. [Winnicott, 1970c/1984, p. 220]

Evidently, Bowlby never subscribed to this doctrine.

Still, this issue of frequency of sessions in itself could hardly have provided sufficient grounds for Winnicott's outright opposition to Bowlby's candidature. After all, already at the time Winnicott was proving quite flexible in practice about the desirability—even feasibility—of full-scale child analysis according to the classical pattern in cases where family attitudes or circumstances provided contraindications to treatment. In prefacing his report a couple of years later on a series of cases that he had seen in his capacity as director of the Child Department of the Institute of Psychoanalysis, Winnicott wrote:

It will probably be agreed that it is wrong to extol the value that analysis would have, if applied, in a case where analysis is not applicable. Parents who come to consultation are feeling guilty about their child's symptom or illness, and the way in which the doctor behaves will determine whether they will calmly return to taking responsibility which they can well take, or anxiously hand over responsibility to the doctor or clinic. It is obviously better that the parents should retain such responsibility as they can bear, and especially is this true if analysis cannot be given a chance to lessen the actual illness of the child. [Winnicott, 1942/1958, p. 71]

In other words, Winnicott then held a more categorical view than did Bowlby over what constituted child analytic treatment—it had to be of a certain frequency in order to sustain the transference—and what its therapeutic benefits were, while sharing with him a recognition that if this ideal of treatment could not be realized for practical reasons to do with family circumstances, it was better to adopt other measures. What apparently Winnicott did not acknowledge at this stage—surprisingly, in the light of his later views and practice—was the efficacy of once-weekly psychotherapy for children, such as Bowlby had instituted as the standard provision from the beginning of his Child Guidance Work.

A probable clue to the deeper cause of Winnicott's opposition is provided by something he wrote towards the end of his life in another paper having a markedly retrospective character:

> Psycho-analysis, in its beginning, had to emphasise the powerfulness of feelings and of conflicting feelings and had to explore defences against them. . . . The Psycho-analyst was always fighting the battle for the individual against those who ascribed troubles to environmental influences. [Winnicott, 1969e/1986, p. 251)]

The next paragraph has a distinctly autobiographical ring:

> Gradually the inevitable happened and psycho-analysts, carrying with them their unique belief in the significance of details, had to start to look at dependence, that is to say, the early stages of the development of the human child when dependence is so great that the behaviour of those representing the environment could no longer be ignored. [p. 251]

Not long before writing this, in addressing the 1952 Club (an informal scientific grouping of senior Middle Group or Independent analysts), Winnicott made a similar observation, this time in more unbuttoned fashion:

> the psycho-analysts were the only people for about ten or fifteen years who knew there was anything *but* environment. Everybody was screaming out that everything was due to somebody's father being drunk. So the thing was, how to get back to the environment without losing all that was gained by studying the inner factors. [Winnicott, 1967c/1989, p. 577)]

"Without losing all that was gained by studying the inner factors"—could this be the nub of his objection to Bowlby's paper? Supporting evidence that this was, indeed, the case comes from a later series of criticisms Winnicott was to make in public and private about several of Bowlby's later offerings. Repeatedly he complains that Bowlby appeared to dismiss the importance of the child's internal dispositions, through his almost exclusive emphasis on external factors. Typical is a comment in a letter to Joan Riviere written shortly after Bowlby had presented his paper on "The Nature of the Child's Tie to His Mother" (Bowlby, 1958b): "It was certainly a very difficult paper to appreciate without at the same time giving away almost everything that has been fought for by Freud" (cf. Rodman, 2003, p. 241).

Bowlby himself, particularly in his early papers, gave no sense of deliberately transgressing the Freudian canon. On the contrary, he appealed in support of his thesis to Freud's own earlier commitment to elucidating the objective bases of the patient's psychoneurotic disorders, declaring in his membership paper:

> My own approach to the role of environment in the causation of neurosis has of course been from the analytic angle. For this reason I have ignored many aspects of the child's environment such as economic conditions, housing conditions, the school situation, diet and religious teaching. [Bowlby, 1940, p. 155]

Evidently, for Bowlby the quality of objective maternal care, though an "environmental factor", was not external to the child in the same way these others were. In his eyes maternal provision was in some sense intrinsic to the way in which the child not only behaved but also experienced the world. The real question at issue between himself and his critics was whether the *objective* quality of maternal care was the primary factor in understanding and dealing with a child's disturbance, or whether it was secondary to the child's own intrapsychic processes the quality and force of which were only partially related to it. And here Bowlby's view seems to have been consistent and unchanging: the objective quality of care was central not only to the child's mental health but to his experience of himself and the world. Occasionally, he would refer to *extra-psychic* as distinct from intra-psychic factors in childhood disturbance, an either/or disjunction that has no counterpart in Klein, Riviere, or Winnicott. Yet he never regarded these factors as *extrinsic*. Echoing a dictum of his one-time mentor, the psychologist Cyril Burt, he claimed for the child analyst to know about the state of the mother when treating the child was like the nurseryman needing to know about the soil in which the seeds were planted. Towards the end of his life he gave his most unambiguous statement of which of these factors, the extra-psychic or intra-psychic, he personally regarded as the more significant:

> Most of what goes on in the internal world is a more or less accurate reflection of what an individual has experienced recently or long ago in the external world. . . . If a child sees his mother as a very loving person, the chances are that his mother is a loving person. If he sees her as a very rejecting person, the chances are she is a very rejecting person. [Bowlby, Figlio, & Young, 1986, p. 43]

The clear implication, therefore, is that for Bowlby it is the objective experience of the actual quality of the maternal provision that is ultimately formative of the child's inner world, rather than the vicissitudes of the instinctual dispositions with which the child is initially endowed and to which the objective experiences of care may be only contingently related.

The position of Joan Riviere on this issue could not have been more different. In the face of the objections of Bowlby and later of Winnicott, she insisted that it was not a case of her ignoring the environmental factor, as she perceived it. On the contrary—she, too, had felt that she had a mission to declare something important about the responsiveness of the infant to its actual care when in 1936 she had presented her paper "On the Genesis of Psychical Conflict in Earliest Infancy" before a sceptical audience of Viennese analysts, as representative of the British (Kleinian) School. There, she drew attention to the fact that the "infant world of the psyche", though narcissistic in character, was nevertheless determined by the infant's reactions to the actual taking in and expelling of nourishment. In this sense "it was based on sensations and ruled by feelings" and could, thus, be called "experience-based". Only, for Riviere, as for Klein, these sensations and feelings were initially "entirely autistic, not only lacking in objectivity, but at first without objects" (Riviere, 1936) (Some years later, and no doubt as a result of reflecting on the differences that later emerged between herself and her two younger analysands, she corrected the last phrase to "at the very first without awareness of external objects".) In her paper she went on to tease out what she saw as the direct conclusion of the foregoing premise:

> From this omnipotent standpoint ... all *responsibility* rests on the self and all *causal relations* proceed from within the self. ... I said that this world was without objectivity; but from the very beginning there exists a core and foundation in *experience* for objectivity. ... I wish especially to point out therefore that from the very beginning of life ... the psyche responds to the reality of its experiences by interpreting them—or, rather *mis*interpreting them—in a subjective manner that increases its pleasure and preserves it from pain. This act of a *subjective interpretation of experience*, which it carries out by means of introjection and projection, ... forms the foundation of what we mean by *phantasy life*.
> [Riviere, 1936/1991, pp. 276–277]

For Riviere, then, infant *experience* was subjective, just as for Bowlby it was objective. Riviere was prepared to concede that these experiences had their *origins* in external, objective events, whereas Bowlby, for his part, could acknowledge that the objective experiences of maternal care—or the lack of it—were transmuted by the child's own subjective reaction to them, this transformation depending to some extent on internal factors in the child. But for each the root cause—and, in that respect, the responsibility—for the health or pathology of the young child was differently situated.

And what of Winnicott? He appears to have taken an intermediate position between the two, although what was to become his own distinctive viewpoint was as yet not clearly articulated. On the one hand, he shared with Riviere the sense that what counted principally for the analyst and clinician was how the infant registered and reacted internally to the quality of its care: it was, in that sense, a subjective experience. Moreover, there was a further sense in which for the infant the experience of maternal care was necessarily subjective, the product of its own internal states. This was because the infant's reality testing was as yet undeveloped. Nevertheless, even at this stage when he was most under the Kleinian influence, Winnicott did not share Riviere's belief that what the mother "meant" for her infant could be understood simply, in oral terms, as the supplier or withholder of nourishment. For him, as for Bowlby, this instinct-dominated view represented a quite inadequate depiction of the complexities of mother–infant interaction. Yet, unlike Bowlby, he was not prepared entirely to downgrade the instinctual factor in favour of the environmental. His position at the time is summed up in this carefully balanced statement written a year or so later, probably in close consultation with his analytic mentors (cf. Rodman, 2003, p. 123):

> as Melanie Klein has shown, there is a constant interchange and testing between inner and outer reality; the inner reality is always being built up and enriched by instinctual experience in relation to external objects and by contributions from external objects (in so far as such contributions can be perceived); and the outer world is constantly being perceived and the individual's relationship to it being enriched because of the existence in him of a lively inner world. [Winnicott, 1941a/1958, p. 61)

One can deduce, therefore, that Winnicott's opposition to Bowlby's membership paper and candidature stemmed from his objection to the latter's apparent discarding of the concept of an internal world that provided not just a theatre where the child's externally mediated conflicts were played out, but a crucible in which character, dispositions, behaviour were moulded from the active, fluid convergence of different, often contrary, instinctual elements. This, in his view, impoverished concept of unconscious mental life was to remain Winnicott's primary objection to Bowlby's formulations here and elsewhere, even when he was prepared to move much closer to the latter in acknowledging the impact of the environment, facilitating and otherwise, on the psyche of the growing individual.

To sum up, Bowlby was proposing to regard the environmental factors relating to the infant's upbringing as *immediate* causes and explanations of a child's later character, dispositions, behaviour, whereas for Riviere, as for most of her fellow analysts, they were *remote* causes. For Winnicott, on the other hand, they were neither immediate nor remote, but *proximate* causes.

The "affectionless character"

Relatively little has so far been said about the accounts of Bowlby and Winnicott specifically concerning delinquency or "the antisocial tendency". However, the foregoing discussion of their different views on the "environmental factor" may help us to a better grasp of the reasons why they started somewhat in opposition to one another, then gradually appeared to become more closely aligned, without ever achieving complete unanimity.

Bowlby never altered his early view about the preponderant influence of actual experience over unconscious instinctual impulses in forming a child's dispositions and behaviour, despite the fact that he was to shift the initial focus of his research interests away from delinquency and maladjustment towards early childhood separation and its effects, and subsequently towards research on the function and vicissitudes of attachment behaviour as a whole—the topic for which nowadays he is best known, at least among fellow scientists and clinicians. Winnicott, in contrast, did substantially alter his theoretical understanding about the nature and importance of the environmental factor in human development, even while maintaining unchanged his predominantly clinical orientation and outlook, based on his abiding belief that the psychoanalyst *qua* scientist ought primarily to be concerned and content with what could be deduced from the study of the individual case. Moreover, this shift in understanding on Winnicott's part owed as much to his reaction to Bowlby as it did to his wartime experiences with evacuated children and their carers.

I shall now explain and elaborate on these twin assertions.

As we have seen, Bowlby's first work on the causes of juvenile delinquency predated the actual wartime evacuation programme. When he wrote it in 1938, however, plans for the mass evacuation of children were already being mooted, and this no doubt provided him with an added incentive to draw attention to the deleterious consequences of early maternal separation, particularly its effects on society. His initial researches established to his own satisfaction—though his results began to be widely challenged a quarter-century later (cf. Rutter, 1972)—that a clear correlation could be established between premature and prolonged separation and extreme forms of disturbed, sociopathic behaviour, such as were manifested by those he termed "affectionless characters". There were 14 such instances in his cohort. These youngsters were characterized by serious and chronic stealing (as well as other forms of disruptive, delinquent behaviour), by an inability to form and maintain loving relationships, and—for Bowlby the most striking characteristic—by a marked indifference to the feelings or opinions of others, accompanied by an absence of responsibility, shame, or guilt. Bowlby's preferred epithet to describe them, naval rather than clinical, was "hard-boiled" (Bowlby, 1944/1946, pp. 49–52).

Though he distinguished between different types and degrees of disturbance among his forty-four young thieves, Bowlby offered few hints about the nature of his therapeutic practice in regard to them, nor any discussion of the efficacy or otherwise of psychotherapy, even though, as he indicated, all these cases initially came to his notice as referrals for assessment and treatment at the London Child Guidance Clinic. There are occasional passing references to ongoing weekly therapy sessions, but no indication is given of any change in the dynamics of the child and the family as a result of such intervention. It is clear that Bowlby's outlook, even at this early stage in his career, focussed primarily on the need for preventive work rather than remedial intervention. Even more urgent, in his estimation, was the need for the government to fund proper research on a national scale into the causes and conditions contributing to the onset of juvenile delinquency:

> The arrest of the criminal, the administration of justice and the punishment or reform of the offender requires a tremendous organisation of police, courts of law, probation officers, remand homes, approved schools, Borstals and prisons, costing the country tens of millions of pounds a year. If a fraction of 1 per cent of this sum were devoted to research into the springs of delinquent conduct it is virtually certain that very considerable sums would be saved, and, what is far more important, thousands of people now condemned to spend a large part of their lives in gaol enabled to live happy and fruitful lives. [Bowlby, 1944/1946, p. 3]

It is clear also from reading this early paper that what most struck the young Bowlby as psychiatrist and scientist was not just the presence of maternal separation as a factor in the lives of these young children, but the seemingly close correlation existing between the type and timing of separation and the likely form of a child's subsequent maladjustment. Others, including the psychologist Cyril Burt, with whom he had briefly collaborated as a research student, had already hypothesized a general connection between broken homes and delinquency. (Burt was doubtless to be numbered among those scathingly referred to by Winnicott as "the perennial screamers" about the importance of such factors as broken homes and the need to do something about them.) Bowlby's distinctiveness lay in making specific links, first, between delinquency and the rupture of the child's tie to his mother and, second, between the nature and severity of the child's disturbance—and consequent delinquent tendency—and when and how maternal separation first occurred. The critical period of infancy in this respect, he suggested, was between six months and three years. Prior to that the infant had not reached a stage of sufficiently differentiating the mother as a person from her role of basic provider of warmth and sustenance:

> In practically all these cases—of affectionless characters—the separation that appears to have been pathogenic occurred after the age of six months and in a majority after twelve months. This suggests that there is a lower age limit, before which separations,

while perhaps having undesirable effects, do not produce the particular results we are concerned with here—the affectionless and delinquent character. [Bowlby, 1944/1946, p. 40]

At this point Bowlby inserted a cautionary note to the effect that more research was needed into the differential effects of separations across the first 18 months of life. Still, this did not prevent him from categorically claiming that there was a lower threshold beyond which, whatever other disturbance the child might subsequently display, delinquency of the sort shown by the "affectionless character" was not likely to be manifest. This was a far-reaching claim. By the time he came to write his report on the effects of separation for the WHO a decade later, Bowlby had become acquainted with the researches of Goldfarb (1943, 1945) and Spitz (1945, 1946), both of whom drew attention to the long-term consequences of the infant's loss of the mother during the very first months of life (Bowlby, 1951, pp. 52–53). Significantly, however, while acknowledging the importance of such work, he did not incline to these authors' view that the psychological damage to the child of very early separation—i.e. during the first six months—might be intractable, as he had claimed was the case with the affectionless character.

There were two reasons for this. In the first place, Bowlby believed that deprivation suffered by the infant after the midway stage of the first year of life was likely crucially to affect that child's capacity to invest emotionally in persons, to love, to trust, to feel secure in entertaining and expressing ambivalent sentiments. This was because separation at this stage would interfere with the dawning awareness of the reality of her dependence on others—particularly of the person of the mother. Prior to this, he believed, the infant was largely dominated by instinctual needs and impulses the strength and immediacy of which rendered the given more real than the giver. In the case of the seriously deprived infant, especially when institutionalized in earliest infancy, Bowlby believed that the frustration of instinctual need was liable to be manifested in retardation and personality distortion. However—and this was Bowlby's second ground for distinguishing between the pre- and post-6-months period—he differed from Goldfarb and Spitz in believing that the negative effects for such infants could be reversed, provided they were given the opportunity of early adoption.

Winnicott and "the antisocial tendency"

Winnicott's considered response to Bowlby's early work was slow to take shape and complex once it had evolved. Moreover, his conclusions on a theoretical level about the effects of deprivation are intertwined with his experiences of the evacuation programme, as well as being influenced, not just by his reaction to Bowlby, but also by his gradual distancing himself from the doctrinal stance of Klein and Riviere on the matter of the "environmental factor", a process that was to some extent independent of the former.

I shall consider the impact of the evacuation on Winnicott's thinking first. He would later claim, as we have seen, that this experience "woke him up" to the importance of environment. From this, one might deduce that through the plight of evacuated children Winnicott merely became alerted for the first time to the importance of the child's real tie to the mother, the negative effects of separation, and the need to preserve it even at the risk of threatened danger. Such a conclusion was, indeed, the principal message of the Cambridge Evacuation Survey conducted by Susan Isaacs and others in 1941, to which Bowlby contributed, and whose published results Winnicott subsequently reviewed (1941b). The authors' emphasis was on the need for planners and policy-makers to ensure that where evacuation was absolutely necessary, everything possible was done to ensure continuity of care and experience between home and placement for the evacuated child: if he could not live at home, then the least damaging option was a setting that replicated the conditions of the child's home as closely as possible.

Winnicott did not contest this general conclusion, yet what he constantly highlights in his own writings and recollections of this period was his growing realization of the benefits of good-quality child care that was being provided by parent substitutes *in non-family settings* as an indirect consequence of evacuation (cf. Winnicott, 1970c/1984, p. 221). His primary task as consultant psychiatrist to the Oxfordshire Evacuation Programme was to provide help for the staff of hostels catering not for the settled trouble-free evacuees, but for the troubled and troublesome youngsters whose behaviour rendered them impossible to cope with in ordinary family settings. Moreover, it is clear from his vivid description (Winnicott, 1970c/1984, pp. 220–221) of his first encounter with David Wills' group of young misfits, temporarily housed in an old Poor Law Institution in Bicester in 1940, that these "casualties" were not simply reacting to a sense of dislocation and deprivation through having been evacuated. Although he called them "evacuation failures", it was obvious that their unmanageability had preceded their evacuation, and that the experience of moving from an urban environment to live in other people's homes in the Oxfordshire countryside had merely aggravated its disruptive effects. Yet, while the physical dislocation suffered by these young people had accentuated problems already present, so also, in Winnicott's view, had it fortuitously provided an opportunity for remedial action: "I was struck by the way in which this wartime provision solved the peacetime problem of management of the early antisocial case" (Winnicott, 1948a/1984, p. 77).

He found that the intervention of a group of properly managed and supported adult figures who were not the child's parents or actual parent substitutes but were capable collectively of taking on the essentials of a parental role as wardens—namely, of providing a pattern of consistent loving care, management, and control in a way that the child's own parents had earlier failed to do—enabled a therapeutic process to unfold that was efficacious for such individuals in a way that psychoanalytic treatment had proved not to be. This realization of the possibility of therapy through management of the child's living environment is what Winnicott truly "woke up to" as a result of his experience of evacuation. By the end of the war he and his future second wife, Clare Britton, with whom much of this consultation work on the Evacuation programme was associated, had jointly evolved the concept of *primary home care* to cover what they regarded as being the essential ingredients of such beneficial residential provision (Winnicott & Britton, 1947).

On the face of it, therefore, Winnicott's response to the evacuation programme was to make him aware of the importance of "environment" in quite a different sense from Bowlby's. The latter consistently viewed the facilitative environment for the child in family terms, and especially as involving the maintenance of the child's tie to the mother. "Better a bad home than a good substitute" was a constant Bowlby refrain, uttered first in 1938 and repeated with added authority and emphasis in his powerfully influential *Child Care and the Growth of Love* (1953). Winnicott, on the other hand, always resisted the simple identification of the person of the mother with the security of the maternal environment, arguing that such an equation discounted, or insufficiently recognized, the importance of the subjective factor of the infant's experience—"imaginative creation"—of the mother and the mother's subjective contribution to the coming into being of such an experience. For Winnicott, it was at least open to question whether a home environment where parental pathology stifled the infant's possibility of "creating the mother in fantasy" was to be regarded as preferable to a substitute home or hostel care in which such childhood potential was enabled to flourish.

There is an irony here. Winnicott never had direct, first-hand experience of residential work with disturbed youngsters, whereas Bowlby did have this: As a young man, having recently left the navy, and uncertain about the course of his future career, Bowlby had gone to work as a teacher, first in a progressive boarding school and then, when that proved unsatisfying, in a newly opened therapeutic school. Though generally reticent about the details of his experiences there, Bowlby was to declare much later that this interlude had been an important formative influence upon him, giving him a conviction that young people's lives could be changed for the better by caring, understanding, and involvement. This, he acknowledged, had helped to shape the direction of his future career, as well as giving him his first acquaintance with psychoanalysis (Smuts, 1977). Despite some reservations about the actual running of this special school, he did not doubt its potential in helping disturbed youngsters, some of whom were also delinquent. Yet rarely did Bowlby give recognition in his writings to the importance of residential provision for young people as an alternative to adoption or fostering in cases where a child could not be brought up or maintained in the family home.[3] Indeed, it fell to Winnicott to warn him about the consequences for the future of residential establishments resulting from his very public stance on the negative effects of separation of young children from their mothers (Winnicott, 1954a/1987, pp. 65–66). Winnicott feared their wholesale closure. It is true that in writing his 1951 WHO report, later published in abridged form as *Child Care and the Growth of Love* (1953), Bowlby felt obliged to admit that residential therapeutic care of disturbed children had a role, if not as something intrinsically desirable, at least as a practical necessity for the foreseeable future. In developing this theme he made a number of positive references to the conclusions reached by Winnicott and Britton on the basis of their consultative work with the wartime hostels for difficult evacuees—material that they had already presented to the government-appointed Curtis Committee charged with looking into the future care provision of young children after the war. Indeed, it seems quite possible that the inclusion of their contribution in Bowlby's final report may have been urged on him by Winnicott himself, who may even have had a hand in its drafting.

If Winnicott's discovery of the value of hostel care as distinct from substitute family care may seem a surprising dividend of his wartime experiences, scarcely less so was his new-found belief in the possibility of therapy through the management of disturbed youngsters, and the need for such provision for young delinquents whose antisocial behaviour had its roots in early maternal deprivation. The link between the nature of the disturbance and the preferred type of remedial provision is not self-evident—it is not a connection that Bowlby wholeheartedly made. Nor is it obvious in the light of Winnicott's own emphasis on the importance of "primary maternal preoccupation", both as a factor in the emotional development of the child and as an essential requirement of remedial treatment when things go wrong, that he should have been so strong in his advocacy of this sort of environmental therapy. Nevertheless, there was an overall consistency in his outlook, as well as a readiness to explore the implications of clinical material with rigour and to pursue them wherever their conclusions seemed to lead, that the more overly "scientific" Bowlby did not always show in equal measure. Part of the difference is attributable to personal style. Where Bowlby preferred to seek correlations and would wait for the evidence to accumulate over time, Winnicott sought *causal relations* based on data and hypotheses from his analytic work, working backwards, as it were, from the individual presenting case to its supposed, unconsciously determined roots.

It is not that Winnicott wished to dismiss Bowlby's researches as lacking in value. On the contrary, he took seriously Bowlby's finding that children suffering separations in the second half of the first year or later were particularly liable to become delinquent, whereas those suffering separation at an even earlier stage did not, developing other forms of disturbance or psychological arrest instead. For him this assumed the status of a basic axiom. What he did not feel that Bowlby's work had convincingly shown was *why* the deprived child was prone to delinquency—or "the antisocial tendency"—as distinct from other forms of symptomatic behaviour. Bowlby had conjectured that this predisposition was due to a mixture of craving "for libidinal satisfaction" and angry, vengeful protest on the part of the child, both dispositions being largely unconscious in origin. Bowlby had gone on to speculate that the earliness of onset and the extent of the child's deprivation had together affected his capacity to develop a superego. On the basis of these two hypotheses Bowlby had accounted for the delinquent's initial tendency to steal from his mother before extending the scope of his thieving outwards; his indifference to the feelings and possessions of others; and his incorrigibility (Bowlby, 1944/1946, pp. 50–52).

Winnicott's 1956 paper on "The Antisocial Tendency" can be seen as in part a rebuttal, in part an attempted revision of this theoretical, or rather, conjectural part of Bowlby's thesis. His starting point—which he puts in italics for emphasis—is that "*the antisocial tendency is not a diagnosis*". What Winnicott means by this is not just that the term "antisocial tendency" is—deliberately—broad and vague, but that "delinquency" does not itself specify a clinical condition. Rather, it denotes a disposition to behave in defiance of the constraints of society. Such behaviour may well have a neurotic motivation, but at root it has to be regarded as an expression of, and reaction to, "the deprived complex" (Winnicott, 1956a/1984, pp. 122–123). Up to this point Bowlby may have been in partial agreement. But now Winnicott draws an inference that is quite foreign to the latter's account. The implicit protest of the deprived complex is, he says, a sign of *hope*. This becomes for Winnicott a fundamental and recurring premise. Through his compulsive stealing the antisocial youngster is expressing a desire for, and belief in, the retrieval of the early lost object, the non-available mother, and it is "vital" that society recognizes and responds to "the moment of hope" in the delinquent's behaviour: "Over and over again one sees the moment of hope wasted, or withered, because of mismanagement or intolerance" (p. 123). This may sound whimsical, even sentimental, on Winnicott's part, and one might guess that Bowlby's reaction to it would have been rather scathing. Yet Winnicott is insistent that it is he who is being realistic and hard-headed, not those who choose to regard delinquency exclusively in terms of its negative impact. What he seems to have particularly objected to in Bowlby's account was the latter's tendency to treat delinquency as if it were a disease entity, from which both the individual sufferer and society needed to be rescued. (Bowlby was fond of drawing parallels between ridding society of formerly endemic illnesses such as tuberculosis through the successful programme of mass inoculation and the possible eradicating of juvenile delinquency by comparable measures of social prophylaxis.) In this respect, Winnicott's outlook remained much closer to the traditional analytic conception of delinquency as a pattern of unconsciously determined but potentially meaningful behaviour requiring to be understood and relieved, rather than removed. (Stealing, including his own "stealing" of others' ideas, he always regarded, indulgently, as a "gesture".)

Nevertheless, by insisting that the youngster is typically displaying hope in and through his antisocial behaviour, Winnicott was adopting a paradoxical stance, and certainly one difficult to reconcile with the profile of "the affectionless character" as described by Bowlby. No doubt it was meant to sound provocative and challenging—he had first expressed this view publicly in an address to magistrates in 1946—and perhaps there was an element of intentional exaggeration behind its initial utterance, given that at the time the whole pattern of children's future welfare was a topic of active political debate. It is also the case that here in 1956 he somewhat modified the generality of this claim by suggesting that the hopeful element expressed though the antisocial act might well go unrecognized and unresponded to, with the result that the deprived individual was liable to become more, rather than less despairing and thus the pattern of delinquency become still further embedded.

Leaving aside the motives Winnicott may have had in declaring his view in this way and simply examining its content, I believe that there are two discernible weaknesses in his account of the delinquent, both possibly occasioned by the fact that in the decade or so between the end of the war and writing this important paper Winnicott's actual clinical encounter with delinquency had become somewhat attenuated. One concerns the range or scope of his claim; the second and more substantial one concerns the applicability of the notion of hopefulness to the class of "affectionless characters".

By 1945 Winnicott had become firmly convinced that residential therapy, not psychotherapy, was the treatment of choice for persistent sociopathic youngsters (Winnicott, 1946b/1984, pp. 117–119). Nevertheless, there were children displaying "an antisocial tendency" whom he continued to treat individually, or whose treatment by other colleagues he supervised. These were typically children in whom the manifestations of an "antisocial tendency" were transient rather than endemic. One such case was that of Philip, aged nine, movingly described in his paper "Symptom Tolerance in Paediatrics" (Winnicott, 1953d). He was referred to Winnicott by his desperate parents after the headmaster of his prep school had decided to expel him following a sudden bout of unexplained and unacknowledged stealing. Winnicott was able to link the boy's stealing, and its associated symptom, enuresis, to a period of family disruption occasioned by wartime and his father's absence on active service. His treatment of the case involved a programme of intermittent therapy sessions for the boy, encouragement of the mother to provide a regressive experience, with supervision of this likewise provided by him, together with his own active intervention in decisions about the boy's future care—such as persuading the headmaster to keep a place open for the boy's eventual return to school. This was therapy through management, certainly—and of a sort that he was later to employ widely in his private work. Yet it was very different from the sort of therapy through management that he had been advocating for young delinquents in residential hostels.

In situations such as that of Philip the element of hope—as well as of despair—expressed through the child's antisocial behaviour can readily be recognized, as can a degree of latent deprivation. But he is a very different case from those comprising Bowlby's original array of affectionless characters. Where Philip's character was highly neurotic and accompanied by a marked degree of guilt and depressive anxiety, so-called "affectionless characters" were distinguishable from the rest of the 44 thieves by the very absence of these traits. Moreover, if "delinquency" was proving an elastic term in Winnicott's fingers, one that could be stretched from the persistent and purposive young criminal at one end to the neurotic child displaying an intermittent bout of dissociative stealing at the other, likewise was "deprivation" being extended. Evidently Winnicott wanted to employ the term "deprivation" in his 1956 "Antisocial Tendency" paper to cover not just actual long-term physical separations or sustained withdrawals of affective care by the parents, in the way that Bowlby originally envisaged, but any physical or psychological rupture occurring at a critical time in a child's upbringing that required for its relief a period of regression and restorative emotional provision. In short, he was using clinical examples where hope in the child and desire for repair in the parents were manifest, as indicators of the presence of hope among delinquents in general. Yet this was a large and unsubstantiated claim. Certainly, in his original communication Bowlby had not signalled hope in the youngster, or even hopefulness in the therapist, as important elements of the presenting picture. On the contrary, he had repeatedly emphasized the relative intractability of the condition, frequently employing the criminologist's term "recidivism" to describe the delinquent's state (a word never to be found in Winnicott's clinical vocabulary).

So why did Winnicott give the impression in 1956 of believing, and wishing others to believe, that his conclusions about the nature and management of the antisocial tendency represented simply an extension of Bowlby's? How was it that he did not recognize that his own claim about the omnipresence of hope in the delinquent was not only absent from Bowlby's work, but was not even consistent with the latter's position? The answer, I believe, lies in the largely unexamined use of the term "deprivation". Bowlby never defined the term in his 1940 paper. We must assume that he meant it to be understood in its commonly accepted meaning, as denoting the absence or loss of some attribute or amenity that belongs to, or is necessary for, the growing child—in this case, specifically, the presence of the mother. Note that Bowlby did not differentiate terminologically between absence and loss, as Winnicott was to do. Nevertheless, in practice, Bowlby did differentiate them in one important respect. For in describing the particular distinguishing marks of his cohort of "affectionless characters"—those he also termed "chronic" delinquents (Bowlby, 1944/1946, p. 38)—he indicated that they had to do with the earliness, extent, and absoluteness of the child's loss of the mother. Why, then, does he speak of "loss", not of the mother's absence for such children? The reason was probably that in all but two of the fourteen "affectionless characters" he identified, the mother became absent for the child some time after the first six months of life. Now, we need to recall that in Bowlby's view the person of the mother, as distinct from her function of provider and nurturer, was not experienced by the infant before roughly the age of six months. So when Bowlby referred to the deprivation suffered by the affectionless child, he was speaking about what in external terms was in most cases the *loss* of something—namely, the physical presence of the mother—yet in another important respect was the *absence* of something never actually experienced—namely, the mother's felt presence. It was precisely the fact that the affectionless delinquent had never had this *experience* of the mother that he was not liable, in Bowlby's view, to depression (had not reached the "depressive position") and hence was prone to the ruthlessness that characterized his behaviour.

While Bowlby never distinguished terminologically between absence and loss, Winnicott did do so: he connected the occurrence of the specific features of delinquency with the child's *experience* of loss, rejection, or absence of the mother after the first six months of life. With deprivation "there has been a loss of something good that has been positive in a child's experience up to a certain date and that has been withdrawn" (Winnicott, 1956a/1984, p. 124).

Winnicott then went on to differentiate between such deprivation and "privation"—a distinction that, as I have already said, Bowlby does not make. Privation denotes for Winnicott not just an actual, physical absence, but the non-experience of "something good". So Winnicott is claiming that the antisocial individual differs from the psychotic or psychopathic in that his behaviour expresses—and protests at—a loss of something once sensed as good and needful. Hence for him the importance of discerning the element of hope behind the antisocial manifestations of the delinquent.

If one accepts the validity of the distinction Winnicott makes between privation and deprivation—and there is, indeed, merit in it—then it is at least arguable that on such terms Bowlby's "affectionless characters" could be said to suffer from privation, not deprivation. In which case, paradoxically, they would appear not to be displaying "the antisocial tendency" that Winnicott is treating in his paper, which, by definition, is always the result of—experienced—deprivation. Either that, or else Winnicott is being too sweeping in his claim that the antisocial tendency and hope are as intimately connected as he claims. For some antisocial individuals—namely, the "affectionless thieves"—do not express hope through their delinquent behaviour, only indifference or despair.

As far as the two protagonists are concerned, the difference in outlook or emphasis between them over this issue was never properly articulated, still less resolved. By the time Winnicott began to propound his new formulations about the antisocial tendency, Bowlby's principal focus of research had moved away from the topic of delinquency to the wider question of separation and attachment. Consequently, continuing dialogue or debate over the meaning and aetiology of the delinquent act seems not to have taken place. What is more, Winnicott's twin submissions in his 1956 paper—namely, that delinquency bespeaks deprivation rather than privation, and that the antisocial act is bound up with the expression of hope—went virtually unchallenged within the psychoanalytic community, possibly because he had appeared to link his own views with those earlier propounded by Bowlby as if they were a mere extension of them. As for the latter, his views about the correlation between delinquency and deprivation were by then taken almost as standard and incontrovertible by his analytic colleagues. They may not have shared his interest in the subject, or even thought that it was a proper object of serious psychoanalytic research, but they did accept that what Bowlby had to say on the matter of delinquency was correct and soundly based.

Nevertheless one person, though not herself a psychoanalyst, did recognize a divergence between their two positions and attempted to reconcile them. Moreover, in doing so, she also succeeded in developing further the dynamic understanding of the deprived, delinquent child. This was Barbara Dockar-Drysdale, founder of the Mulberry Bush School. In 1953 she introduced the term *frozen child* as an alternative to Bowlby's affectionless character. While not referring explicitly to Bowlby's 1946 monograph, she used epithets strongly reminiscent of those used by him to describe "affectionless characters": frozen children were manipulative, destructive, ruthless, disavowing any sense of guilt, and apparently indifferent to others (Dockar-Drysdale, 1953/1993, p. 9). In another paper a few years later, she explained her preference for the epithet "frozen" in terms of hopefulness: "'affectionless' sounds final, but a thaw can follow a frost" (Dockar-Drysdale, 1958/1993, p. 17). In her Glossary she defined the frozen child as one "who has early been broken off, rather than separated, from the mother" (p. 157). Such an individual—unlike, for instance, the "false-self child"—has *not* had the "experience of something good that has then been withdrawn", in Winnicott's terms. In short, he suffers from privation rather than deprivation.

It is to be noted that with Dockar-Drysdale, the element of hope is located not in the antisocial child, but in the care-giving adult. He or she has to carry the expectation of a different outcome or prospect for the child that the latter cannot carry, until the child has sufficiently "thawed" as to be able to sense for himself the possibility of a new beginning. I believe that this was a much more plausible proposition than Winnicott's original claim about the hopefulness of the antisocial child being expressed through his delinquent activity. Significantly, when Winnicott was later invited by Dockar-Drysdale to provide a preface to her first collection of papers, he picked out the term "frozen child" for particular approbation:

> "*Affectionless child*" has proved to be a useful clinical description, but the term *frozen child* gives us the defence organization that has value to the child in that it brings invulnerability, an idea which carries with it the idea of potential suffering. [Winnicott, 1968c, p. ix]

Nevertheless despite Dockar-Drysdale's contribution, Winnicott still continued in later years to insist that the antisocial tendency is linked inherently with deprivation and that "environmental disturbances distorting the emotional development of the baby do not produce the antisocial tendency, but distortions of the personality which result in illnesses of the psychotic type" (Winnicott, 1968b/1986, pp. 91–92).

The social dimension of delinquency

Possibly Winnicott's persistence in proclaiming the essential hopefulness underlying the antisocial act stemmed from the implications of a second important theme developed in his 1956 paper—namely that "the antisocial tendency compels the environment to be important" (Winnicott, 1956a/1984, p. 122). The environment referred to here is not primarily the maternal or familial environment, but the public environment, society. Winnicott's view is that the antisocial delinquent youngster actually provokes—unconsciously intends—the world of adults to take notice of his deprivation. As he had put it ten years earlier, in his address to a group of Magistrates: "The antisocial child is merely looking a little farther afield, looking to society instead of his own family or school to provide the stability he needs if he is to pass through the early and quite essential stages of his emotional growth" (Winnicott, 1946b/1984, p. 116). This is rather different from Bowlby's perspective, who argued that society needed to attend to the social problem of the delinquent by demonstrating concern on his behalf, not in the least implying that the delinquent himself insisted on such concern.

Once more one may discern here a recurrent difference of outlook and emphasis. Bowlby shows himself as not only the scientist but also the socially committed, politically aware spokesman and advocate. For him society, through its instruments of government, is the potential provider and support, particularly of its most needy citizens. From his university days on he was and remained a committed Socialist, and he regarded the advent of the Welfare State, and in particular the advent of the National Health Service, as an unalloyed blessing. Winnicott, on the other hand, was more reserved in his attitude, at least towards some aspects of these developments in government-sponsored social welfare. With his independent West Country Methodist background, he was suspicious of signs of encroaching regimentation and control on the part of government departments over the practice of doctors and therapists. He even wrote a hectoring letter to his fellow Liberal, Lord Beveridge, in which he demanded: "How can I reconcile my admiration of your new work on behalf of our democratic value, and my hatred of you because of your irresponsible suggestions in respect of doctors?" (Winnicott, 1946a/1987, p. 8).

Nevertheless, both a new situation and a new opportunity presented themselves in the immediate post-war period. As I have argued elsewhere (Reeves, 2001, 2002), evacuation and its aftermath confronted the British Government for the first time with a sense of what nowadays might be called "its duty of care" towards its citizens—a sense of responsibility for welfare that found clear expression in the foundation of the Welfare State, but in essence went far wider in its implications. Bowlby and Winnicott both recognized and tried to capitalize on this burgeoning sense of the participant function of Government in mental health, having both seen at first hand the benefits for the physical health of children of national public health measures, particularly inoculation, that had been instituted between the wars. Yet the model of participation envisaged was different. For Bowlby the responsibility in the social sphere was for government initiatives first and foremost to promote and safeguard the functioning family. The relationship was to be administratively supportive. For Winnicott, on the other hand, the relationship of society—he was less fond of referring to "government"—to the family was to be interactively supportive, "facilitative" in the way that good-enough parents were towards their growing child: above all, non-intrusive. Particularly in the case of the antisocial tendency—which, Winnicott was fond of insisting was a part of normality—society had to constitute the "object" which was non-subjective, "the Outside World" towards and on which the young person needs to act and react as a third element in a triangle encompassing himself and his immediate family.

Both men were listened to and taken seriously by Government during the immediate post-war years, since each was felt to be speaking in an idiom that administrators could understand. And at that time Government was surer about the problems, actual and anticipated, in regard to the nation's children, than about the way to solve them. Bowlby and Winnicott had proved themselves. Both had palpably contributed to making the wartime evacuation process less damaging and socially divisive than it might otherwise have been. It is difficult still to judge to what extent Bowlby's admonitions, first in his monograph *Forty-Four Juvenile Thieves* (1946), and later in his widely circulated WHO Report, contributed to a "mother's-place-is-in-the home" culture during the 1950s or whether this culture was mainly due to economic factors and the experience of full employment. Undoubtedly the immediate post-war period appears, in retrospect, to have been one of notable social harmony in Britain, quite different from the aftermath of the First World War. And for this Bowlby perhaps deserves some measure of credit. As for Winnicott, his positive contribution in the sphere of post-war social policy lay probably in the saving of numerous residential facilities for disturbed and deprived youngsters from risk of closure. It is doubtful whether his beliefs about the hopefulness of the antisocial youngster and of the need for society willingly to accept and endure the pain and punishment of the young person's natural aggression were ever given much credence among politicians or magistrates. Nor do these concepts seem to have significantly penetrated the teaching and training of social workers, in spite of the fact that Winnicott, along with his wife Clare, kept up an unremitting routine of lecturing and supervision at the London School of Economics and elsewhere during the last two and a half decades of his life (Kanter, 2004b). His theories about the importance of transitional objects, opportunities for creativity, and of the need for substitute care to be personally centred, became widely accepted. But his thoughts about the antisocial tendency were largely ignored.

By the 1960s, other voices were being listened to by Government, voices that challenged some of the underlying presumptions of both men concerning the centrality of the family unit, and of the mother's role within it. The rise of feminism, the need for a more flexible workforce, and the economic attractions for women of earning a wage, together with the relative social emancipation this afforded, all conspired with the concurrent social fragmentation of the nuclear family to render their work seemingly outmoded. In the process Bowlby and Winnicott became once again increasingly viewed as a pair: joint upholders of a former and now less desirable status quo. History, when unconsidered, distorts. This chapter has set out to show that although to some extent the two men sang the same tune, they were never quite in unison.

Notes

1. While Winnicott's series of BBC radio broadcasts both during and after the War have become well known through later publication in book form, Bowlby shorter series in 1948 has been largely forgotten.

2. According to van Dijken (1998), who had access to some of Bowlby's private correspondence, Edward Glover, writing on behalf of the Training Committee at the Institute of Psychoanalysis, had taken exception to Bowlby's preparedness, while still an Associate member, to treat an adult patient privately by "psychotherapy" but "using psychoanalytic techniques"—i.e. less than the 5-times-weekly norm—claiming that doing so contravened the permitted practice of those not yet fully qualified. Bowlby's opinion was that the patient was not in a position to undertake full analysis. It is not certain whether or not Bowlby heeded Glover's warning.

3. Notwithstanding Bowlby's reservations about removing young children from their home environment, the author has had sight of referral letters written by Bowlby in the late 1940s from the Department for Children and Parents to the Mulberry Bush School, a residential therapeutic unit in Oxfordshire that had only recently opened.

CHAPTER THREE

Reflections on Donald Winnicott and John Bowlby

Bruce Hauptman

These reflections delve deep into the recesses of my memory: thirty-five years ago. Some elements are as fresh to me as if they had happened hours or days ago: they have that sort of power and clarity of experience, "imprinted" on my brain. Others have been mulled over, reviewed, lectured about, influenced by new ideas, experiences and discussions, and, most important, clinical applications, successes, and failures. Those perhaps suffer from hindsight revisionism, a form of natural distortion that occurs when an amalgam of original and new elements contends for place in one's memory, leaving an admixture, possibly or hopefully made richer by the infusion of rethinking and reformulating, producing a richer ideological compost. The attempt to put into practice what I learned and assimilated so long ago has stood the test of time. It is upon that footing—hopefully a reasonably solid one—that I comment here and offer my humble observations about my experience with these two respected and important figures.

I was first drawn to the writings of Donald Winnicott during my residency in general psychiatry in the mid-1960s. Sol Nichtern—a paediatrician-turned-psychoanalyst, one of my supervisors at Hillside Hospital in Queens, New York—spoke with great enthusiasm and admiration about a book, *Through Paediatrics to Psychoanalysis*

(Winnicott, 1958). He knew I was interested in working with children, and he advised me to spend time studying in England because of the breadth and richness of writing that was coming from such centres as Tavistock and Hampstead, and because he was finding writings by Anna Freud (1945), Winnicott (1945a, 1957a, 1957b, 1958), and W. R. Bion of particular clinical usefulness. Nichtern was a clinician who was able, through his own eclectic training and experience, to impart interest and excitement about clinical work, rather than emphasizing research and theory, which, by its nature, was removed from clinical encounters.

I completed my general psychiatry training in 1967 and was summarily drafted into the US Navy at the height of the Viet Nam era. I spent two years in Chicago running a recruit evaluation unit as my primary responsibility. It sensitized me to the complexity of diagnostic issues as well as prognosis, needing to make quick decisions regarding the disposition of new recruits who often exhibited emotional issues. Wartime forged different structures and needs and at times accelerated learning and innovation, as one learned reading Bion and Winnicott and Bowlby. This experience amplified my desire to go to England, and I spent considerable time during those two years arranging for grant moneys and getting accepted as a Senior Registrar at the Tavistock Adolescent Unit, then under Derek Miller's direction (Miller, 1969, 1973, 1983).

The year in England, plus numerous subsequent trips back to seminars and conferences, was extremely important for me professionally. I had an opportunity to be exposed to and study with several groups of psychoanalysts, many of whom were barely known in the United States. John Bowlby and his colleagues, and Arthur Hyatt-Williams at the Tavistock, exposed me, respectively, to attachment theory and Kleinian psychoanalytic theory and practice (Segal, 1973). Bowlby (1970a, 1970b, 1973, 1979, 1980, 1981), the Robertsons (Robertson, 1962; Robertson & Robertson, 1989), and Murray Parkes (1972; Parkes, Stevenson-Hinde, & Marris, 1991) lectured on various aspects of the abject consequences that befell children reared away from their primary caregivers. With references to Karl Popper's philosophy (1963, 1965), Niko Tinbergen's studies in ethology (1951, 1958), Harlow's primate studies (1958), Mary Ainsworth's attachment research protocols (Ainsworth, Blehar, Waters, & Wall, 1978), James and Joyce Robertson's extraordinary cinematography (Robertson,

1962; Robertson & Robertson, 1989), and John Bowlby's own early WHO monographs and articles (1940, 1944, 1951, 1953, 1958a, 1958b, 1966) regarding the clinical consequences of children being removed from their mothers leading to delinquent development or severe disorders of relationships and affectional development, I found myself immersed in what appeared as a treasure trove of "data" from a respected authority whose entire professional life at the time that I met him was immersed in the science of attachment.

Early on in my year in London I was invited to attend a seminar by the author of *Through Paediatrics to Psychoanalysis* (Winnicott, 1958) that, I was told, would focus on a new book Winnicott was writing about squiggles (Winnicott, 1971d). My mentor in New York had introduced me to squiggles, and I found this new projective/therapeutic technique fascinating as a way of learning about the fantasy life of children as well as communicating with and treating them.

I found myself in an educational environment that exceeded my expectations.

John Bowlby, during my year at the Tavistock (Dicks, 1969), was personally helpful and always available to assist me with administrative problems. In fact he was of great help to me after I returned to Boston and needed his support in getting credit for my year at the Tavistock towards sitting for Board Exams in Child Psychiatry. I was impressed with how he had developed a curriculum that was dominated by the various aspects of teaching attachment theory. The Robertsons captured our attention with their dramatic *cinema vérité* depiction of devastating moments in the lives of a small number of young children who were removed from their mothers for one reason or another. The films were intense and highly emotional and created an atmosphere where one could scarcely question what seemed to be the inevitable impact of separation: an indelible pathological impact upon the emotional state of these children as captured on the screen. Murray Parkes (1972) related issues of the impact of bereavement upon adults who had lost a close relationship: disbelief, numbing, protest, anger, despair, detachment—an emotional cascade with a predictable development that paralleled events in the young child, although with different ultimate outcomes due to the adults' maturity. John Bowlby himself focused on well-wrought presentation of others' work, a collection of research methodology from humans (Mary Ainsworth: Ainsworth, Blehar, Waters, & Wall, 1978), animals

(Harlow, 1958; Tinbergen, 1951, 1958), feedback theory, and philosophy of science (Popper, 1963, 1965, 1972). The curriculum at the Tavistock was mostly aimed at documenting his life's work. Clinical material seemed to have little place or relevance here.

Dr Bowlby himself seemed little interested in clinical material. Questions posed by students that might raise questions regarding attachment theory were "parked". Parking of queries became a shorthand to those of us in the seminars that we had inadvertently stumbled onto an area that he did not wish to open up: whether or not it was a question regarding the validity or applicability of attachment theory, we quickly understood that any questions other than requests for clarification were quite unwelcome, and that we were to sit back and be recipients of knowledge and information.

This approach to science, as well as the promulgation of theory that would serve as a basis for explanation of clinical events and thus offer particular help in dealing with patients, was unfortunate. I found myself "shutting down" once I understood the basic ideas. The basis for providing good family experience for the developing infant and child seemed clear and quite rational. The horrors of institutional child rearing were well known on both sides of the Atlantic in regards to mortality and morbidity statistics. The attachment paradigm was interesting to me, especially the predictive nature of Mary Ainsworth's clinical experiments: it seemed to validate Winnicott's clever and simple paediatric examination paradigm laid out in the article I had read in *Collected Papers* on the "Observation of Infants in a Set Situation" (1941a). In that article, anxiety, or lack of, in a one-year-old was being assessed with a technique that, with remarkable simplicity and sophistication, opened the door for attention to potential trouble as well as possibilities for intervention.

The lack of ability to question Dr Bowlby was worrisome to me. It was as if I questioned a religious person on some aspect of his practice and was being met with suspicion as to *my* motive for raising the question, rather than a sincere attempt to better understand or question some aspect of a theory . . . a theory is a theory, not a fact or belief. I eventually stopped asking questions, and when each of the three volumes of *Attachment and Loss* came out, I perused them with limited interest: not that they did not have some useful information, but that as works that could be translated into clinical practice, they were of limited value to me in my work.

Winnicott, on the other hand, provided a constant stream of evocative questions, ideas, insights, and reflections. I found myself eagerly awaiting each of the Tuesday evening meetings at his home; I would not allow anything to get in the way of attending them. The underlying theme of the meetings was a presentation of cases from a book he was preparing: *Therapeutic Consultations in Child Psychiatry* (1971d). Each week brought discussions of success or failure. It did not matter if the technique failed with a particular child. What mattered was that one felt oneself part of an ongoing process—an exploration seeking knowledge. This seemed more real in terms of attempts to understand human nature than Bowlby's "science". It is interesting that Winnicott would gravitate to Gillespie's *The Edge of Objectivity* (1960). The foreword by James Clerk Maxwell in his 1871 Inaugural lecture as Professor of Experimental Physics at the University of Cambridge highlights the difference between these two men—Bowlby and Winnicott—when he says that "the history of Science is not restricted to the enumeration of successful investigations. It has to tell of unsuccessful inquiries, and to explain why some of the ablest men have failed to find the key of knowledge" (Gillespie, 1960).

One Tuesday evening, someone in the group raised the issue that since Bowlby had just lectured us regarding the "fact" that a young infant did not attach until six or eight months, how did that fit with Winnicott's writings on primitive emotional development or, for that matter, Melanie Klein's writings on earliest infant experience? We seemed to have found a flaw in Bowlby's theory, or at least a serious question. Winnicott listened politely and attentively. He said he would put off discussing the issue that night but would, at our next Tuesday meeting, invite a colleague of his to join us for a discussion of the issue, and she would present some material.

The next Tuesday we were greeted by Winnicott and a middle-aged woman, who announced that she had little to do with children: however, her area of expertise was with horses. She proceeded to present material around the birthing of foals and how, almost instantly upon birth, there was obvious recognition by the newborn foal of its mother, and father. While not questioning Bowlby's theories about human development, theories that were heavily influenced by animal observation, especially in primates, Winnicott had offered a "suggestion" of competing possibilities: to whit, there is much we don't know about, and, thus, don't try to draw universal conclusions from limited data and conjecture—a powerful and gracefully delivered lesson. The lesson was to be respectful of theories but not wedded to them to the point of making clinical judgements and decisions based on them. The seminar raised more questions than it answered, and that, in my opinion was what Winnicott's aim was: to make you think. In all of his writings I find a resistance to develop a global theory of the human condition.

It is noteworthy to me that the closest to a unified theory that Winnicott came to present is found in *Human Nature*, which was not published in Winnicott's lifetime but posthumously and was perhaps never intended for publication by him because he recognized its incompleteness.

This brings to mind reading the philosopher W. V. Quine (1936). In an essay entitled "Truth by Convention", Quine writes: "the less a science has advanced, the more its terminology tends to rest on an uncritical assumption of mutual understanding. With increase of rigor this basis is replaced piecemeal by the introduction of definitions" Quine (1936/2004, p. 1). What about the definition of the concept of "separation"? Both Bowlby and Winnicott rely heavily on the term. When Bowlby speaks of separation, it is inevitably to focus on the potential for dysfunction. Others use the term more broadly, with less pathological connotation. The term, as originally derived, connotes "the birth of the self". This is not a determinant of developmental psychopathology but, rather, a developmental statement, for better or worse. Winnicott seems aware of the broader aspects of separation in introducing the separation paradigm with the birth of a foal.

Winnicott's openness, his lively mind, and dedication to his work was constantly refreshing. Another example I can cite comes from a lecture of his that I attended. The lecture was given to a group of psychiatrists. During the discussion, a clinician in the audience described working with a ten-year-old child. He had worked with the child for an extended period of time, and sessions were becoming less and less productive. At one point the boy turned to the clinician and said, "it's time for a dream". The implication seemed to be that the boy would describe a dream. Winnicott turned to the clinician and said, "Well, did you tell him one? I always keep a few dreams around for such a moment." The implication was that the child needed to hear something from the clinician before he could continue, something that would address how the clinician was responding to the child, so the child would know if he was being heard and understood. The understanding that the child was seeking could come from the clinician's dream material. It would reveal something of the clinician's state of being. Knowing that, and knowing that it was safe, the child could continue and perhaps reach a more meaningful place in his relationship with the clinician and, hence, in his own self-understanding and integration. This corresponds to Winnicott's discussion (1967b) of the mother's face as a mirror for the child: when the child looks at the mother, ideally the child sees himself (1969e). The mother serves as a holding environment, a reflection, so that the child can further integrate himself. This example also illustrates the function of the "Squiggle game", a deceptively simple game that allows for complex communication between the child patient and therapist, rapid access to deep emotional levels, which are often precluded because of the child's anxiety in communicating with this unknown person, the therapist (1971d). As with the dream and the "Squiggle game", the child patient has a need to know that the clinician is a safe person, as adjudged by some reflections from the clinician's own fantasy life. Then, and only then, can the child proceed and feel the safety and security of the therapeutic "holding environment" (Winnicott, 1986a).

It has been many years now since my sojourn in London. Since that year I have returned a number of times for meetings and seminars. During my year in London I was fortunate in being able to visit several Winnicottian-influenced education establishments: George Lyward's school for delinquents (Bridgeland,1971, pp. 161–167; 1987; Burn, 1953; Lyward, 1958), David Wills' school (Bridgeland, 1971, pp.161–167; 1987), Otto Shaw's The Red Hill School (Bridgeland, 1971, pp.161–167; 1987; Shaw, 1969), The Cotswold Community (Balbernie, 1966, 1971; Rice, 1968), and the school with which Barbara Dockar-Drysdale was involved, the Mulberry Bush School (Dockar-Drysdale, 1953, 1958, 1991, 1993).

Visiting these programmes had a profound impact on me: a direct and vital application of Winnicott's work to educational/therapeutic environments. The idea that the intervention of a group of people properly trained and supported who were not the child's parents or actual parent substitutes but were capable of taking on the essentials of a parental role could provide a pattern of consistent loving care, management, control, education, and therapy, one that the child's own parents had earlier been unable to provide because of the complexity of the child's needs or severity of the child's manifest disturbance, enabling the therapeutic process to unfold that was efficacious in a way that other forms of treatment were not—that is, realization of therapy through a child's living and specialized school environment, medical and special educational provisions, supporting the parents, and integrating all aspects of intervention, hence creating a holding environment: a heavily therapeutic one, but a holding environment nevertheless.

Those three programmes carried the stamp of Winnicott's thinking.

After my exposure to Winnicott and Bowlby and my opportunity to see several therapeutic programmes in England operating with rich strains of Winnicottian ideas giving guidance, direction, and support, I returned to Boston and was immediately struck by the paucity of therapeutic programmes for young children. In fact, in the early 1970s the numbers of young children seen at the several centres in Boston with which I had contact were few.

The Community Therapeutic Day School

In 1973, shortly after I finished my child psychiatric training at the Massachusetts Mental Health Center and Boston Children's Hospital, I wrote for a grant to the National Institute of Mental Health to start a therapeutic school for young children. I was excited with the prospect and used my visits to schools in England as prototypes for the sort of therapeutic/educational programme I had in mind. Visions of Winnicott's lectures and writings streamed through my mind: the idea of a holding environment: not a hospital, with its sterile medical facade, but, rather, more like a progressive school, a therapeutic milieu that took account of a wide range of disturbed/disordered children. It was to bring to bear a wide range of therapies and embrace concepts of the holding environment, the diagnostic and therapeutic significance of theories of privation and deprivation, in terms of when to attend to the environmental provision and when to study and treat aspects of the child that he/she was born with and which constituted a formidable barrier to development. Some issues of privation were seen in neurologically vested developmental conditions as well as physically rooted learning disabilities. Deprivation was seen in children whose families and communities had started off all right but had then failed them. Psychoanalytically oriented psychotherapies dealt with the children's reactions both to their environment and to their biological conditions and the manner of abnormal developmental twists that carried them through life. Issues of deprivation often necessitated measures to strengthen the family, if that was possible, or to find an alternative. Issues of privation would need attention to specific disabilities via appropriate therapies. In 1974, while at Harvard, I was given the opportunity to set up a school for young children with serious psychiatric and neurological conditions—children with psychosis, autism, serious behavioural disorders, children with psychosomatic conditions, severe learning disabilities, and schizophrenia, post-traumatic stress disorders, and even disorders of attachment. We established The Community Therapeutic Day School with a grant from the National Institute of Mental Health, under the auspices of the Boston Children's Hospital and the Massachusetts Mental Health Center. The School is now approaching 30 years of age.

Many of Winnicott's papers were used to teach staff a way of conceptualizing the child's condition, as well as helping a family deal with their child's atypicality and/or distress. Winnicott's language gives parents as well as clinicians powerful tools to see their children and to become partners in their children's treatment and education. The "good-enough mother", with its implications of a certain "lack of perfection", is vital. One does one's best and, with certain children, realizes one's limitations because of the intensity of the child's needs. Papers on "The Use of an Object" (1971c) and "Transitional Objects" (1951c) provide important insights into the evolution of relationships from earliest emotional development through to the development of the self (Winnicott, 1948b, 1958, 1960b, 1963c, 1965d, 1970b) and give an appreciation of how relationships facilitate and are the essence of how emotional development takes place. The role of the mother's face as a mirror to the child is stressed (Winnicott, 1967b): What does the child see when looking at the mother if not itself? (1969e, 1971c). And if not itself, what is ailing in the relationship that the child needs to attend to the mother's needs before it can be taken care of? (Winnicott, 1935, 1953a, 1959b, 1960b). And, of course, we read and think about Winnicott's extraordinary article for assessing the nature of health in a one-year-old child: "Observation of Infants in a Set Situation" (1941a; Jackson, 1996). This simple but elegant paediatric evaluation of child and mother–child relationships goes to the nature of attachment as well as the health in a relationship—or the lack of it—and thus captures the state of early emotional development in the young child. Papers like "Hate in the Countertransference" (1947), the use of squiggles to capture the state of playfulness and health of older children (1968e, 1968f, 1971c, 1971d) and to tap into their dreams, Winnicott's perception of hope in "The Antisocial Tendency" (1956a), all of these works (1988b, 1971c, 1988a) form a bedrock of ideas on which the Community Therapeutic Day School operates (Winnicott, 1968c). As it enters its 30th year, it has a staff of almost 40, serving 30 children in the day programme and an additional 60 children supported heavily in state school. The children in the programme range from age three to twelve. They may attend the school for a year or two, or eight or nine, depending on their needs and the rate of progress towards understanding their needs as well as the needs of their families. Some children can return to mainstream school, and occasionally a child needs a residential treatment programme to continue the treatment process.

What Winnicott's legacy has provided is a rich collection of ideas and concepts, ways of thinking about child health and pathology, ways of providing intensive care and treatment for those children and families, as well as keeping oneself healthy and supported in the process so that the work can go on as long as necessary.

Winnicott's humility in the face of difficult problems was rare and refreshing. I remember sitting through his discussions from the book *Therapeutic Consultations in Child Psychiatry* (1971d), which he was writing at the time, where he was describing his use of the "Squiggle game" for therapeutic and diagnostic purposes, and his ability to talk about his failures (1965d) as well as successes. One learns from both and sometimes with more clarity from a failure, as it allows one, with humility, to see a misunderstanding or misconception that rendered one unable successfully to carry forward a programme or treatment for a child—hopefully not to make the same error again.

Just as each of the English schools that I visited some 35 years ago carried the mark of the people who had set them up, so the Community Therapeutic Day School carries its mark too. Each of these programmes is highly individual: what ties them together is a respect and appreciation for Winnicott's way of thinking, his way of getting others to think, supported by ideas that he had carried to a certain point, and was turning over to us the task of carrying the ideas further or, even proving them wrong or partially flawed in the process. That was all part of his way of application of scientific methodology applied to the study of human nature, a study that could only be viewed as works in progress.

Winnicott's writings and principles sustain it with a philosophic underpinning, acknowledging the school as a holding environment. The school adds therapeutic modalities largely unavailable in Winnicott's time, including a range of special educational techniques to ameliorate learning disabilities, occupational and physical therapy services, speech, language, reading, and communication remediation, psychopharmacological intervention, as well as neurological interventions utilizing advanced imaging and electroencephalographic techniques. The importance of Winnicott's substantial body of work supports therapists in understanding and working with the children. Winnicott's openness, encouraging others to think, creativity, and his writings, which suggest, but do not dictate, ways of conceptualizing and working with difficult life problems have been "metabolized" by me and by those with whom I work. They provide a way of thinking about human nature, without dictating its boundaries, but by establishing ways to work with children and their families that offer hope.

Editorial afterword

The ethos of the thriving therapeutic community school for children that Bruce Hauptman describes is a tribute to Winnicott's influence. Joel Kanter (2004b) has drawn attention to the significant way in which Clare Britton and Donald Winnicott influenced each other, and Clare's stature in the field of social work. When it comes to case management, education, and residential community treatment, the Winnicotts' ideas were useful to many workers, including Harold Bridger (1985; Amado, 1995; Fees, 1999, 2002; Trist & Murray, 1999), R. D. Laing and colleagues at The Arbors, Josephine Lomax-Simpson and the Messenger House Trust homes and groups (Fees, 1998), the Cassell Hospital therapeutic community established by Tom Main (1983, 1989), Peper Harrow for disturbed adolescents (Rose, 1990a,

1990b), and the Cotswold Community (Balbernie, 1966, 1971) "which derives much inspiration from Donald Winnicott" (Rayner, 1990). Aside from Derek Miller, who freely used what he had learned from Winnicott and David Wills in developing adolescent in-patient and day-patient psychiatry in Michigan and Illinois and whose work has been influential in that field world-wide (Miller, 1969, 1973, 1983), in the United Kingdom, child and adolescent psychiatrist Tom Pitt-Aikens, who attended Winnicott's Squiggle Seminars, used Winnicott's principles in inpatient psychiatric practice. So did Mary Ellis, consultant psychiatrist to Feltham Borstal for assessment of adolescent offenders: she attended both the groups I ran for doctors and for senior medical and other staff in HM Prisons services (Issroff, 1974). The Winnicotts' notions, observations, and ideas about practice permeate the working of various therapeutic communities. Christopher Reeves has written about the contribution of psychodynamic theory to therapeutic education in a residential setting (1983, 1990) and the necessary conjunction of Winnicott and Barbara Dockar-Drysdale who established the Mulberry Bush School and was constantly in communication with Winnicott (Dockar-Drysdale, 1953, 1958, 1968, 1980, 1991, 1993; Fees, 1995; Reeves, 2001, 2002). George Lyward's school for highly gifted social misfits deemed "educationally unfit" adolescents was another special community important to Winnicott, and vice versa (Bridgeland, 1971; Burn, 1953; Lyward, 1958). Lyward showed me a card he had received from Winnicott—up the edge was scribbled: "important to me to know you're there".

Kanter (2004b) draws attention to the fact that most of Winnicott's publications were addressed to non-psychoanalytic audiences, but are quoted in the psychoanalytic literature. Many psychoanalysts appear not to realize the enormous influence the Winnicotts have had outside the world of psychoanalysis. Clare Winnicott's independent contribution, both at the Home Office and at the London School of Economics (LSE), is highly regarded by her many themselves influential old students. Donald Winnicott lectured at the LSE on Kay McDougall's Course for Mental Health and to educationalists and social work trainees, as well as succeeding in sharing his ideas with the general public who listened to his BBC broadcasts. An important facet to understanding the scope of Winnicott's commitment to the environmental factor in development and therapy is what was learned during the war. Winnicott was influenced by visits to Q-camps/Hawkspur, and he paid tribute to David Wills (1941) for revealing educational aspects of therapy and management to him (Winnicott 1970d).

Bruce Hauptman's personal tribute demonstrates how Winnicott's legacy affects The Community Therapeutic School in Lexington, Massachusetts. This establishment is related to the communities mentioned that undertake environmental therapy and "containment" work; its remit extends, however, to dealing with an ill and developmentally handicapped population that present medical, educational, and behavioural challenges. The community school is also a child psychiatric clinic that functions as a day-hospital unit for children, combining neuro-psychiatric, medical, and psychodynamic assessment and short- and long-term care and treatment. In the United Kingdom Winnicott's ideas are not as well known, nor are they applied in child and adolescent psychiatric units as in the model Hauptman describes and the experiences of the various community schools mentioned suggest they should be.

CHAPTER FOUR

Bowlby and Winnicott: differences, ideas, influences

Judith Issroff

Few would disagree that Winnicott and Bowlby were perhaps the two most influential pioneering British child psychiatrists and psychoanalysts of the past century, although technically Winnicott was a community paediatrician, not a psychiatrist, and Bowlby had worked in a residential school and been a teacher who had read psychology prior to taking his medical degree. Without aspiring to comprehensive or in-depth considerations of the broad scope of their work and its developments, because its range was great, this chapter touches on a number of topics and looks in greater detail at their respective attitudes, styles, links to others, mutual provocations, differences, and influences.

Contributions and interests

Bowlby and Winnicott were among the first to recognize that human infants enter the world predisposed to participating in social interaction. Their work addressed both healthy "securely attached" development with its consequent reflection in the inner world and the ravages caused by neglect, deprivation, and insensitive parenting. They showed how these early experiences pave the way for understanding a developing dependent infant's and child's absolute need for continuity of "good-enough" care (Bowlby, 1940, 1953; Winnicott, 1945a, 1945b, 1945c, 1949d, 1967b, 1984, 1986b, 1987a, 1988a, 1988b). Accordingly, they traced the adverse developmental consequences of loss of appropriate personal environmental provision, trauma, and mourning.

Bowlby's focus was on the way actual life experience became internalized and affected the inner world in communication patterns (Bowlby, 1991), rather than on the fantasy life elaborated. While Winnicott never ignored the actual influence of the environment at any stage of life and was, on the contrary, involved in exploring ways in which it could be made use of as a means of containment and management to effect therapeutic changes if possible, his prime interest was in the way the inner world engages with and thereby is affected by external events. He was endlessly fascinated by the elaboration and play of conscious fantasy and unconscious inferred phantasy in all areas of his implicit metapsychological structures (Issroff, 2001), whether they were derived from internal bodily activities and interacting introjected objects (selfobjects) or from outer-world stimuli. Winnicott regarded an individual only as part of a community of others (Reeves, 2004). This is demonstrable in his favourite diagrams, his constant pictures of Janus-faced circles, enclosed and enclosing, representing spheres in Brownian movement, containing, intersecting and overlapping with, and rebounding off others, like the individual within the family, within the group, within society, within the world. His approach reveals an intuitive understanding of molecular energetic resonance, chaos theory (Gleick, 1987), and quantum physics (Bütz, 1998; Gribben, 1984; Spruiell, 1993; Zohar & Marshall, 1994, 2000). Winnicott's ambitions were in line with those of contemporary physicists in search of a theory of everything (TOE) (Gribben, 1998; Wilbur, 2001). There is an interesting parallel between Winnicott's thought and that of Amit Goswami (1995), physicist and Eastern philosopher, who argues cogently and convincingly as a scientist for what he terms "monistic idealism"—the way in which it is consciousness itself that brings physical reality into being. The viewpoints are similar, and the very different ways in which they arrive at this conclusion complement each other.

As previously mentioned, along with their other notable contributions, Bowlby and Winnicott laid the foundations for preventive psychiatry, for primary mental health care, and towards understanding human development with an emphasis on health. Personality and social disorder, psychosomatic problems, and actual psycho-socio-spiritual functional breakdown were not absent from their attention, particularly Winnicott's (e.g. Winnicott, 1961b, 1963c, 1964c, 1969a). He was also preoccupied with philosophical problems related to the nature and construction of reality in all its paradoxes and contradictions. He sought his data everywhere. His manifold interests are revealed in Harry Karnac's compilation of his works (Abram 1996; Rodman, 2003; Winnicott, 1996) and in the forthcoming Routledge edition of Winnicott's collected works that Jan Abram is editing, but I hope this will contribute to an appreciation of how they extended during his lifetime beyond his publications.

Definition of attachment theory

Bowlby (1977) defined attachment theory as a way of understanding the propensity of human beings to make strong emotional bonds to particular others, and of explaining the many forms of distress and personality disturbance that occur after separation and loss. The threat and experience of separation cause a sequence of anxiety, protest (anger), despair (depression), and, finally, emotional detachment. The concepts are essentially concerned with explaining why human beings tend to make strong, selective, and enduring bonds and how discontinuity—to link to Winnicott's terminology—creates emotional pain and consequent psychopathology. Bowlby always strove to explain clinical observations, but also to achieve greater coherence and accuracy in correlating observations made in both clinical and empirical settings (Diamond & Marrone, 2003, pp. 1–12). Bowlby's publications are listed by Holmes (1983, pp. 228–243).

Asocial behaviour

Both men made pioneering contributions towards our understanding of delinquency—addressed by Christopher Reeves in chapter 2. From their work derive ideas about the prevention, management, and the possibility of treatment in certain cases where there has been a good-enough beginning, so that, as Winnicott pointed out, the aetiology lies in deprivation rather than privation. In this way both contributed to the field of forensic psychiatry (Pfäfflin & Adshead, 2003): Bowlby in his important study of the "frozen" affectionless, unempathic characters who have suffered privation in "Forty-Four Juvenile Thieves" (1944), Winnicott (1968b) in perceiving theft as a sign of hope in deprivation and the delinquent act as having a signal function that requires an appropriate response if future recidivism and distortion of character is to be avoided.

Kahr (1996a, 1996b, 2001a, 2001b, 2003, 2004b) has eloquently and enthusiastically spelt out his appreciation of Winnicott's contributions, their extent and importance, and edited the first book of an intended series devoted to Winnicott's work and its influence in relation to the field of forensic psychiatry (Kahr, 2001a).

Winnicott's distinction between psychoanalysis proper, psychotherapeutic interventions, and management of cases

Psychoanalysis proper—sessions five times a week directed towards facilitating the emergence and inspection of subjective phenomena—was, for Winnicott, equated with "doing as much as possible" (1971c). At times this might be augmented by arranging for a suitable supportive environment (Winnicott & Britton, 1947), or a planned regression, or treatment mainly managed by a parent at home (e.g. 1965a; or *The Piggle*, 1977). Winnicott was a practitioner dedicated to attempting to help those whom he encountered to manage and ameliorate their personal predicaments. So he also did what he called "as little as possible", exemplified in a therapeutic consultation in child psychiatry (Winnicott, 1971d), or by something as commonsensical as arranging to facilitate communication between different services to bring about a semblance of integrated support and care when he responded to a letter in a newspaper; or when he sent an imprisoned youngster authentic Buddhist wisdom texts because such texts had proved themselves useful traditionally over thousands of years (George Allyn, personal communication). Had he lived longer, according to Clare Winnicott (1982), then perhaps many more cases might have been published that demonstrate this not infrequently efficient, effective, and economical way of working in child psychiatry. This is also my personal experience in the "right" case where the child's environment can welcome and support change rather than re-traumatize. Technically I regard such interventions as "psycho-operative" in their depth-plumbing and often sustained ameliorative impact (Issroff, unpublished casebook). There is evidence that Winnicott planned another course of case presentations in a letter to Josephine Lomax-Simpson in which he apologizes to her, saying that there were already twenty participants and he could not deal with a larger group in his home (letter in the PETT archives). These illustrative case presentations showed how Winnicott derived his theories and demonstrated his remarkable technique and gifts. Had he lived, I am confident that there would have been further such series of presentations and publications.

The impact of Winnicott's war-time work with Clare Britton on his ideas about therapeutic efficacy of case management—another area of applied psychoanalysis—cannot be underestimated. The way he viewed this demonstrates how comprehensive a view he took of the importance of education, social work, and the child in a specific environment. These aspects all overlapped with his applied psychoanalytic therapeutic interventions using informed, supported, and understanding case management in residential situations. Winnicott said: "For me watching [Wills] work was one of the early educational knocks which made me understand that there is something about psychotherapy which is not to be described in terms of making the right interpretation at the right moment" (Winnicott, 1970d, in his Memorial Lecture to the Association of Workers for Maladjusted Children honouring therapeutic environment–educationalist David Wills, 1941, with whom he had worked during the war).

Relationship to official British psychoanalysis

At a time when the psychoanalytic emphasis was on intra-psychic imputed structures and their functioning as perceived in the analytic situation, both Bowlby and Winnicott questioned accepted doctrines. They both took for granted that the outer world influenced the inner, and vice versa: Sutherland (1983) has succinctly articulated that "philosophy for the helping professions". Marrone (1998) notes that Sutherland lived in the Bowlby household as one of "the tribe" after the

Second World War. He and Bowlby worked together in establishing and developing the Tavistock Institute and Clinic (Dicks, 1969; Trist & Murray, 1999) so it is not surprising that Bowlby shared this interactional inner–outer model and philosophy for the caring professionals.

Bowlby's "feisty independence", as Grosskurth termed it, was in evidence already in 1935, "when, as a promising young man, then in analysis with Riviere, he was invited to participate in the discussion following Klein's paper: 'A Contribution to the Psychogenesis of Manic-Depressive States'" (Grosskurth, 1986, p. 402) He reported that several patients he had seen at the Maudsley Hospital who were suffering from depression had experienced a recent bereavement. This, he thought, supplemented the idea Klein was advancing. She and Riviere thought otherwise. As Bowlby recalled to Phyllis Grosskurth:

> At that time I had not realized that my interest in real-life experiences and situations was so alien to the Kleinian outlook, on the contrary, I believed my ideas were compatible with theirs. Looking back on the years 1935–1939, I think I was reluctant to recognize the divergence. That became crystal clear only after the war, especially as I became increasingly shocked by their intransigent attitudes. [Grosskurth, 1986, p. 402]

While the originality of Bowlby and Winnicott was never in doubt, its relevance to accepted doctrine and practice was questioned. Their recognition of the significance of environmental factors throughout life generated ambivalence and distrust in the British Psychoanalytical Society. Despite this, at some stage or another both men occupied responsible high official positions there and in other professional capacities (King, 2004).

Bowlby was on good terms with many of his critics. He was Training Secretary from 1944 to 1947 and Deputy-President under Winnicott from 1957 to 1961. He had helped to keep the Society together after the war, when the split between followers of Anna Freud and Melanie Klein—the Controversial Discussions—threatened to tear the organization apart (King & Steiner, 1991; Karen, 1994, p. 115). Bowlby was aware that "in the natural course of things" he "might well have been elected the next president", but "it had become clear there would be too much opposition and, with my agreement, those supporting me did not propose me" (Smuts, 1977). After the criticism—not only by Winnicott—with which his papers were received, Bowlby stopped attending meetings of the Society. "Unread, uncited, and unseen, he became the non-person of psychoanalysis and was lost to his peers for the better part of the next three decades" (Karen, 1994, p. 115). Upset by the hostile reception Bowlby received at meetings, David Malan rose to his defence (Malan, 1990). Afterwards he went away "somewhat terrified about the consequences of being so passionate a supporter of John's position" and wondered whether he would be "excommunicated" at once. Interestingly, along with John Bowlby, Winnicott also wrote to thank Malan.

Darwin foresaw the hullabaloo his discoveries and theories would bring about and withheld publication for as long as he could. Richard Bowlby describes his father, on the other hand, as naive: never anticipating the rejection and criticism to the point of enmity that his reformulations of psychoanalytic theory generated.

Winnicott was pre-eminently a conciliator. As Padel pointed out:

> Winnicott did perhaps more than anybody else to keep the British Society together at a time in the 1950s when antagonisms between the followers of Anna Freud and those of Melanie Klein were still most bitter. Thanks for his profound respect for Freud and his discoveries, and thanks to his deep affection for Melanie Klein [whom he welcomed for putting the closeness of child and mother before any other feature of human experience], Winnicott did so much to reconcile the two wings of the British Society that, after his first presidency, senior officers of the Society could at last be chosen from those two wings, and not, as over the previous 15 years, only from the middle group. Winnicott was a natural peace-maker. [Padel, 2001, p. 269]

But was it only that?

Rycroft referred to Winnicott as "a crypto-prima donna" (1992, p. 4) and discussed his "self-ablation" (1985; Roazen, 2004). Why was Winnicott so reticent—as was Rycroft—in not making explicit what he surely recognized as his own originality? Was it part of his almost over-tolerance of human behaviour? Or was it his inability to deal with aggression in the negative sense in his attempts to perceive creative, positive ways of evaluating destructiveness?

In the larger world of psychoanalysis some psychoanalysts might still quibble with Kahr's assertion that Bowlby's concepts have "now become cornerstones of the psychoanalytical process, both nationally and internationally" (2004a, p. xvi). Nonetheless, the work of Bowlby and those in his tradition is widely valued and much discussed. The Adult Attachment Interview[1]—which, interestingly, has never been published by the authors (Marrone, personal communication; Steele, 2002)—is used increasingly in assessment interviews and in work on troubled mother–infant relationships, for instance, in the mother–infant department of the Anna Freud Centre and by Acquarone (2005). Attachment theory has been developed to enable us to understand how attachment and nonverbal communication link brain and body, not just within individuals but between them (Pally, 1998; Schore, 1994, 2004a, 2004b; Thomson Salo, 2001; Trevarthen, 1998). The significance of Bowlby's work on the importance of attachment, relationality, separation, loss, and mourning is acknowledged and respected.[2] Notably, as formidable and original a practitioner and observer-critic of psychoanalysis as Charles Rycroft was an early admirer of Bowlby's work on *Attachment and Loss* (1970a, 1970b, 1973, 1979, 1980, 1981). Although he was greatly influenced by Winnicott's thought (Arden, 2004, p. 59), Rycroft considered Bowlby's contributions among the most significant to psychoanalysis during his lifetime. Once he remarked to Arden that

> he and Bowlby were ploughing the same furrow from opposite ends. Bowlby was right to stress the importance of an intimate continuous relationship for the infant's well-being, but he was unconcerned with symbolism and imagination. They both understood that only satisfaction of instinctual needs in infancy can lead to a love of reality. [Arden, 2004, p. 66]

There are psychoanalysts who still regard Bowlby's contributions as too deviant to be useful psychoanalytically. Winnicott's are often not altogether understood, but, rightly, he is regarded as more mainstream, and as enormously important by many. However, there are still a great many analysts to whom his work remains as if inaccessible—I think mainly through unfamiliarity and/or dogmatic adherence to some other "total" theoretical approach system within which a particular analyst was trained. Theories and habitual practice might at times require modification were Winnicott to be assimilated/accommodated properly in all the complexities, ramifications, and subtleties of his approach to psychoanalysis and psychotherapy in theory and practice.

It is not easy to "translate" Winnicott into a different language without distorting or missing his intent (Ogden, 2001). His style is succinct and exact even when sometimes apparently obscure to someone who is not ready to grasp the complex and even contradictory nuances at that stage. For instance, as already mentioned, when he presented his late discoveries, many distinguished American and British analysts did not comprehend his complex and subtle views on how the sense of reliable external and internal realities is established, and his distinction between ordinary object relating and "object use" (Winnicott, 1968a, 1968h; see also Davis, 1992). His overlapping but distinctive concepts of the sense of continuity-of-being, the "female element present in all men and women and children" (Issroff, 2001) and the "true self", also confuse many—especially those who themselves function with what he termed "false" "split-off intellectual functioning" (Winnicott, 1959a, 1960b, 1971c, 1989a, pp. 127, 158, 195, 214, 565), or hyper-use of "male" (ego) personality elements (1971c), or have saved themselves from anxiety by a "flight to sanity" (1949b/1989, p. 547). This is not the place to enter into theoretical exposition, but once one has the clinical experience of a context in which these ideas make sense, they are most useful. Part of the problem is that all of Winnicott's work needs to be read as a whole (Issroff, 1983, 2001), and, as he ruefully said in 1965 to Paul Roazen (2002), many analysts appeared to have read only his paper about transitional objects (1951c). To this I would add, from my reading of the first book of papers devoted to the subject (Grolnik, Barkin, & Münsterberger, 1978), that in so doing many totally missed the emphasis on the subjective meaning of such a specially endowed "*quelque chose*", as he referred to his own in a letter to Clare Winnicott in 1946 (C. Winnicott, 1978): they objectified it entirely—one of his criticisms of Bowlby's approach. However, I think that now, four decades later, many more analysts have read considerably more of Winnicott's work, whether in the original or in some translation that may or may not be good enough—the Hebrew I read certainly would compound any reader's misperceptions. As Bettelheim (1983) has pointed out, the problem exists also with our understanding of Freud in translation.

It is not only the theories and languages we use that affect our comprehension (Deri, 1984): assimilation–accommodation of an idea also depends on personal developmental receptivity. Those who follow a dogma will always perceive what their limited or fixed theoretical lenses enable them to discern and nothing outside that range. This Bowlby well grasped when he advised us to have as many theories as possible at our disposal in order to examine clinical data.

Both Bowlby and Winnicott were devoted to using language that anyone could comprehend. Bowlby used to say that if one wrote anything, one should always try to say it in ways that "any intelligent eight-year-old could understand"; he said that one should always think of to whom one wanted to say what, why, where, and how before one began to say it. Winnicott's chosen aim was to make analytic thoughts available to the general public, "so that who runs may read"—as he put it in his letter to his sister Violet when he was trying to explain to her why he was choosing this field (Winnicott, 1987, Letter 1, 19 November 1919, p. 2). Winnicott's still steadily selling wartime radio broadcasts and lectures to the public on a variety of topics—compiled in *The Child, The Family, and The Outside World*—are masterpieces of sophisticated communications to the ordinary public (Winnicott, 1957c, 1964a, 1984, 1986b, 1987a), as is *Talking to Parents* (1993) and *Home Is Where We Start From* (1986b). When reading his work, it is useful to note whom he was addressing, as he discussed similar topics in many different settings, developing his variations on ideas and themes (Issroff, 1983). However, there are areas of his work that are far from easy to comprehend on first reading. In this context we may recall Pontalis' sage comment: "When a psychoanalyst will not let go of what could seem to others as either a confused empirical intuition or a superfluous theoretical refinement, he is often handing over the essentials of his thinking" (1981, p. 144). As Winnicott worried away at several primary themes for years, gradually the theories he was putting to the test in clinical experiences and then clarifying, sometimes almost poetically, do become clearer. One can see this well demonstrated in, say, Hernandez and Giannakoulas' excellent paper (2001) about "the construction of potential space" and in several other works that appreciatively analyse the immense significance and revolutionary psychoanalytic cogence of his contributions (such as Bonaminio, 2001; Bonaminio & Di Renzo,

2005; Eigen, 1991, 1996; Fromm & Smith, 1989; Davis, 1985, 1992; Giannakoulas, 2005; Ogden, 1999, 2001; Taylor Robinson, 2005).

Language mattered to Winnicott. He used language creatively and poetically, arriving at theoretical clarifications, as, for instance, when he chose to use the word "ruth" as opposed to "ruthless" when refining his disagreements with Melanie Klein and discussing the development of the sense of concern and guilt (Winnicott, 1958), or in drawing a distinction between "fantasy" and "fantasying" (Fielding, 1988; discussed further below). In a letter to Melanie Klein he insisted that "the only way language will be kept alive is by people presenting what they discover in their own language" (Winnicott, 1987b, Letter 25).

Both Winnicott and Bowlby have been subjected to not infrequent misreadings. Karen (1994, p. 117) suggests that this was widespread "because much was circulated by word of mouth or picked up from inaccurate secondary sources". The radically different use of language and novelty of concept removed their ideas from usual psychoanalytic parlance and made demands on readers that could disturb their habitual ways of understanding. Thus their writing was perceived as too foreign for easy comprehension or unclear within circles who believed in a particular ideational focus.

On reading Winnicott and Bowlby

When reading Winnicott it is useful to try to deduce the question he had in mind as the starting point for any particular piece of writing. Sometimes this is not difficult: his title and opening remarks lead one along without effort. Occasionally his question is more like a Zen *koan*: not readily soluble by mere logic, but leading to a moment of almost revelatory insight or enlightenment when one eventually grasps what he was getting at, sometimes many years later—as when he left me thinking with a cryptic, "what about the creativity of salivation?" (Issroff, 1975 and 1993, are examples of what my delayed comprehension enabled me to grasp). Usually I find it helps to read him slowly, and repeatedly: if one has a degree of familiarity with the major questions with which he grappled, one is better able to pick out the variations on his themes. Ogden (2001) relishes and reads Winnicott aloud to his students.

Bowlby is always quite clear about the questions in his mind. His writing is admirably lucid and logical. He chose what he considered to be strategically most accessible to objective research as the question to examine within a cybernetics feedback loop-systems theory approach: he focused his attention on addressing affectional bonds, their nature, making, breaking, and the impact of loss. He did not study what he regarded as the "sexual behavioural system" (Southgate, 1990) or what Lichtenberg (1989) developed as "motivational systems" in his theorizing. Bowlby discarded Freud's original energy models, referring to them as "steam-kettle"–"pump" models.[3] However, in view of his advice to address data with as many theoretical models as possible in mind, I suspect he would agree that there is a place for both, and one does not discredit the other in our world of behaviours that have a circumscribed repertoire determined by many causes, similarly to the way symbolization processes condense the many strands of association and meaning in dreams. It is likely that there is a final common pathway we discern and can explain with various valid and complementary, conceptual explanatory metaphors. That these overlap is becoming evident in our understanding of, say, brain function (see simplified referenced summary in Zohar & Marshall, 2000). When Bowlby quite deliberately, after due consideration, "parked" a question, as a psychoanalyst he was aware that he left aside a great deal that he knew concerned his fellow psychoanalysts. But in his mind this was "a strategic decision", and by making it, he aimed at and succeeded in illuminating an extremely important—indeed, crucial—area. As he hoped it might, what he put forward did lead to sound investigation and has been highly fertile and fruitful in contributing to our increasingly "reliable" and "public knowledge" (Ziman, 1968, 1978, 2000).

The kinds of philosophical questions that preoccupied Winnicott—such as "How is it that the world becomes real and experienced as outside of psyche-soma?" or "How does the mind locate itself in the body and vice versa?" (e.g. Winnicott, 1971, 1988)—were not likely to have distracted the pragmatically chosen-task-focused Bowlby.

Bowlby attempted a radical reformulation of psychoanalytic theory; however, in the view of Winnicott and the majority of psychoanalysts at the time and today, in the process he apparently lost sight of many essential intrapsychic and interactional features of human beings in all their complexity.

Influences on Winnicott

Winnicott built on Freud and extended his ideas (Winnicott, 1989a, p. 499; see also Bertolini, Giannakoulas, Hernandez, & Molino, 2001; Issroff, 2002a; Green, 2000; Grolnik, 1990; Ogden, 1985, 1986, 1989, 1999; Roazen, 2002; and many others). Late in life Winnicott's constant bedside reading was Freud (Clare Winnicott, 1991). He commented: "I am somewhat addicted to [Freud's] footnotes and quotations which he perhaps allows to go further than he can go in terms of theory as it obtains at the time of his [Freud's] writing" (Winnicott, 1969f/1989, p. 244). Winnicott was referring at the time to what Freud had written in 1939. For instance, he said he felt that Freud himself "would welcome new work that makes sense" (p. 244) of footnote such as the one referring to Breasted's (1906) calling Amenhotep "the first individual in human history" (Freud, 1939a, p. 21) "in terms of a universal in the emotional development of the individual, namely the integrative tendency that can bring the individual to unit status" (Winnicott, 1969f/1989, p. 244). Winnicott's own theory, extending as it did to the preverbal and pre-unit-status phases of life, discussed this and exemplifies what I think Rycroft (1985) meant when he discerned Winnicott's "self-ablative" tendencies.

I do not think Winnicott would have minded me playing with this remark of his and suggesting an underlying narcissistic addictive involvement with himself as "footnote" to Freud. After all, one can play with the notion that he was one of Freud's psychoanalytical grandchildren via Strachey, his first analyst, so to speak.

Much of what Winnicott wrote was stimulated by, but diverges from, other psychoanalytic authors, not only Melanie Klein (Phillips, 1988). I have already pointed out that in some important and unacknowledged way Bowlby mystified Winnicott—his incomprehension of Bowlby's approach surely must have provoked and influenced his own thinking. He admitted that if he read something worth reading, then by the end of the first page he was excited enough to be writing something of his own—or, if not, he might fall asleep. During that sleep he might dream something and when interpreting his dream, he might discover something that would lead him to formulate new theory—as mentioned earlier (see Winnicott, 1963a; see also 1950 letter to Clare Winnicott in Winnicott, 1989a, pp. 16–17). Winnicott wrote:

> "Sleep"
> Let down your tap root
> to the centre of your soul
> Suck up the sap
> from the infinite source
> of your unconscious
> And
> Be evergreen.
>
> [Winnicott, 1989a, p. 17]

Winnicott appeared to be less dependent on the work of others than was Bowlby: he worked with his own observations, although always reacting to, elaborating on, and re-interpreting what he discovered and made a part of his own thinking.

Influences on Bowlby

Mary Ainsworth, ethology, Darwinism, and systems theory all affected Bowlby's thinking, and probably so did Fairbairn and the Hungarian school of psychoanalysis—but how much did Winnicott?

Bowlby relied greatly on research like that of Mary Ainsworth (Ainsworth, 1962, 1967, 1969, 1985a, 1985b, 1990; Ainsworth et al., 1978), who established the inter-connectedness between an adult's care-giving ability and quality of attention and attachment behaviour in adults and children (Egeland & Sroufe, 1981; Erickson, Sroufe, & Egeland, 1985; Sroufe, Waters, 1977; Steele, 2002), and a child's ability to explore from a secure base (Bowlby, 1973, 1979, 1980, 1981). This topic—of the need for proximity to the attachment figure when bonded securely, "as if on an invisible elastic string with limited range", as Bowlby used to remind us—was also addressed elsewhere in the psychoanalytic world: Michael Balint built on fellow Hungarian Imre Hermann's (1943) discussion of instinct theory in terms of tensions between clinging and exploratory drives. This work led Balint to distinguish two distinct personality types in ocnophils and philobats (Balint, 1952, 1959, 1968), stay-at-homers or explorers in relation to their secure attachment base. Balint was surely aware of Bowlby's work: at the time these ideas were being delineated, both men were on the staff—although in different departments—of the Tavistock Clinic and Institute of Human Relations School of Family Psychiatry and Community Mental Health. Bowlby never mentioned Balint's work to us, but it is unlikely that he would not have been aware of it. Was Bowlby aware of Hermann's ideas, I wonder? He knew and would not infrequently refer to the work with institutionalized infants of Rene Spitz (1945, 1946), which drew on Hermann's as well as Charlotte Bühler's tutelage (Karen, 1994, p. 92), for Spitz (1960) responded to a paper of Bowlby's.

Fairbairn (1952) was an object relations and interpersonal conceptual pioneer who saw biological drives as aspects of relational needs, and Bowlby must have been familiar with his views, especially because, as already mentioned, he and "Jock" Sutherland—who was analysed and influenced by Fairbairn—lived in the same household and were Tavistock colleagues until Sutherland (1980, 1983, 1990) left to establish the equivalent Scottish organization.

Developments from Bowlby's work

The annual John Bowlby memorial lectures established in 1994 under the auspices of the Centre for Attachment-based Psychoanalytic Psychotherapy (CAPP) have addressed various significant developments deriving from Bowlby's work, summarized by Laschinger, Purnell, Schwartz, White, and Wingfield (2004). They include important contributions from Colin Murray Parkes on bereavement and mourning (1972); the development by Molly Main of the Adult Attachment Interview (Main & Hesse, 1990; Main & Solomon, 1986; Main & Weston, 1981; Steele, 2002), used in the study of the unconscious processes that underlie the attachment behavioural patterns identified by Mary Ainsworth (1962, 1967, 1969, 1985d, 1985b; Ainsworth et al., 1978); and studies elaborated by Daniel Stern and his colleagues in the sphere of mother–infant interaction (Brazelton & Cramer, 1991; Bretherton, 1987; 1991; Stern, 1985, 2002) and in their relevance to psychoanalytic processes (Stern, 1998; Stern et al., 1998). Allan

Schore's most important integrative work in neuro-psychoanalysis, which demonstrates how the quality of attachment behaviour affects infant brain development and later personality qualities (Schore, 1994, 2001a, 2001b, 2004a, 2004b), also draws on Winnicott's ideas. Psychoanalyst Stephen Mitchell (1999; Mitchell & Aron, 1999) links attachment theory to other "relational matrix" psychoanalytic ideas that move away from drive theory; Peter Fonagy and Mary Target use attachment research and develop Bowlby's notions of internal working models into their concept of "mentalization" (Fonagy, 1999, 2000, 2001; Fonagy & Target, 1995, 1996; Fonagy, Target & Steele, 1997; Target & Fonagy, 1996); while Diamond and Marrone (2003) prefer a "reflective" feedback influence in their relational discussion. Sroufe and his colleagues in Minneapolis have carried out major studies, including longitudinal ones, in several areas (Sroufe, 1985; Sroufe, Carlson, Levy, Egeland, 1999; Sroufe & Fleeson, 1986; see also Grossman, Grossman, & Waters, 2005; Harris, 2004; Hopkins, 1990).

Echoing the work of transference–countertransference interactions pioneered by Ferenczi (1955) in psychoanalysis, Beebe and Lachmann (1998) have worked on the way the mutual non-verbal influence and regulation that develops in parent–infant interactions is reproduced in the adult therapeutic relationship. Daniel Stern's collegial Boston psychoanalytic group has also worked on this (Stern, 1998; Stern et al., 1998). In an attachment relational and trauma *context*, among others, Rothschild (2000), White (2004), Mollon (2004), and Orbach (2002) have turned their attention to the body in clinical practice.

Major differences in approach

While deeply involved with the complexities of inner world development and the way in which it engages with the outer world and vice versa, Winnicott distinguished both the area of potential space and the transitional areas (Hernandez & Giannakoulas, 2001) and he studied the way in which someone develops a capacity to make use of others: "use of an object", from "object relating"—that is, attachment behaviour, the major chosen area of Bowlby's attention. To me this seems very clear, yet Vicki Hamilton (1996a) has a fascinating and different understanding of Winnicott's (1971c, pp. 86–94; see also Davis, 1992) chapter on the topic. I think both our ways of working with this particular extremely important Winnicott contribution are valid and complementary. But I am inclined to a more simplistic view—especially on the basis of my clinical experience: the negative transference can be endured as a manifestation of object relating and transference attachment style. Only after the covert and overt transference attacks have been survived can an analysand/patient really make use of the analyst and analytic therapy (Issroff, 1979, in preparation-c).

As a trained psychoanalyst, Bowlby never altogether ignored the inner world, but he chose to try to reformulate aspects of psychoanalytic thinking in testable and refutable ways, thus turning his attention largely to the environmentally observable aspects of human behaviour. In this sense he was more of a primatologist, deeply influenced by ethology. Winnicott (1959b/1989, p. 429) said quite bluntly that "for the analyst the ethology contribution is *a dead end*" (emphasis in original). He liked ethology "because of what it tells us about animals". In contrast to Bowlby's deliberately focused work, Winnicott's thinking was far more complex, subtle, imaginative, wide-ranging, and flexible: "nothing short of everything" commanded his attention. Bowlby's ambitions and aspirations may have been quite as great, but their very nature limited his legacy—or did they, on the contrary, ensure recognition of its real merit? According to his son, Richard, Bowlby's wife Ursula used to say that if you touched or scratched him, you would find attachment theory running in his blood.

Example of how their ideas may be applied in understanding a group dynamic situation

As an example of how I "make use" of Winnicott's ideas, I would like to consider aggression in a group setting and Winnicott's "Use of an Object" theory (1968h). The group as a group, and each group member individually, has to find his or her way both to relate to and to make use of the leader and other members. This takes time and repeated testing of the extent to which destruction—in fantasy—can be withstood. Perhaps on another level this is necessary in order to build trust, and is also part of identity formation and of role differentiation in group dynamic terms. The ability to make positive personal use of significant people must be distinguished from inter-relating—cross-identification was the term Winnicott favoured—transferential projections onto and projective and introjective identifications with each other. In the light of his last major contribution (Winnicott, 1968h, 1971, pp. 86–94), "aggressive" attacks within the group, both on leader and on group individuals or factions, can be understood as part of the process of achieving a reliable and useful external object relationship (see also Groarke, 2003). With this understanding it may be far easier for a group leader, or an analyst, or a teacher in a classroom situation, to deal with the sometimes overt and difficult-to-handle hostility in a "fight–flight" group situation.

Winnicott's attitude towards "aggression" is completely different from a Kleinian approach (Segal, 1973), which might, for example, view such behaviour as a manifestation of envy. Winnicott's statement about this Kleinian concept, which he began to record in 1962, was only published in 1989, and so Segal (1973) was not able to take it into account (Winnicott, 1989a, pp. 447–464).

In Abraham's classical developmental level terms—conceived as a progression from oral incorporative–explorative, to urinary, to anal controlling, to genital developmental stages—aggression is often thought of in terms of anal sadistic attacks, or as genital-level Oedipal strivings. After traumatizing events, aggressive behaviour in a group or individual can also be understood in terms of reconstructive re-membering by repeating through re-enactment via identification with the aggressor or with role reversal (Anna Freud, 1945).

In terms of Bowlby's attachment, separation and loss theory (1973, 1979, 1988a), the expression of aggression could be viewed as an attempt to overcome feelings of helplessness in reaction to separation from an important attachment figure, whereas in terms of Mahler's theory, aggressive behaviour might be interpreted as strivings towards separation–individuation (Mahler, 1975); it might also be looked at in the light of Lichtenberg's (1989) motivational systems theory and distinguished from assertiveness, as Bowlby, too, insisted on a distinction.

I have mentioned these diverse attitudes towards dealing with manifestations of aggression in a group or individual setting in order to illustrate how and why I think Winnicott's almost optimistic way of viewing the expression of imaginative attacking behaviour can be understood. Making use of Winnicott's theory of object use to withstand the attacks of "negative transference", whether interpreted or merely understood, can enable the aggression to be borne and survived by a group therapist no less than in an individual setting.

There can be little argument about the novelty and potential usefulness of Winnicott's (1968h, 1971c, pp. 86–94, 1989d) observation that the more sophisticated ability to make use of an object is a later stage of development, which is not always achieved and which must be contrasted with the innate capacity of relating to (objective) others—which latter is studied and detailed in Bowlby's attachment theory (1973, 1979, 1988a). Group settings and group work provide excellent opportunities to observe these distinctions.

As psychoanalysts and scientists

Winnicott

Winnicott recognized the importance of recording and understanding complex and particular individual data from subjective and objective perspectives. His cautious attitude to broad statistical data may have originated in something similar to whatever led to his acknowledged horror of the mandala—

> a truly frightening thing for me because of its absolute failure to come to terms with destructiveness, and with chaos, disintegration, and the other madnesses. It is a defensive construct against that spontaneity which has destruction as its next door neighbour . . . an obsessional flight from disintegration. [1964d/1989, p. 491]

There are aspects of the way in which Winnicott reacted to Bowlby's style of focused work that make me wonder whether he held similar views, amounting to a real distaste for any systematic narrowing of focus that unavoidably over-simplifies the complexities of the individual human condition. "It is necessary that we remind ourselves that human nature is too complex for evaluation by the statistical method" (Winnicott, 1953b/1989, p. 424).

As we well know, our individual life experiences are singly and cumulatively at least as important as is our genetic endowment.

Garmezy (1992) has argued "The Case for the Single Case in Research"—illustrated par excellence by Winnicott, who often quotes his patients because his reference points and research domain are clinical concerns within the analytic setting. A model masterpiece of this kind was given in "Deductions Drawn from a Psycho-Therapeutic Interview with an Adolescent" (1964b): "just the picture of one girl" (p. 340). I quote from Winnicott's general opening remark: "A great deal can be got from an examination of adolescence as *a whole phenomenon. . . . If it be true that one cannot generalise from one case it is even more true that one cannot see the individual in a broad survey*" (p. 325, emphasis added). This point, too, could be perceived as aimed at the unnamed John Bowlby, along with others who rely on such statistically significant "evidence-based" samplings for accepting validity of data. Winnicott's subtle understanding of the inter-relationship of inner world's use of outer reality affected his attitude to observation, experimentation, and the "respectable" sciences to the unequivocal acceptance of which Bowlby aspired.

Bowlby himself was quite clear that if two adequately trained independent observers perceived something, that event or observation could be considered an "objective" reliable "fact". Nonetheless, unlike Winnicott, Bowlby did not consider the clinical situation as one from which reliable data could be obtained—reliable data for him were a sufficient statistical number of replicable, preferably predictable observations. In my view, Winnicott's integrity as an observer who repeatedly tested his own hypotheses and those of others in the clinical situation over many years of practice does point to a scientific attitude and basis for the generation of useful theory (Rustin, 2005; Ziman, 2000). Large statistical data have never been necessary for physicists, for instance, and I see no need to resist the evidence of but one observation when, in Popperian scientific formulations, but one refutation is sufficient, and "proof" of a theory is only to be stated in terms of probabilities. Michael Rustin criticizes Popper as a prescriptive philosophical legislator and thinks of psychoanalysis as not as unlike other sciences as people had imagined it to be. "The more complex the idea of science, and the more different kinds of science there are recognized to be, then the less abnormal and peculiar psychoanalysis has come to seem" (Rustin, 2004, p. 117).

Bowlby

> Bowlby was a nuts-and-bolts man. He liked hard data and researchable concepts.... He preferred to work... where facts were facts.... he was more wary of... where faulty and nonsensical notions, products of an overly active imagination, could gain credence and where disturbing feelings could not be easily warded off. [Karen, 1994, p. 110]

He rejected the death instinct—as did Winnicott, whose relationship to the notion was more complex (Davis, 1992; Issroff, 1979; Reeves, 1996). As mentioned previously, Bowlby also rejected drive theory, but

> Bowlby remained committed to psychoanalysis as a discipline that was concerned with certain questions—such as the role of the unconscious in emotional life, the meaning of dreams, and so on—he felt that Freud had asked many of the most important questions. But he argued that every other academic discipline is defined by its realm of interest, not by a particular theory that must be adhered to. [Bowlby, Figlio, & Young, 1986]

Mary Ainsworth (1990) worked with John Bowlby at the Tavistock for three years,

> at a crucial time when the ferment of his theoretical ideas was beginning to take the shape of what has become attachment theory. . . . He was dissatisfied with current psychoanalytic theory. It could not account adequately for observed facts concerning the responses of young children to separation from their mothers and to deprivation of maternal care. He was groping for a way to revive psychoanalytic theory. His clinical work had led him to a deep and abiding belief that the course of individual personality development is largely shaped by real life experiences. As a scientist he recognized that a good theory must not only make sense of data already observed, but also should be capable of guiding observations into new and profitable directions. It must then be open to extension, refinement, and/or revision in order to accommodate itself to the new data yielded by further exploration.
>
> Like Freud, Bowlby believed that psychoanalytic theory ought to be compatible with established branches of science. Whereas Freud chose the energy model of Helmholzian physics upon

which to base his theory, Bowlby chose biology and evolution theory, having hit upon a new branch of biological science—ethology—as a relevant starting point for his updating of psychoanalytic theory. It was a happy choice. Like all top-flight theorists Bowlby drew heavily upon the relevant accumulated knowledge of his day—not only upon psychoanalysis, ethology and evolution theory but also upon developmental psychology, cognitive psychology and systems theory. His genius lay in the way he put it all together. [Ainsworth, 1990, pp. 12–13]

It is Mary Ainsworth's conviction that "Bowlby's attachment theory began with a sudden flash of insight, sparked by ethology, that led to a scientific revolution, the understanding of personality development".

Winnicott

Winnicott explained his own approach when writing about Marion Milner's *On Not Being Able to Paint* (Milner as Joanna Field, 1951a). First he quoted Follett (1924):

> Concepts can never be presented to me merely, they must be knitted into the structure of my being, and this can only be done through my own activity. [Winnicott, 1951a/1989, p. 390]

He then singled out the theme of Milner's book, as

> to do with the subjective way of experiencing and the role of this in creative process. Thus the book is in one sense a plea for the recognition of subjectivity as having its own place and way of functioning, just as legitimate and as necessary as objectivity, but different. As applied to education, it is pointed out that subjectivity must be understood by teachers, otherwise the objectivity aimed at must be in danger of fatal distortion. . . .
> The concept of the role of subjectivity which emerges has two main aspects, one to do with illusion, the other with spontaneity. Both are connected with what [Marion Milner] calls the interplay of differences, out of which creativity proceeds, but if interplay is to be allowed in oneself one must be prepared for mental pain. . . . At a comparatively late stage of emotional development, what is familiar in psycho-analytic literature about unconscious conflicts between love and hate in interpersonal relationships is relevant,

and indeed this paved the way for all other statements. Such conflict involves the problem of the preservation of the loved object from hate and from erotic attacks (whether in fact or in fantasy) and creation is seen in this setting as an act of reparation. If one considers earlier stages in emotional development of the individual, one must use other language, such as the statement that magical creativity is an alternate to magical annihilation. [pp. 390–391]

Is this perhaps a statement relevant to the way he apportioned or ignored the work of others? Or behaved with his first wife—preserving her from hate and "erotic attacks"? (See Issroff, in preparation-a.)

Then he states a fundamental assertion of his own, well exemplified in every aspect of Winnicott himself:

If I understand [Marion Milner] aright she wishes to make a yet more fundamental statement about creativity. She wishes to say that it results from what is for her (and perhaps for everyone) the primary human predicament. This predicament arises out of the non-identity of what is conceived of and what is to be perceived. To the objective mind of another person seeing from outside, that which is outside an individual is never identical with what is inside that individual. [Winnicott, 1951a/1989, p. 391]

Here he states explicitly what he claims Marion implies:

But there can be, and must be, for health . . . a meeting place, an overlap, a stage of illusion, intoxication, transfiguration. In the arts this meeting place is pre-eminently found through the medium, that bit of the external world which takes the form of the inner conception. In painting, writing, music, etc., an individual may find islands of peace and so get momentary relief from the primary predicament of healthy human beings. [p. 391]

. . . wish-fulfilling illusion may be the essential basis for all true objectivity. If these moments of fusion of subject and object, inner and outer, are indeed more than islands of peace, then this fact has very great importance for education. For what is illusion when seen from outside is not best described as illusion when seen from inside; for that fusion which occurs when the object is felt to be one with the dream, as in falling in love with someone or something, is, when seen from inside, a psychic reality for which the word illusion is inappropriate. For this is the process by which the inner becomes actualised in external form and as such becomes the basis, not only of internal perception, but also of all true perception of environment. Thus perception itself is seen as a creative process. [pp. 391–392; cf. Goswami, 1995]

Following this theme through to posthumously published "Dreaming, Fantasying and Living" (*Playing and Reality*, 1971c, pp. 26–32), Winnicott provides material about the contrast between fantasy, fantasying, and dreaming in the realm of inner reality. In a patient he described, there was clearly

> an essential difference ... between fantasying and the alternatives of dreaming on the one hand and of real living and relating to real objects on the other. With unexpected clarity, dreaming and living have been seen to be of the same order, day-dreaming being of another order. Dream fits into object relating in the real world and living in the real world fits into the dream world in ways that are quite familiar. By contrast however, fantasying remains an isolated phenomenon, absorbing energy but not contributing-in either to dreaming or living. [Winnicott, 1971c, p. 26]

Fielding (1988, p. 9) points out how Winnicott redefined the word "fantasy" as opposed to "fantasying" and recognized that he used the word in quite an unusual way:

> Fantasy is not something the individual creates to deal with external reality's frustrations. This is only true of fantasying. Fantasy is more primary than reality, and the enrichment of fantasy with the world's riches depends on the experience of illusion. [Winnicott, 1945c/1958, p. 153]

Turner (2004, p. 134) discusses the history of illusion in Winnicott, Milner, and Rycroft. He quotes Virginia Woolf (from *Between the Acts*, 1945, p. 125): "Death, death, death, when illusion fails". It is likely that Bowlby's apparent dismissal of the realm of illusion most confounded Winnicott.

In his 1951 paper on transitional objects—a notion he developed from his dream about his *quelque-chose* doll about which he wrote to Clare Winnicott, as she mentions in her reminiscence (1978), Winnicott studied the substance of illusion. The paper was delivered to the British Psychoanalytical Society: Adam Phillips (1988, p. 119) regarded it as "quietly scandalous" with "coded message" when Winnicott stated,

> We can share a respect for *illusory experience* ... we may collect together and form a group on the basis of the similarity of our illusory experiences. This is a natural root of grouping among human beings. Yet it is a hall-mark of madness when an adult puts too powerful a claim on the credulity of others, forcing them to acknowledge a sharing of illusion that is not their own. [Winnicott, 1951c/1958, p. 231]

Axiomatic to Winnicott's thinking was the notion that every bodily experience was accompanied by a nascent unconscious imaginary or fantasy component, as is now, in the wake of newer brain imaging techniques, commonly accepted by neuroscientists (Winnicott, 1949b, 1988b). I do not think that Bowlby's "internal working models" hypothesis particularly considered this (on "internal representations" see Diamond and Marrone, 2003, chap. 4), but psychosomatic problems are part of his study of Darwin (Bowlby, 1992).

Winnicott talked about "the infinite richness that is subsumed in the word "fantasy". It not only allows for all degrees from conscious to unconscious but it also has room for the concept of an infinite series of fantasies co-existent and possibly dissimilar or opposite" (Winnicott, 1987b, Letter 158 to Donald Meltzer,). He says elsewhere:

> Fantasy means—to some people a manipulated affair rather like what a child's comic is to a child. But fantasy goes deep into the personal inner psychic reality.... It is all the time making the individual's actual experience rich and real to them. In this way everything under the sun can be found in the individual and the individual is able to feel the reality of whatever is actual and desirable. [Winnicott, "This Feminism", 1986c, p. 189].

> Whereas a great deal of dream and of feelings belonging to life are liable to be under repression, this is a different kind of thing from the inaccessibility of fantasizing ... which is associated with dissociation rather than repression. [Winnicott, 1986c, p. 189]

He came to perceive dreaming when awake as a defence against dreaming—of no symbolic value (1971a).

He reports his interpretation to his patient, saying "that fantasizing was a dead end. It had no poetic value. The corresponding dream however had poetry in it, that is to say, layer upon layer of meaning related to past, present and future and to inner and outer and always fundamentally about herself" (Winnicott, 1971c, p. 35), fantasizing perceived as the activity that "paralyses the ability to dream" (Fielding, 1988).

Contrast this subtlety and complexity of conception with Bowlby's language of object-seeking behaviour, inner working models, and plans. These examples of Winnicott's way of examining phenomena that are so very different in approach from Bowlby's are addressed with scholarly enthusiasm in many articles, such as, for example, by Bonaminio (2001), or Hernandez and Giannakoulas (2001), and by Madeleine Davis in "Destruction as an Achievement in the Work of Winnicott (1992), and "Winnicott and Object Relations" (1995), among others. Winnicott followed his mentor's, Lord Horder's, advice to listen, observe, and take notes—to the extent that when a Winnicott centre was set up in 1982 and Clare Winnicott was interviewed (C. Winnicott, 1982), she could report that a paediatrician informed her that his case notes—not the treatments—were still being used as models for teaching purposes half a century later.

In "Winnicott and the Spatula Game", Madeleine Davis (1993) discerns the seeds of many of his ideas—including in his understanding of the infant's stage of hesitation before handling the spatula—in relating fantasy to its effect on behaviour. She points out how astonishing it is that as a 27-year-old doctor who had just become a consultant in clinical medicine, Winnicott could make such creative use of the clinical situation that he found waiting for him in an extraordinary synthetic moment of creation when he recognized the way an infant behaved with the ordinary spatula as a sequence of behaviour. In this sequence he noted the healthy infants' slight hesitations when handling the tongue depressor while he talked with their mothers. From these observations he derived inferences that he tested clinically for decades and that he could turn into a clinical diagnostic tool (Jackson, 1996), and reliable data on which to build theoretical hypotheses, because they were repeatedly observed across a great number of cases. Note that this began in 1920—a decade before he encountered Melanie Klein. "To Winnicott, children who become disturbed, whether psychoneurotic, psychotic, psychosomatic, or antisocial, showed difficulties in their emotional development in infancy, even as babies" (Davis, 1995). His later theory developed in his detailed "Observation of Infants in a Set Situation" (Winnicott, 1941a), written when he was already at work and observing evacuated children and their hostel staff in Oxfordshire, where he saw the antisocial tendency expressed in full force (C. Winnicott, 1982; Winnicott & Britton, 1947). Surely this is the work of a practical clinician scientist (Rustin, 1997, 2003) documented in the best possible way?

Bowlby

Bowlby was more interested in intra-psychic processes than his detractors realize. While Winnicott's criticisms may have been at play in his mind without his consciously acknowledging them, Bowlby told Marrone (personal communication) that he developed and refined the concept of an internal working model while being in the multidisciplinary study group in Geneva, after contact with Piaget (Flavell, 1963). When Piaget created the School of Sciences at the University of Geneva in 1956, he attended some meetings at the WHO when Bowlby was there, so Piaget's influence on Bowlby should not be overlooked, any more than that the concept of internal working models is also firmly rooted in the psychoanalytic theory of representation, as Diamond points out (Diamond & Marrone, 2003, chap. 4; Jacobson, 1965; Tuttman, 1981). Not only did Bowlby develop the "internal working models" of self and other built on how a child experienced significant intimate people in life, but also what he called "defensive exclusion", and he explored aspects of repression and dissociation. Southgate (1990) has revealed that, in the latter years of his life, Bowlby was very supportive of and interested in ways of working with people who suffered from dissociative problems following massive trauma, including childhood sexual abuse.

But, as Karen comments: "if the inner world of Bowlby's child, buttressed as it was by research with lower animals, was more scientifically substantiated, it was less complex, less rich, less tormented and passionate than that conceived by some of his peers, especially the Kleinians" (1994, p. 112) and Winnicott, who was decidedly himself and not a Kleinian.

Were they important to each other?

While it is clear that Winnicott had reservations about Bowlby's approach, it is equally clear that Bowlby did appreciate Winnicott, while himself avoiding that kind of approach.

Winnicott's explicit criticism of Bowlby's work

While Bowlby, although he did not much cite him, was straightforward in his appreciation and admiration of Winnicott, this appears not to have been reciprocated. My last encounter with John Bowlby took place at the Tavistock Institute in his honorary retirement office near the library, the day before he went into hospital for his final operation. One of the things he said—recalled in my chapter 1—was: "You know, Winnicott was always of the greatest importance to me."

I do not know whether Winnicott himself knew this, or whether he reciprocated this respectful attitude, but when Winnicott opposed Bowlby's membership of the British Psychoanalytical Society, he was uncharacteristically forceful, ruthless, even hurtful during his attack on Bowlby's 1939 membership and later papers. I suspect this may well have influenced Bowlby to develop his concept of internal working models, for he always took everything Winnicott said as of deep significance.

I have also narrated the incident of Winnicott's action-criticism and feigned boredom at a lecture. Nonetheless, talking to the Association of Workers for Maladjusted Children in October 1970, towards the end of his life, Winnicott remarked that "John Bowlby has done more than one man's share of drawing the world's attention to the sacredness of the early holding situation and the extreme difficulties that belong to the work of those who try to mend it" (1970c/1984, p. 225–226). He went on to describe his further understanding, adding,

> It always has to be remembered that where the child is hopeless then the symptomatology is not very troublesome. It is when the child is hopeful that the symptoms begin to include stealing and violence and ultimate claims which it would be unreasonable to meet except in terms of the recovery of that which is lost which is the claim of the very small child on the parents. [Winnicott, 1970c/1984, pp. 225–226]

At the outbreak of war, Winnicott, and Bowlby, together with Emmanuel Miller, had written to the *British Medical Journal* about the evacuation of small children (Bowlby, Miller, & Winnicott, 1939; see also chapter 2).

Although he recognized that they were both making some similar and some different important statements when giving evidence to governmental commissions like that which resulted in the Curtis

Report (Kanter, 2004b; see also chapters 2, 5, and 6 herein) or to the World Health Organization, Winnicott was highly critical of Bowlby's work in private. He criticized the latter's membership paper in some detail (see criticism in Winnicott, 1959b; see also Karen, 1994; King, 2004) and was against his election to membership of the British Psychoanalytical Society. When he reviewed Bowlby's *Maternal Care and Mental Health* (1951), Winnicott voiced his reservations to a wider readership of interested professionals. He wrote: "The danger is that by forcing facts on a public that is not willing to suffer there may be reactions and counter-reactions and a new kind of muddle" (Winnicott, 1953b/1989, p. 426). Winnicott wrote directly to Bowlby in 1954 to express his concerns (Winnicott, 1987b, pp. 423–432). To Joan Riviere, who had also been Bowlby's analyst, Winnicott wrote on 21 June 1957: "It was certainly a very difficult paper to appreciate without at the same time giving away almost everything that has been fought for by Freud" (Rodman, 2003).

Anna Freud wrote to Winnicott that Bowlby "sacrifices most of the gains of the analytic theory, such as the libido theory, the principles of mental functioning (the pleasure principle), ego-psychology etc. with very little return". She supposed Bowlby was "put off by the antedating of complex mental events in the Kleinian psychology, but that is no real excuse for going too far in the other direction" (Rodman, 2003, p. 241). Nonetheless, she thought he was "too valuable to lose". She argued that Bowlby was too focused on environmental events in themselves—"as analysts we do not deal with happenings in the external world as such but with their representations in the mind" (A. Freud, 1960, p. 54). Bowlby's third paper on mourning, in *The Psycho-Analytic Study of The Child* (1960b), was published with the written criticisms of Anna Freud (1960), Max Schur (1960), and Rene Spitz (1960). As always, the Kleinians were extremely hostile and dismissive; as Karen puts it: "Klein's followers exhibited neither Anna Freud's frozen cordiality nor the gentlemanly restraint that Bowlby always maintained despite his obvious and sometimes disagreeable self-certainty" (Karen, 1994, p. 114).

When Bowlby read his paper "Grief and Mourning in Infancy" (1960b) to the British Psychoanalytical Society in 1959, Winnicott again delivered a detailed and lengthy critique, this time from the chair (Winnicott, 1959b). While he was careful to express his appreciation of Bowlby's advocacy for the avoidance of unnecessary breaks in the mother–infant relationship, Winnicott disliked the "propaganda element" that could lead to a "fashion in child care" and "the inevitable reactions which follow propaganda and over-conversion" (Winnicott, 1959b/1989, p. 427). He was very uneasy with regard to Bowlby's views about grief. Winnicott gave "a personal opinion" about how unsatisfactory he found Bowlby's chapter on theoretical problems (pp. 424–425). He hoped Bowlby would re-write it. He objected on the grounds that "only confusion can result in the minds of those who are new to psychology by a statement that some psychic machinery 'is the ego', especially as the word 'ego' is used variously by various groups of people". And he added that, to his mind, "there is a poverty of treatment in this theoretical chapter which lets the book down". Winnicott pointed out that "there are very complex internal factors that cannot be dealt with in a book like Bowlby's at all". He notes that although Bowlby mentions psychoanalysis, he has not quoted Freud in his bibliography and that "the unconscious is not ignored but is not brought to the fore" (p. 426). He

> feared that readers who are new to the subject [of deprivation and delinquency] will think that the antisocial child can be largely explained by the presence of a thinking difficulty, *in fact, the trouble is very much to do with affect, and to do with unconscious guilt and with such things as the fear of madness and fear of loss of identity and of contact with external reality*. [Winnicott, 1959b/1989, emphasis added]

If Bowlby "really maintains what he has written in this chapter, then [Winnicott] must express disagreement with him". But it is typical of Winnicott, who may, nonetheless, have been somewhat tongue-in-cheek, that he thought "that either he [Winnicott] had got hold of the wrong end of the stick or else Bowlby had slipped up on this chapter, which he will re-write" (p. 425). Did this remark provoke a response in the apparently self-confident John Bowlby?

Winnicott mentions the stages "of grief, of protest, and of the denial of grief and depression which hardens into the manic defence". For him, "the term 'manic defence' covers all the processes of the denial of mourning which is nevertheless retained as a theoretical depression" (p. 430; see also Winnicott, 1935). Winnicott states that Bowlby has not taken into account "the deeper effect of object loss or neglect of ego support" that he (Winnicott) has "stated in terms of the primitive emotional conditions", using the terms "loss of contact with external reality", "loss of relationship between psyche and soma", and "disintegration"—all post-traumatic dissociative phenomena in contemporary ICD–10 and DSM–IV terminology. He thinks that Bowlby has not been careful in the statement of his central thesis on which the whole of the rest of his paper depends—namely, Bowlby holds that loss of mother-figure habitually gives rise to the processes of mourning during the emotional development of infants at the stages before and during the gradual establishment of their capacity to mourn. For Winnicott, mourning implies emotional maturity and health: "mourning is an achievement" after "a long series of delicate mechanisms at the end of which the infant arrives at the capacity to mourn" (1959b/1989, p. 430). This ability is not to be taken for granted as being always there, as Bowlby implies.

Further, Winnicott predates what Bowlby has put forward to Melanie Klein's "discovery of the gradual transformation of grief into hardened indifference". He acknowledges his differences with Melanie Klein but says that "Bowlby makes me rally to her support, even if she doesn't need or want me", and he adds that he feels similarly about Anna Freud, because she "knew that babies separated from mothers at an early age were unable to achieve anything so normal as grief" (Winnicott, 1959b/1989, p. 428).

In addition, Winnicott was critical of Bowlby's apparent unawareness of

> the change-over from a relationship to a subjective object to a relationship to an object that is objectively perceived... This disillusionment process belongs to health, and it is not possible to refer to the infant's loss of object without referring to the stage of disillusionment, and to the positive or negative factors in the early stages of this process which depend on the capacity of the mother to give the baby the illusion without which disillusionment makes no sense. [Winnicott, 1959b/1989, p. 429]

> Bowlby has not seemed to leave room in his statement for symbolism and the establishment (in health) of objects which stand both for the self and for the mother [p. 431]

> During the period to which Bowlby makes special reference, six months to three to four years, the child is in the process of change-over from a subjective object to one that is objectively perceived [p. 432]

[This links] with the concept of the establishment of the reality principle.... It would be wrong to deduce that the subjective object can be lost with impunity.... It would appear that the subjective object of the first few months can be changed in the eyes of the onlooker and yet possibly not changed for the infant. ... the loss of the subjective object is a major disaster, something that belongs to the order of things which are described by the words "psychotic anxiety", or "the basic fault" of Balint's [1968] nomenclature, or a failure of ego-support during the time when the infant's ego only has strength because of reliable support from the mother-figure, etc. [p. 432]

Winnicott further asserted that, in "Grief and Mourning in Infancy",

Bowlby has signally failed to show how he applies his views of early infantile reflexes to the area of development represented by the film *A Two-Year-Old Goes to Hospital* [Robertson, 1962; Robertson & Robertson, 1989].... The complexity of two years is tremendous if we remember the whole elaboration of unconscious fantasy and unconscious conflict. [p. 429]

He is critical of Bowlby's

implication that there is a very simple object-loss phenomenon rather like the failure of a reflex because of the absence of stimulus.... Dr Bowlby is talking as if there were no such thing as fantasy in early infancy.... Unconscious conflict seems to have no place in Bowlby's psychology, and he seems to give no room for the concept of the object dying and reviving within the infant, that is to say in the psychic apparatus, that which is lodged by the healthy infant in the functioning body. As a consequence of these omissions there seems to be no place in Bowlby's psychology for a description of those infants who because of gross mismanagement in the very early stages do not get near to anything as healthy as the capacity to mourn and perhaps do not even become integrated at any stage. [pp. 431–432]

I have quoted extensively from these important notes published in 1989, almost two decades after Winnicott's death, because they enable us to understand the gulf between Winnicott's and Bowlby's psychoanalytic lives, and why Winnicott could not understand Bowlby, because, as he wrote tartly, "the matter which Bowlby is examining is so very much richer than he seems to suggest that I fear we may lose sight of all that reaction to loss may mean by getting engaged in some controversy about ravens or ducklings". It is probable that Winnicott never actually said the latter in public, for the editors note that Winnicott had pencil-marked "only extracts read actually" on the version from which this is quoted (pp. 426–427, fn 3).

In his 1953 review of Bowlby's *Maternal Care and Mental Health* (1951), Winnicott aligned himself with "those of us who are clinically minded and slightly scornful of figures" (1953b/1989, p. 423) because "we should remind ourselves that human nature is too complex for evaluation by the statistical method" (p. 424). "For the purpose of statistical enquiry simplifications have to be made, but no harm is done provided that there is a return to the complex from the simplified before the construction of new theory." Winnicott is wary because "statistics are valueless unless based on data which are beyond reproach, and indeed it is just these data which are so difficult to collect in our specialty".

Social workers who studied at the London School of Economics in the social work programme that was entirely the territory of Donald and Clare Winnicott spoke of learning about Bowlby's work straightforwardly and appreciatively from them. So whatever differences they may have had—at least in their roles as educators it is clear that without ambivalence they recognized that their respective ways of addressing the same problems were directed towards the same ends. Kahr (2004b) refers to correspondence between them that he has read as always congenial and collegial. And Pearl King's memoir (2004) does not highlight strife, whatever private feelings existed.

Yet while Winnicott refrained from attacking Bowlby in public except at the Psychoanalytic Society when he opposed Bowlby's membership paper, to Anna Freud he wrote: "I can't quite make out why it is that Bowlby's papers are building up in me a kind of revulsion although in fact he has been scrupulously fair to me in my writings" (letter in Cornell archives, quoted by Grosskurth, 1986, pp. 405–406). Perhaps he, too, felt that Bowlby "took the poetry out of analysis", as Arthur Hyatt Williams put it, and he probably agreed with Susan Isaacs Elmhurst that "Bowlby is too mechanistic. He treats humans as though they were animals, which is just what they aren't" (Grosskurth, 1986, p. 406). In fact, Winnicott's criticism was formulated decisively and clearly. In view of the above quotations, there is no need to speculate as to why Winnicott's ways and works took so little from Bowlby's work. Rather, I wonder why Bowlby seems equally to have been so little influenced by Winnicott—if he actually did mean it when he took leave of me with his spontaneous, apparently sincere confession that "Winnicott was always of the greatest significance" for him, and, more so, if Richard Bowlby could say to me with confidence that his father always felt that they were singing the same tune but that Winnicott knew "intuitively", in Bowlby's estimation, what his father, John Bowlby, had to amass evidence to discover. Bowlby might have been influenced by Winnicott's unpublished 1939 opposition to his membership paper: remarks made at the time may have played a significant role in influencing Bowlby's conceptual development of "internal working models". After all, he used the terms "intra-psychic" and "extra-psychic", remained a psychoanalyst, identified himself as one still in 1988, and is likely to have developed his "inner working model" terminology because he did, of course, recognize the specificity of the human primate.

Brett Kahr (personal communication, 2004) has told me that he has seen Winnicott's personal copy of Bowlby's WHO *Maternal Care and Mental Health* (1951) in the New York archives and had been amused by the frequently scribbled "taken from me", "mine", annotations where Winnicott believed Bowlby had used his ideas without citing him. This unreferenced pre-emptive use of the ideas of others is one of Winnicott's own self-confessed habitual "faults" (1967c/1989, pp. 569–582), but it is likely to have contributed to his aforementioned highly critical 1959 discussion of Bowlby's "Grief and Mourning in Infancy" (Winnicott, 1959b), and in his critical review of Bowlby's *Maternal Care and Mental Health* (Winnicott, 1953b). Nonetheless, Winnicott did appreciate "the specific trend in Dr Bowlby which makes him drive on towards a translation of the psycho-analytic findings of the past half-century into social action" (1953b/1989, p. 423).

Is one more important than the other?

This is an idle question, because both men are important—but some have raised this question. I consider it difficult to decide which of these towering figures has had and will continue to have the greater influence on the development of their common and respective fields.

The contribution of each in its way is immense, and the ramifications of their respective contributions continue to reverberate and stimulate diverse avenues of fertile exploration in many fields.

Peter Rudnytsky (1991) and others consider Winnicott to be the most important psychoanalyst since Freud, while Charles Rycroft viewed Bowlby's contributions as "the most important advances in psychoanalysis during [his/Rycroft's] professional lifetime" (1992, p. 4). Rycroft considered *Attachment and Loss* (Bowlby, 1970a, 1970b, 1973, 1977, 1980) to be Bowlby's *magnum opus*, and he explained his reasons in *Psychoanalysis and Beyond* (Rycroft, 1985). Peter Fonagy's (2001) appraisal and overview of Bowlby's work related to psychoanalysis is ample testimony to Bowlby's importance: "Attachment theory is almost unique among psychoanalytic theories in bridging the gap between general psychology and clinical psychodynamic theory" (Fonagy, 2001, p. 5). Diamond and Marrone (2003) locate the work within wider contexts with admirable clarity. Early attachment experiences lead to the development of thinking, referred to as "metacognitive knowledge". Fonagy and his co-workers (Fonagy, 2001; Fonagy & Target, 1996, 1997; Fonagy, Target, Steele, 1997; Target & Fonagy, 1996) linked this idea to the concept of "mentalization". Diamond and Marrone (2003) prefer the concept of "reflective function" rather than "mentalization" and explain why (in chapter 7 of their book).

Commenting on "Bowlby and Kohut: Where Science and Humanism Meet" (Maratos, 1986), Bowlby "warmly welcomed ... efforts to build bridges ... in a field still plagued by inbred schools of thought which fail to communicate with each other" (Bowlby 1988b, pp. 81–82).

Himself a prodigious interdisciplinary integrator, Allan Schore (1994, 2001a, 2001b, 2004) drew attention to the way in which Bowlby integrated the biological and psychological realms. Schore asserts:

> Perhaps the most important scientist of the late twentieth century to apply an interdisciplinary perspective to the understanding of how early developmental processes influence later mental health was John Bowlby. Over two decades ago he asserted that attachment theory can frame specific hypotheses that relate early family experiences to different forms of psychiatric disorders, including neurophysiological changes that accompany these disturbances of mental health. It is thus no coincidence that attachment theory, the

dominant theoretical model of development in contemporary psychology, psychoanalysis, and psychiatry, is the most powerful current source of hypotheses about infant mental health. [Schore, 2001a, p. 13]

The flourishing and productive fields of research into the centrality of affect attunement and regulation, along with its connection to brain and personality development, resilience, and attachment disorders and their ramifications for health or social malfunction and psychopathology, are solid evidence of Bowlby's wise choice of focus for his major life work. Winnicott's work also emphasized these matters, while the number of works in the wide array of fields involved in the reaches of human thought that make use of some insight or other of Winnicott's grows exponentially and mirrors that of Sigmund Freud himself (Bertolini et al., 2001; Kahr, 2002; Rudnytsky, 1993; Wyatt-Brown, 1993). One seldom attends a meeting in related fields where Bowlby and Winnicott are not mentioned. The work of both men continues to influence researchers, thinkers, and our understanding across a wide spectrum of endeavour.

Relationship to early Freudian drive theory

I was told that on their way to hear Bowlby speak, Winnicott once said to Jennifer Johns that he had never understood Bowlby. I do not know what he meant by this comment, but I suspect that it was his way of implying his own lack of fellow-feeling for a psychoanalyst who apparently showed so little appreciation of the inner life of the imagination, basic Freudian theoretical constructs like drive theory, or the role of subjectivity and the importance and richness of interplay of inner and outer worlds. Bowlby was explicitly dismissive of "the steam kettle energy model", as he referred to it. Yet it is this early Freudian model that Phil Mollon has used in his important new book (2004) to integrate psychoanalysis with a span of references to well-validated clinical work: EMDR (eye movement desensitization and reprocessing), EFT (emotional flooding technique), TFT (thought flooding technique). Mollon refers to ancient and newer techniques of energy and body work, some of which are not universally accepted. Some are based on what Eastern practitioners have long described as energy channels, meridians, and chakras: techniques such as *shiatsu, chi gong, tai chi,* and acupuncture are linked to recent studies and ideas about electromagnetic and holographic energy transfer (Pribram, 1971), and revolutionary knowledge and ideas about brain–body–psychic functioning acquired with the new tools available to researchers that have brought about the recent knowledge. In this significant "landmark" book, along with early Freud, Mollon uses Bowlby's language of attachment theory, internal working models, executive regulatory control systems, and Kohut's psychoanalytic contributions to give new life to the usefulness of Freud's conceptualizations (Mollon, 2001). He criticizes in detail the at times too narrow and rigid contemporary psychoanalytic technique that over-uses incomplete here-and-now transference-based interpretations without reference to developmental and traumatic events of the kind that Bowlby deemed so significant. As revealed in numerous publications, the subtleties of Winnicott's technique did not fall into the type of psychoanalysis to which Mollon raises pertinent objections. Of course, Winnicott never did discard Freud's theories, including this early one, although he transformed them in relation to his clinically derived discoveries; perhaps he could not understand how Bowlby came to discard them.

Bowlby as strategist, Winnicott as experience-based theoretician

Both men were highly original thinkers. Winnicott's questioning perceptive intelligence lurched and sparkled, constantly spread-eagled in non-linear intuitive ways. Like an amoeba, he budded off notions destined to move in unpredictable ways and take on new shape and life from his central thinking core. This basic dissection he set out in *Human Nature* (1988b), which he started writing in 1956 as "A Primer of Psychoanalysis" that he intended for medical and allied practitioners, with the model of an anatomical dissection consciously in mind. He was revising when he died, and he never completed his dissection of all the strands he was following, leaving some but partially revealed and others that inevitably were partly concealed as he progressed (see Green's, 2000, evaluation).[4] Winnicott did not deliberately choose to follow a certain thread of interest but sported with everything and anything that he discovered. However, for decades he continued to follow through on his seminal theoretical ideas, developing

> his complex structure of ideas always in close contact with experience. Intuition, observation, inference and argument were closely interwoven. In communicating his researches he used his own words, his own personal idiom, always careful not to dismantle the metapsychological edifice of his mentors and ancestry. And yet the language of theory was always in the service of his clinical work, and of the distinctive clinical stance he came to embody.... His is the language of the immediacy of sensation and experience, rooted in an intimate assertion of their priority over more abstract qualities of consciousness. [Hernandez & Giannakoulas, 2001, p. 151]

As the latter point out in their important paper "On the Construction of Potential Space", paediatrician Winnicott's *Clinical Notes on Disorders of Childhood* (1931) was akin to neurologist Freud's "Project for Scientific Psychology" (1950 [1895]), and likewise to the invention of his clinical and conceptual vocabulary, which generated psychoanalytic texts.

However, to reiterate, Bowlby was a remarkable strategist who focused his attention with great determination and clarity on his specific goals. Unlike Winnicott, he radically reformulated psychoanalytic theory, with little regard for the existing metapsychological edifice. This paid off. Bowlby's change of conceptual framework employed concepts not available to Freud, of information and communication theory as well as ethology. They led him to a radical shift in valuation, with far-reaching influence on how we perceive and treat other people: consider, for example, the way parents are expected to be in hospital with their young children rather than being excluded.[5] (On Bowlby's and the Winnicotts' post-war evidence to the Curtis Commission, see chapter 5.)

"Turning point" encounters with Darwin and Freud

For both Winnicott and Bowlby, their encounters with Darwin (1859, 1871) and Freud's writing, especially *On Dreams* (1901a), were extremely significant, stimulating, exciting events that were life-course-changing. Both wrote about the impact of their reading them. Bowlby was fascinated by, and, at the end of his life, wrote about what he considered to be Darwin's psychosomatic complaints (Bowlby, 1992). These have been attributed to the bites of some insect Darwin was tormented by in Patagonia (Adler, 1959). Bowlby's speculations are not necessarily incompatible with those of the medical historian and parasitologist Saul Adler (1959), who put forward the entomology-based illness hypothesis.

Kahr (2004a, p. xiv) recalls Bowlby telling him about reading MacCurdy's *Common Principles in Psychology and Physiology* (1928) as a student, and he suggests that this may have had an impact upon Bowlby's subsequent work because earlier MacCurdy wrote "arguably the first intelligent critical study of psychoanalysis". Reading McDougall (1923) who was an early ethologist, must also have made an impact on John Bowlby.

Ethology

Bowlby ensured that his students were exposed to ethology, read it, and were lectured to by Tinbergen (1951, 1958; Tinbergen & Tinbergen, 1972), Lorenz (Lorenz, Huxley, & Wilson, 1952; Lorenz & Wilson, 2002), and Robert Hinde (1966). This was one of Winnicott's major areas of concern about Bowlby's approach, as Bruce Hauptman's anecdote of one of Winnicott's nonverbal eloquent "happenings" illustrates (chapter 3). To look from the outside at humans as one might observe other primates or animals rather than to explore their distinctive individual human characteristics from the intimacy of the consulting-room could not have diverged further from Winnicott's committed traditional classical Freudian psychoanalytic perspective. In terms of Winnicott's interests, in this respect Bowlby was simply working beside the point. The two men differed fundamentally in their approaches towards human behaviour, in their ways of deepening their—and our—understanding, and in their respective life works.

Bowlby viewed the "Fruits of Attachment Theory" conference (Parkes, Stevenson-Hinde, & Marris, 1991) that honoured his 80th birthday as "testimony to the light that can be thrown on personality development and psychopathology when they are studied in an ethological perspective" (1991, p. 293). In the view of recent studies the evolutionary advantages probably lie in the influence of attachment patterns in regulating affective attunement and brain development (Schore (1994, 2001a, 2001b, 2004 a, 2004b) no less than in securing empathic, caring, compassionate, and cooperative social bonding. A secure attachment is the product of "good-enough mothering" during infancy. It promotes resilience, self-confidence, emotional intelligence and spiritual–aesthetic appreciative dimensions fundamental to well-being that enhance appreciation of life (Valent, 1998, 1999; see also Maslow's "peak experiences", 1970). Such sensual life-enhancing experiences and interests keep us from succumbing peacefully to "the death instinct". As Winnicott (1949d) put it, we know that *to be merely sane is not enough*. Attuned "good-enough" mothering is the efficacy factor in rearing healthy-enough human beings. The common efficacy factor in effective therapies is affect regulation (Bradley, 2000)—dependent on similar processes, "moments of meeting" (Stern et al., 1998). Winnicott (1953b/1989, pp. 424–425) specifically objected to Bowlby's cognitive-thinking emphasis that might mislead readers into neglecting the major role of problems of affect, despite Bowlby's depiction of the affect-flat character in delinquency.

The evolutionary advantages of secure attachment patterns are based in the development of group cohesiveness, empathy, and compassion. Bowlby pointed out that "the urge to keep proximity is to be respected, valued, and nurtured as making for potential strength". This he viewed as "a radical shift in valuation . . . the single most important consequence of the change of conceptual framework, . . . with far reaching influence on how we perceive and treat other people, especially those whose attachment needs have been and still are unmet" (Bowlby, 1991, p. 293). Building on Bowlby's legacy, Harwood, Miller, and Irizarry (1995) have made use of attachment behaviour theory to study cultural meaning systems.

Bowlby thought systematically, and utilized systems theory. During his last public communication he commented,

> with defensive process (blockages to free communication) as a central concept of psychoanalysis, the data requiring explanation are concerned almost entirely with information and its organization, and especially with ways in which it is, or is not, communicated both within a person's own mind and between him and others.

He took care to remind us that

> the biologically given strategy of attachment in the young has evolved in parallel with the complementary parental strategy of responsive care giving—the one presumes the other. For any systems to work together in harmony, efficient communication must exist between them, and for none more so than for the coupled systems of child and parent. [Bowlby, 1991]

This is the area so extensively psychoanalytically explored by Winnicott (1956a, 1957c, etc.), amply substantiated by "infant psychiatry" and developmental research (e.g. Brazelton & Cramer, 1991; Call, Galenson, & Tyson, 1983; Diamond & Marrone, 2003; Fonagy, 2001; Harel, 1986; Murray & Cooper, 1997a, 1997b, 1998; Sameroff & Emde, 1989; Schore, 1994, 2001a, 2001b; Stern, 1985; Trevarthen, 2001; and many others). [Contentiously, Green claims that infant research is of such a different order from psychoanalysis that it is irrelevant to consider a possible contribution from the research (Thomson Salo, 2001, p. 1)].

By now it should be clear that Winnicott's theories and observations arise from a more inner orientation in interaction with what is there, discovered in, or provided—appropriately or otherwise—by the external world: Bowlby's observations are more external.

Winnicott (1949d, 1971c) approached *"the lifeline sense of ongoing-continuity-of-being"* as a central—indeed core—notion to all of his developmental metapsychology. He defined trauma as anything that disrupted this sense of ongoing continuity-of-being, whether it arose from outer impingements that breached an infant's defensive shield and capacity to cope or from inner need or agitation that was not met by "good-enough" environmental provision when a developing infant is dependent on the environment to meet its needs if trauma is to be prevented. Bowlby approached the same problem not introspectively, but from the "objective" external perspective that resulted in his major studies and publications on attachment, separation, and loss.

Using Winnicott's conceptualizations, any separation and loss would have a disruptive traumatic impact on the inner sense of continuity-of-being. Both men were familiar with and used the notion of the child's capacity to keep an image of a significant other person in mind and emphasized the importance of a like ability in their significant attachment figures, notably their mothers. It is the smaller child's incapacity to do this that Bowlby understood. This was convincingly demonstrated through the observations and moving evidence of James and Joyce Robertson's films (Robertson, 1962; Robertson & Robertson, 1989), such as *Mother Goes to Hospital*.

Bowlby's recognition of "compulsive caretakers" is a designation that has useful clinical implications: not infrequently he spoke about people who vicariously made good their own early deprivations by taking care of others, often in professional roles. Winnicott identified a "caretaker self" as part of the "false self" (1960b), or in the words of one of my analysand's, "façade self" development that protects the subjectively significant designation of the feeling state of "true self" or "real self" (Issroff, 1979).

Winnicott's contributions outside Bowlby's area of attention

Moshe Halevi Spero (personal communication, 2004) wrote to me that he thinks that when Winnicott described the "female element present in all men and all women and all children" (Winnicott, 1971c), he was "*trying* to talk about a psychological aspect of himself that he truly did not comprehend, and that his female psychoanalysts and Strachey did not help him much" with this. Perhaps Spero is correct, but I am inclined to disagree. Writing to Clare in 1950 about getting in touch with his own early transitional object (1951c), to which he referred as "a *quelque chose* of my own", Winnicott

> knew retrospectively that it must have been a doll. But it had never occurred to me that it wasn't just like myself, a person, that is to say it was a kind of other me, and a not-me female, and part of me and yet not, and absolutely inseparable from me. . . . If I love you as I loved this (must I say?) doll, I love you all out. [1989a, p. 17]

He had dreamt about this doll, "felt enriched", and went on to write about *transitional objects* (p. 17).

I think Winnicott was in touch at the deepest level with inarticulable, mainly right-brain-based experiences when he described the *"female element"*, a concept that overlaps with other attempts to delineate what he also experienced as incommunicable parts of the self, such as the inner sense of continuity-of-being (Winnicott, 1971c). He, himself, was dissatisfied with this "female element" terminology. He told me jokingly that in private he referred to the "female elephant" and specifically distinguished this notion from bisexuality, with which he appears to have been very much at ease. He wrote, "For me, the anima is the part of any man that could say: I have always known I was a woman" (Winnicott, 1964d/1989, p. 485). Winnicott wrote of the deep, usually unconscious fear of woman/women that he considered to be present in everyone as a reaction formation to hatred of having been born (Winnicott, 1970a).

Winnicott kept health in mind

Health is a developmental achievement dependent on genetic factors and the environment's facilitation of their expression—but "health cannot be derived from illness. . . . In order to treat illness one must know about health." Winnicott's thinking can be considered as "a meditation on health, on its manifestations—the capacity to play, for friendship and for cultural and interpersonal living—and its origins" (Spurling, 1996, p. 60). Winnicott endeavours to see the health and positive aspect in any process, from stealing as a sign of hope (Winnicott, 1968b), to the use of string to tie things together as a concrete-operational attempt to re-establish continuity (Winnicott, 1960c), to the transference situation (Spurling, 1996). This clinical situation is "a space of illusion which can be constituted and sustained only by the therapist's willingness to *believe* in the transference"—a required quality of attitude during the encounter. Spurling considers "this vision of health . . . uncompromising in Winnicott's work" and points out how in his conception of health and illness there is no path from one to the other, nothing of paradox and transition as in other phenomena he studied. "The difference between the emotional and cultural richness of health and the poverty of illness is a qualitative not quantitative one" (Spurling, 1996, p. 60). Winnicott appreciated richness of personality. He did not mind "making a fool of himself" or fooling around. Clare Winnicott (1982) tells how immediately he established rapport with a newcomer at the door, remarking: "How nice of you to come to see me wearing your red shoes." As Spurling points out (1991, p. 60), "either one has a capacity to play, or one does not, one is either a good-enough mother or one is not. There is no continuum as with Freud between normal and neurotic. Or with Klein between the paranoid–schizoid and depressive positions" (Segal, 1973). In fact, with Winnicott to be merely neurotic is a developmental achievement approaching being very nearly healthy.

He also pointed out, importantly, that nothing in all the pain, anguish, and suffering encountered in psychiatric hospitals amounts to that experienced by those who have achieved health and maturity.

Oedipal issues

It seems safe to conjecture that Winnicott had significant unresolved Oedipal issues. Perhaps his father's authoritarian and powerful position as mayor of Plymouth played a part in Winnicott's non-identification with him, or in a reaction formation against exercising the kind of power he might have exercised rather than remaining largely a ceremonial figurehead (King, 2004) when in influential positions such as the presidency of the British Psychoanalytical Society.

Is there a clue to this in Winnicott's wonderfully all-encompassing re-statement and exploration of "Oedipal issues"/"triangular relationships" in *Human Nature* (1988b)? I am tempted to reproduce this, but will merely suggest that anyone unfamiliar with his comprehensive and imaginative statement read it. Here he emphasizes the need for containment of phantasized power of parental genitality and the possible nature of the damage that might be caused by fantasized talion/revenge for taking either parent's place in relation to the other (1988b).

The destructiveness fantasies he perceived in taking up such positions may perhaps have affected him in his actual disinclination to exercise the powers he might have done when holding office, something he admitted to me with regret and is evidenced in Pearl King's recollections (2004). It also undoubtedly affected his personal life (see Issroff, "In Search of Alice Winnicott", in preparation-a).

Pioneers in social and preventive psychiatry

As discussed in chapter 1, Bowlby ran a seminar for those of us who were 1967/8/9 Registrars, Senior Registrars and Visiting Fellows—international distinguished visitors such as Ken Adams, Gert Morgenthal, Bruce Hauptman, Edward Ziegler—in the Tavistock Departments of Child Adolescent and Adult Psychiatry. Six of us attended. The seminar examined the issue of preventive psychiatry and long predated the thinking in the HAS Report that currently influences child psychiatry and other attempts better to integrate services for children and primary care provision in the United Kingdom (Williams & White, 1996). Our training encompassed what today are considered Tier 1–4 types of provision. Bowlby sent trainees out to acquire experience in children's homes for looked-after children, schools for "maladjusted children", ordinary schools, and special communal schools like Summerhill and George Lyward's (Burn, 1953). We observed in nursery schools and visited Dockar-Drysdale's therapeutic community (Dockar-Drysdale 1953, 1958, 1991, 1993; Reeves, 1996, 2002). Our exposure ranged from infant–mother observation (Middlemore, 1941) to work with police, whom Bowlby viewed as practical front-line workers in crisis-intervention preventive psychiatry terms. We ran groups for probation officers, visited and worked in prisons (Issroff, 1974), with social service practitioners and GPs. All this happened long before liaison work became recognized as part of the necessary fields of engagement of any child, adolescent and family psychiatrist. Bowlby ensured that we also learnt about what was then known as "minimal brain damage" and how it affected infants' behaviour and maternal–infant interactions and, hence, attachment bonding. Prechtl and Beintera (1964) lectured to us about innate reflexes in newborn infants and their examination in order to determine the extent of the minimal brain damage that, we learnt, most babies sustain during birth. Of course the knowledge-base today validates how correct Bowlby and Winnicott were in drawing attention to the way infants engage with their—maternal—caretakers as of no less importance than the quality of mothering they receive in the feedback loop of interactions (Beebe & Lachmann, 1998; Stern, 1985, 1998; Schore, 1994, 2001a, 2001b, 2004a, 2004b; Trevarthen, 2001) and in affecting their resilience, whatever their innate temperament.

(Bowlby's influence is exemplified in Appendix E, which describes international and trans-cultural work I undertook in the Middle East—e.g. Issroff, 1994a, 1995b, 1998b—and as a UNICEF consultant in post-civil-War-devastated Mozambique—e.g. Issroff, 1998a, 1998b, 1999a, 1999b, 2004, in preparation-c—and other activities directly influenced by that seminar.)

Bowlby's vision of the role of a child psychiatrist

Bowlby held that almost a quarter of our time should be spent on trying to disseminate professional knowledge to the wider public as well as to other workers. He recognized that there would never be a sufficient number of adequately trained professionals to deal with the need and amount of damage and disturbance prevalent in post-war society. Accordingly, a quarter of our time ought to be allocated to sharing professional knowledge and supporting and training others in allied fields. We did not then have deMause's (1982, 2001a, 2001b, 2002) compilation of the recorded history of childhood, or, as mentioned earlier, he might have realized that we are still only on the cusp of the quite recent change from universal prevalence of neglect, abuse, torture, exploitation, and slavery to the passing of statements and legislation that condemns these practices. Effective implementation of policy statements is a separate matter.

We should remember that both Bowlby and Winnicott were born before women had the right to higher education or the vote, and the rights of children were not yet on the agenda. Bowlby wanted us to be aware that the average age of weaning in the human primate is three years; he has us read Julian Huxley's honeymoon study of *The Courtship Habits of the Great Crested Grebe* (1968), Karl von Frisch's superb study of how bees communicate (1967), Jean Liedloff's "continuum concept" regarding proximity (1977, 1986), and all the primatologists from Harlow's aberrant, privation-suffering Rhesus monkeys clinging to their cloth surrogates and subsequently being unable to mother their first infants (1958; Harlow & Harlow, 1966) to George Schaller's year with the gorillas (1971), and the writings of Eibl-Eibesfeldt (1971, 1989) and Desmond Morris (1967, 1970, 1978). Studies of human beings (Ainsworth, 1962, 1967; Schaffer & Emerson, 1964; Tinbergen,

1951, 1958; Tinbergen & Tinbergen, 1972) were high on the reading list. Of course he drew on anthropology and recommended we read at least *The Golden Bough* (Fraser 1890). He was delighted with Eibl-Eibesfeldt's photographic ingenious research studies that revealed the universality of affective signals in facial expression in different peoples around the world: he had a camera apparently pointing into the distance while he was actually taking photos, at a ninety-degree angle to the direction in which the camera ostensibly pointed, of the puzzled on-lookers who congregated. John Bowlby wanted us to understand budgetary constraints and the nature of authority, and to be able to run organizations (Sofer, 1973). We were expected to train others, plan projects and do research, review books, and carry out interdisciplinary activities in the various places mentioned. A quarter of our time was spent in actual clinical work with patients, and deliberately he pointed out that we could become swamped by clinical work and lose sight of the fact that there would always be more cases in need than professionally trained people to cope adequately with that demand. That was one of his arguments to stress how important our other activities were in his view. He in no way discouraged us from pursuing psychoanalysis and psychoanalytic training, including child psychoanalysis and psychotherapy—quite the contrary. He was equally concerned that we be exposed to everything already mentioned, and also family and individual work, group work, and group relations training (Trist & Sofer, 1957), as well as the Law (Goldstein, Freud, & Solnit, 1973, 1979) and ethics. Theoretically, we read also cybernetics, information theory, and research methodology. It was expected that we learn to try to think and write clearly, and plan to use our time well—including the explicit expectation that we put our training to good use.

Differences in their contributions to psychoanalysis

Bowlby set out to reframe psychoanalysis in a way that disregarded previous models—much as Freud himself considered what he had theorized and revised/revisited as rather scaffolding than building. Winnicott's complex ideas were expressed in his own idiom, but, as I have already noted, he was careful, as Hernandez and Giannakoulas equally carefully note, not to dismantle the metapsychological edifice of his mentors and ancestry.... His is the language of the immediacy of sensation and experience, rooted in an intimate assertion of their priority over more abstract qualities of consciousness. It is a language predicated on an attempt to make the symbolic dimension of words coincide with their material referents, in a sort of verbal replica of his methodological approach. [2001, p. 151]

Another of Winnicott's radical contributions is that "subjective creation and subjective destruction are *both* essential to the acceptance of subjectivity *and* of reality" (Hernandez & Giannakoulas, 2001, p. 149). I am not alone in recognizing that Winnicott developed his own implicit rather than explicit, complex, non-Freudian, non-Kleinian metapsychology.

Winnicott's work has yet to be examined closely in relation to its overlap with the major contributions of Charles Rycroft (1991, 1992; Bourne, 2004; Pearson, 2004) and Kristeva in relation to language, drive, semiotics, fantasy, image, illusion, symbolization, and symbol. Kristeva's writing (2003) seldom seems to be linked to clinical evidence but is steeped in written texts and critical literary analyses. Yet Kristeva's thinking undoubtedly overlaps with that of Winnicott whom she quotes, but rarely. Her contributions are important, challenging, seemingly speculative but widely informed also by literary, anthropological, and linguistic training as well as her continuous psychoanalytic experience.

Rycroft (1985) underplayed—while possibly not underestimating, yet modestly never "pushing"—his own largely unrecognized "ablative" contributions to psychoanalysis (Bourne, 2004, Pearson, 2004; Rycroft, 1991, 1992, 2004). Winnicott's work reflects

> how the statement and explication of problems raised by the clinical situation are in fertile relation to a very demanding effort at theorizing. Events and processes, observation and theory, evidence and inference all appear in a new perspective. [Hernandez & Giannakoulas, 2001, p. 152]

It is this characteristically and specifically human area, the actual subjective and cultural verbal and image-communicated domain of psychoanalysis, that Bowlby's contributions almost totally fail to address. The notion of "internal working models" exists, but in no way does it touch on Winnicott's major contributions—for example, what

Hernandez and Giannakoulas have deemed his "radical intuition" that "creative illusion is as vital to the subjective existence of the presented object as destructive illusion is to its being placed outside omnipotent subjectivity" (e.g. as detailed above in the excerpts from Winnicott's remarks, 1951a, when he discussed Marion Milner's "*On Not being Able to Paint*").

Here the difference between Winnicott's undoubted interests and Bowlby's apparent indifference is most marked: Gert Morgenthal and I were assisting a Bowlby and Dorothy Heard-directed ethologically grounded research project observing toddlers playing in a looked-after children's home. I was most uncomfortable that we were not recording the nature of the play, nor any language content in these children, nor noting when they interacted with observers at all. Bowlby dodged the questions and the argument that we considered weakened the research itself in that we were being asked specifically not to note any of our observations that distinguished these *Homo sapiens* primates from other primates.

For many practitioners the kinds of subtleties of theorizing in the area of semantics may seem abstruse, but, after all, we are human, and psychoanalysis deals with us in our complexities. It is because of this that personally, while appreciative of much that I gained from John Bowlby, it is to Winnicott and his works and those that derive from them and build on them that I return repeatedly, and am always enriched. "Even today, the topics discussed by Winnicott are at the cutting edge of psychoanalytic thinking" (Hernandez & Giannakoulas, 2001, p. 152).

Why do so many psychoanalytic psychotherapists have problems in applying attachment theory to clinical situations?

Hamilton (1987a, 1987b) considered various problems in the clinical application of attachment theory. Juliet Hopkins (1990) states it how it is:

> The infant of attachment theory has been created to explain the behaviour of infants rather than to explain the free associations of adults on the couch. Consequently few psychotherapists have become attached to it. This would not surprise its originator, John

Bowlby, who has recognized our insecure profession's need to cling to established theories and their parental figures rather than risk exploring new territories. Our clinical work is fraught with anxiety and uncertainty, and we need to rely on familiar theories to sustain us as we work. As clinicians we value the security provided by the familiar but in our role as scientists we must risk exploring the new. Attachment theory is centrally concerned with this in-built polarity between the need for security and the desire for exploration and mastery of the environment, a polarity that is most obvious in toddlers but is with us through life. [pp. 16]

She points out that "Attachment theory is becoming the chosen language of an increasing number of developmental psychologists and of professional workers in child mental health in both America [e.g. Sroufe, 1985] and Europe." It is accepted by child psychiatrists and has been adopted by the World Association for Infant Psychiatry (and disorder) (WAIPAD) (Brazelton, & Cramer, 1991; Bretherton, 1987; Call, Galenson, & Tyson, 1983; Cramer & Stern, 1988; Ososfsky, 1987; Stern, 1995, 1998; Trevarthen, 2001). Hamilton (1985) has competently summarized all the theoretical essentials. Hopkins (1990) focuses on "the empirical findings of attachment research with reference to their clinical relevance".

It is no accident that she chooses to quote Winnicott (1957a), who wrote, "by constantly co-operating, analysts and direct observers may be able to correlate what is deep in analysis with what is early in infant development".

Hopkins (1990) and Bowlby himself (1988a) provide lucid, succinct, and useful overviews of the observed infant, the classified patterns of attachment behaviour, and how Bowlby's work on attachment and loss is useful in conceptualizing family patterns and therapeutic communication. To resolve some of the difficulties inherent in the concept of "internal objects" and how they become part of an individuals' habitual behaviour, self-regulation, and person, Bowlby developed the concept of "internal working models", not only of people and patterns of attachment and behaviour, but also of the world that allow for interpretation, prediction, and planning. Defensive obstructions to communication are believed to occur in response to intolerable mental pain or conflict. Hopkins (1990, p. 27) suggests that "it is probably the finding that an infant's security is more dependent on his (actual) parents (and events) than innate endowment or fantasies which is most difficult for some psychotherapists to accept". Accordingly, it is in the area of direct intervention in parent–infant relationships when difficulties are encountered that psychotherapeutic–preventive, and hopefully ameliorative and corrective, intervention is increasingly being directed towards changing the nature of the dyadic attachment patterns to more secure reliable ones actually during infancy, or intervening supportively, preferably using a psychodynamic approach, in post-natal depression (e.g. Crittenden, 1988; Fraiburg, 1980; Kennell & Klaus, 1983; Murray, 1992; Murray & Cooper, 1997a, 1997b; Osofsky & Fitzgerald, 2000; Schmidt-Neven, 1994; Stern, 1998). This is something Winnicott was already practicing seven decades ago, as is evident in some of his case studies—for instance, observations of an infant in a set situation when he described the Spatula game (1941a). Kestenberg and Buelte, in their clinic and in newsletters of parents and infants in Long Island, New York, were other pioneering practitioners and advocates of such practice (Kestenberg & Buelte, 1977). It is becoming accepted as part of infant psychiatry, and there are special training and practice pioneering departments in places such as the Anna Freud Clinic.

As mentioned, Bowlby was fond of the term "compulsive caretaker" to describe vicarious self-caretaking behaviour, identification with role reversal in a reparative effort for past deprivation. But however useful in conceptualization, Bowlby's work is not used much clinically in mainstream psychoanalysis.

Example of an attempt to bridge and make use of the work both of Bowlby and Winnicott

While not the only one, Fonagy has worked productively with Bowlby's concepts. For instance, he proposes that some personality-disordered individuals are those victims of childhood abuse who coped by refusing to conceive of their attachment figure's thoughts, and thus avoided having to think about their caregiver's wish to harm them (Fonagy, 1999). Continuing defensively to disrupt their capacity to depict mental states in themselves and in others leaves them to operate on inaccurate, schematic impressions of thoughts and feelings. They are then immensely vulnerable in intimate relationships. He puts forward two propositions here: (a) individuals who experience early trauma may defensively inhibit their capacity to mentalize; and (b) some characteristics of personality disorder may be rooted in this inhibition. Ingeniously, Fonagy then uses clinical material to illustrate how he perceives "mentalization" as a mode for therapeutic action as it develops during therapy in the patient through the work with the analyst. This is a clear attempt also to bridge to cognitive behavioural forms of therapy, and a continuation of Bowlby's attempts to reframe psychoanalysis in formulations amenable to research.

Fonagy's work usefully appropriates areas where Bowlby's ideas were under-developed, and he expands his own notions about mentalization. However, to my mind, and without denigrating the usefulness to the links to Bowlby's work that Fonagy has made, Winnicott's work already predates and takes for granted the point to which Fonagy's propositions about the significance of mentalization lead him. It would be rare to find an issue of a psychoanalytic journal in which citations of Winnicott's fertile psychoanalytic conceptualizations are not found. I think it fair to state that all of us who studied with both men, however appreciative we may be in our diagnostic assessments of the Bowlby legacy and its applications in research, make far more use of Winnicott's work in our clinical practice. Hamilton has dealt with this issue, particularly in considering the difficulties in applying attachment theory to the clinical situation (1982, 1987a, 1987b, 1996a, 1996b). Juliet Hopkins has written an extremely clear and appreciative study of Bowlby's applicability in "The Observed Infant of Attachment Theory" (1990), yet her depiction of supervision with Winnicott is far livelier (2002). Her "bridging" attempt is depicted in her 1996 study of the dangers of "too-good" mothering as an obstacle, which interferes with the process of separating and adequate separation. Winnicott himself stressed the necessity for graduated failure in doses with which the developing infant's stage of maturation can cope, implying that he was aware of what she has so usefully elaborated.

While they make use of attachment perspectives derived from Bowlby's work and language, Fonagy and Target (1996; Target & Fonagy, 1996) have pondered and been influenced by Winnicott's contributions and acknowledge that "a normal awareness of the relationship between internal and external reality is not universal, but rather a developmental achievement" (Fonagy, 2000; Fonagy & Target, 1996, p. 218). They invent a new language that tries to reconcile the views of Winnicott and Bowlby and build a theory of development. They point out that a child normally moves from an experience of psychic reality in which mental states are not related to as representations, to an increasingly complex view of the internal world. This more complex view has as its hallmark the capacity to mentalize: to assume the existence of thoughts and feelings in others and in oneself, and to recognise these as connected to outer reality (but only loosely). Initially, the child's experience of the mind is as if there was an exact correspondence between internal state and external reality. Fonagy calls this mode *"psychic equivalence"*, to emphasize that for the young child mental events are equivalent in terms of power, causality, and implications, to events in the physical world. "Equating internal and external is inevitably a two-way process" (Fonagy, 2000). He acknowledges that what he proposes is part of Winnicottian theory. But he insists on using Bowlby's language about a secure base. The emergence of mentalizing is deeply embedded in the child's primary object relationships, principally in the mirroring relationship with the caregiver. The experience of affect is the bud from which eventually mentalization of affect can grow, but only in the context of at least one continuing and safe attachment relationship. The important capacity of accurate mirroring and recognition of the child and the ability of a "mothering" person to think about that child is recognized by Winnicott and spelled out by Fonagy (2000). However, a central question that seems not to have engaged Fonagy or Target—or many others—is Winnicott's preoccupation with how to make contact with the real and with the external (see also Rodman, 2003, p. 319).

Winnicott was always involved with the question of "how to subtract the truth of the subject from a merely relational mediation?" as Groarke puts it (2003, p. 493):

> For Winnicott, through the object that is "always being destroyed" the illusory experience of play becomes the imaginative use of play; self-possession becomes inhabitation; and imagination becomes the embodiment of belief as fidelity. Fidelity describes a particular state of mind, but it may also be understood as a formal condition to the extent that it makes contact with external reality possible. [p. 493]

Groarke emphasizes the return of the external and real in the later works of Winnicott, concluding,

> The infinite affirmation of the thought of the outside confirms the transformative value of disillusionment, where the plenitude of illusion is shattered together with the unconscious destruction of the object in fantasy.... The articulation of affirmation and destruction requires more than a relational paradigm. [p. 493]

Groarke points out how Winnicott "attempts to reformulate the subject–object dialectic as a four-fold structure of relations, recognition, return, and encounter" (Groarke, 2003, p. 492).

Winnicott's language is the best way to read and understand Winnicott, as Ogden (2001) has argued appreciatively and compellingly. But summarized understanding of others is sometimes helpful. Here, juxtaposed with the above excerpts from Fonagy and Target, I want to demonstrate further how totally different Winnicott's work is from Bowlby's, and how Bowlby's and Fonagy's languages in no way do justice to Winnicott's contributions to our understanding of "the structuration of exteriority", as Groarke (2003) terms it. Bowlby takes exteriority as a given. This is a developmental achievement, not to be taken for granted, and a constant process in Winnicott's profound later conceptualizations.

Winnicott's "structuration of exteriority"

At "first, object-relating is described as a subjective experience, where the object becomes meaningful only as a subjective object" (Groarke, 2003, p. 492).

> In a matter of a few months after birth the baby is obviously capable of oral sadistic experience, that is to say, can experience primitive loving in which the motor impulses fuse in with the erotogenic zone satisfactions, and the infant arrives at the eating of the object, and of being eaten if loved. At about the same time this primary object ceases to be a subjective phenomenon, and if all experience becomes directed towards that which is symbolic of the primary object, the infant becomes able to play and to imagine, and experiences the use of the primary object only in dreams. [Winnicott, 1962/1989, p. 453]

This is a pre-Kleinian "depressive position" phase. Winnicott continues:

> In this early phase the baby is developing a memory system and a self-awareness that becomes available for projection. The good enough mother meets this projection; and in this way the baby's experience in relation to the good breast is a relationship to a projection from the self. [1962/1989, p. 453]

The "transitional object" is a subjective found object. The use of the term marks a fundamental shift at the level of relations because by definition it lacks a definite sense of exteriority: "The baby whose mother is not good enough never joins up that which was available for projection with this mother's good breast. The latter fails to take the projection" (1962/1989, p. 453).

Winnicott (1962/1989, p. 453) then discusses the "tantalizing" situation where mothering is only intermittently good enough, the baby's continuity-of-being is impinged on and disrupted, and

> here we have the paradox of a good breast that is a persecutor, a thing that must be destroyed. Thus aggression appears, directed toward the good object, but this aggression is reactive and is not *the aggression of the primitive love impulse which represents an achievement*, a fusion of muscular erotism and the sensory orgy of the erotogenic zones. [p. 454]

Winnicott describes how the subject is destroyed in the unconscious phantasy that accompanies instinctual activity, and, because it keeps reappearing, it becomes placed outside the omnipotence of the phantasy of destruction and so recognized as real and external. "Destruction is seen as constitutive of the real, initially to the to the extent that the subject recognizes the externality of the object" that is there. Groarke (2003) recognizes that "The spectral structure of exteriority is therefore predicted on a world that 'feeds back' an other-than-me". Only then can the subject "make use" of what is there not as an object of recognition, but as an object of encounter with

> an object that returns and gives the subject a taste for the real. It involves an "impulse to destroy" that is neither disastrous nor reactive. Winnicott differentiates the destruction of the object of encounter from both primitive annihilation ("no hope") and aggression relative to the confrontation with the reality principle.

Fidelity to failure overcomes faith in illusion through encounter with a world that fails, but does not inflict harm in retribution for destructive attacks. [Groarke, 2003, pp. 492–493]

Bowlby's work never aspired to grapple with such issues—or, for that matter, with notions such as "true and false self" or "continuity-of-being" or much else that is novel, like Winnicott's appreciation of paradox. Bowlby does deal with the effects of the interruption of continuity-of-being, but he does so without any appreciation or acknowledgement of the existential state itself. We never encounter in Bowlby's *écriture* the kinds of remarks that sting one awake that pepper Winnicott's writing.

Lack of psychoanalytic cross-referencing in Winnicott's work

Winnicott (1959b) criticized Bowlby's studiously referenced paper on "Grief and Mourning in Infancy" (1960b). He implied that through his referencing Bowlby was "anxious to show where he supplants the former analytic writers", and here Winnicott found him "unconvincing" (1959b/1989, p. 427). (I wonder whether this possibly hints at Winnicott's personal rationalization or attempt to excuse himself for his own notable tendency to neglect to cite the work of others?) Winnicott was continuing his firmly held belief that ideas had to be used and made over—a kind of digestive–metabolic notion (pp. 426–428). However, in one of his last talks, entitled "D.W.W on D.W.W." (1967c), he said that he realized more and more as time went on what a tremendous lot he had lost from not properly correlating his work that of others. He felt it not only annoying to other people but also rude, and that it meant that what he had said has been isolated and people have to do a great deal of work to get at it. He said: "It happens to be my temperament, and it's a big fault." At the end of his talk to this select group of British colleagues then in the 1952 club (King, 2004), he said, "I can't cover all that I want to." Awkwardly, he asked them to help join him in a letter "to try and make amends and join up with the various people all over the world who are doing work which either I've stolen or else I'm just ignoring". By then he was getting to the stage where he really "would like to be more correlated". But he didn't "promise to follow it all up because", he said, "I know I'm just going to go on having an idea which belongs to where I am at the moment, and I can't help it" (Winnicott, 1959b/1989, pp. 426–428).

Cross-referencing of Winnicott's work, particularly to the past two decades of experimental observational research in infant and mother and father interactions and development, remains to be carried out systematically—a suggestion for someone's thesis.[6]

Further comments on mutual influence

Much of the time Winnicott was reacting to the ideas of others. While I wonder to what extent his outspoken criticism of Bowlby discussed and quoted above may have influenced the latter's later "inner working models" theoretical developments, I also wonder whether in Winnicott's distinction between "object relating" and "object use" (1968h) we might discern glimmerings of an influence derived from Bowlby's work on attachment bonding? In my perhaps simplistic understanding of this very important distinction made by Winnicott, I think he was possibly referring to the capacity for innate attachment behaviour—including the analytic transference—when he used the term "object relating" and differentiated it from what he saw as a more sophisticated developmental stage when someone is capable of making constructive use of the external world and the "objects"—including other people—discovered there. Winnicott always "complexified" issues rather than attempting to simplify them, as Bowlby strove to do. As I have noted already, Hamilton (1996a) has a more complex and subtle view about this. Both of us may be correct.

Evaluating Winnicott's and Bowlby's respective contributions

Their work as it relates to society

One of the most important of Winnicott's many papers on society is his seminal post-Second-World-War "Some Thoughts on the Meaning of the Word 'Democracy'"(1950; see also Issroff, 1999a). In the wider public arena this paper can be viewed in a continuum with those that deal with his notions of "holding" and "containing" situations, of case management and therapeutic uses of regression. As noted previously,

Winnicott (1950) pointed out that for any society to operate democratically, there is a critical ratio between the x number of relatively mature, relatively undamaged individuals who contain or "hold" the y number of immature and damaged individuals—who are often regressed, or dependent. At some critical point in the x:y ratio, when the mass of immature and damaged people becomes too great for those who are capable of dealing with them sensitively enough, without themselves becoming overwhelmed, society becomes re-organized into totalitarian, fundamentalist–authoritarian, dictatorial structures.

If Winnicott's observation is true—and the evidence tends to support this—the implications for society and social policy are immense. They underline the need for attention and funds to be directed to many neglected issues, among them trauma and its after-impact at all levels.

Bowlby advocated pro-active integrated health programmes: implementation requires prior recognition of the significant roles well-functioning perinatal, mental health, and allied professionals can play. Increasingly they are coming into being in various parts of the world: at least lip-service is paid in various WHO, Universal Human Rights, and Children's Rights declarations to which nations subscribe in principle: at least in theory, these are subscribed to by many national states. The contributions of Winnicott and Bowlby lend weight to our recognition of how important it is for society to provide the kinds of conditions in which "good-enough" parenting and secure bonding can occur, for in conditions of war, famine, poverty, and instability salutogenic attitudes to life (Antonovsky, 1988) are unlikely to develop. Both resilience and the mental, bodily, and spiritual strengths needed for satisfactory negotiation of ordinary expectable life crises and events depend on confident, securely based and bonded early life experiences.

Without trying to force unwelcome facts, we must recognize that there is a need to educate everyone, from politicians, economists, and administrators to the public in general. Not only police, army, therapists, and perinatal hospital staff, but also those who work with refugees and other vulnerable people have to understand—poor conditions for nurture generate poor parenting. We cannot afford to ignore those who have been traumatized or those who are in contact with them who become vicariously traumatized (Issroff, 1999b; Pearlman & Saakvitne, 1995). When allocating budgets or devising working schedules, short-term goals are sufficient to meet the immediate needs of those who are traumatized—and also those of infants, their mothers, and families. Long-term requirements also have to be considered if social cost–benefit analyses are to be made. Society itself is endangered if we do not identify and support on-going human needs for the social structures that buffer and ameliorate the negative spread of the overwhelming, indigestible after-effects of the impact of trauma: namely, affect contagion phenomena (Issroff, 1980, 1997, 1999a). Anything that disrupts continuity-of-being, whether at social, emotional, physical, or relational levels, is traumatic by definition. In our vision for maintaining a peaceful-enough, democratic way of life we need to include "cultural containers"—the worlds of art, theatre, sporting arenas, and music—along with the rest (Issroff, 1999b).

Bowlby's heritage

Bowlby would be justifiably satisfied with the enormous amount of productive and profoundly useful tools and research of substance his work has generated.[7]

Even without his masterly central theoretical contributions to the study of attachment, separation, and loss (Bowlby, 1970, 1973, 1977, 1979, 1980, 1981, 1988c), Bowlby's importance would have been ensured by his study of Darwin (1992) or his participation in multidisciplinary study groups (1957), his WHO report on *Maternal Care and Mental Health* (1951, 1966). As I experienced from training under his direction, Bowlby's thinking about the role and function of child psychiatrists anticipated by decades the HAS (Health Advisory Service) Report (Williams & White, 1996) on which NHS (National Health Service), CAMHS (Child and Adolescent Mental Health Services), and children's services in general have been re-organized. Chapter 5 deals with Bowlby's evidence to the Curtis Commission, along with that of Clare and Donald Winnicott. However, in terms of public policy in the United Kingdom and elsewhere during the past half-century, has the weight of either their respective or their combined contributions received due respect, and has its purport been implemented? (See chapter 6.)

Winnicott's range of influence

Bowlby's contributions occupy a different niche from that of Winnicott's psychoanalytically more complex, richer, and less easily accessible legacy. The breadth, depth, and fertility of Winnicott's manifold observations and thoughts stimulate and are useful to practitioners and thinkers in all areas of human thought, not only psychoanalysis. Winnicott himself acknowledged that he was trying to tackle "nothing short of everything" in human nature—as mentioned, the somewhat altered title of his unfinished autobiography was taken from T. S. Eliot's lines, "Costing not less than everything" (1942, p. 198). His was in every way a closely examined and articulate life, lived to the full in each moment.

Winnicott's understanding of the processes of enrichment of the imagination can be equated with the symbolic abundance of fantasy and dream: "As a function of our humanity we constantly imagine entry into other people's lives and we derive from these exclusions an extension of what we imagine to be possible in life" (Fielding, 1988, p. 12). I do not believe that John Bowlby was deficient in imagination, but I think in his work he deliberately inhibited any such excursions, and to that extent his work for me lacks the deep human resonances in which Winnicott's excels.

Winnicott's and Bowlby's work compared

With the exception of his important studies of Darwin and his remarkable attempt, with Evan Durbin, in *Personal Aggressiveness and War* (1939) to analyse Hitler's speeches and their social influence in terms of animistic beliefs, comparing them to the behaviour of "primitive" societies described in the anthropological literature, Bowlby's work is focused. Winnicott's ranges far, wide, and deep[8]: both looked at infants, mothers, and children, but in very different ways.

Bowlby's work did not stray far from his well-chosen crucially important themes of the secure basis for development, attachment, separation, and loss. As for Winnicott's, John Padel (2001b, p. 269) wrote:

> Winnicott, even long before he met or heard of Klein, firmly believed that the primal closeness of child to mother persisted in

some form in the mind of every individual, he had genius in getting a child to reveal to him what it was in his or her life that had first seriously interrupted that closeness: whether it had been an illness of mother or of child, loss or separation of some kind, acute and unmitigated awareness of another closeness of mother to somebody else, or simply the mother's too limited capacity for love and for the closeness which the child deeply needed.

Elsewhere Padel points (2001a, p. 4) out that "Winnicott was a great clinician, but often expressed his ideas in paradoxes and his theories piecemeal." Did anyone consider John Bowlby a great clinician, I wonder? Certainly no one could ever accuse him of expressing his ideas not clearly or systematically. For him, a mother was a mother. For Winnicott, there was a step that implied a structural change in the infant's psyche: for the infant, a mother exists as an objective "environment-mother" and a subjective "object-mother". An infant relies on the objectively actual environment mother to hold it and to hold the situation while it has an intense experience with its subjective object–mother. Indeed, while for Bowlby there was always a mother and a baby, Winnicott could write:

> As a baby grows, no sense of self emerges except on the basis of this relating in the sense of BEING. This sense of being is something that antedates the idea of being-at-one-with, because there has not yet been anything else except identity. Two separate persons can *feel* at one, but here in the place that I am examining, the baby and the object *are* one ... projective and introjective identifications both stem from this place where each is the same as the other. [1971c, p. 80]

Enthusiast of the then "scientifically" acceptable techniques of ethology, Bowlby could never have allowed himself to arrive at such an observation, speculation, or statement about an area that is for Winnicott a starting point.

In these respects Bowlby and Winnicott might have spoken different languages.

Interviewing professor of comparative literature and anthropologist Vincent Crapanzano, Anthony Molino reminded him of Paul Ricoeur's and what Crapanzano had called Abram Kardiner's "romantic hope" for a unified social science. He asked how Crapanzano saw the agonistic element of dialogue that he had called for: Might it invigorate the cross-currents between psychoanalysis and anthropology? Crapanzano did not see why "science" should be unified. "Why shouldn't . . . sciences be at one another's throats—asserting, debating, challenging? A unified science would be the death of science. It's the debate, the dialogue, the challenges, the multiple angles of vision, the divergent viewpoints, their refractions and mirrorings that make for good science" (Crapanzano, 2004, p. 65). Crapanzano thinks about the pluralization of both anthropologies and psychoanalyses and considers "the tension within and between them" as creative. He perceives the power of their relationship in their disjunction. For him complementarity can only breed complacency. The same comments can be applied to the relationship between the respective works of Winnicott and Bowlby. Let us value their differences and make use of the heritage with which they have immensely enriched us.

Notes

1. The Adult Attachment Interview (AAI) is a semi-structured protocol designed to elicit a subject's recollections about relationships with parents and other attachment figures during childhood. The interviewer asks about childhood experiences with parents, significant separations and losses during childhood, and the current state of the child–parent relationship. Scoring of the interview is based on: (a) descriptions of childhood experiences; (b) the language used to describe past experiences; and (c) the ability to give an integrated, coherent, believable account of experiences and their meaning. The interview is scored from a verbatim transcript using scales that measure whether, in the coder's opinion, attachment figures were: loving, rejecting, neglecting, involving, or pressurizing. A second set of scales is used to assess the interviewee's state of mind and discourse style, overall coherence of the material, thought, idealization, gaps in recall, active anger, derogation, fear of loss, ability to reflect on matters, and so on. The authors discovered that what is important is not only what the subject says but how he/she says it.

2. E.g. Ainsworth, 1985a, 1985b, 1990; Alexander, 1992; Allen, 2000; Belsky & Nezworski, 1988; Brazelton & Cramer, 1991; Bretherton, 1987; Cortina, 2003; Crittenden, 1988; Diamond & Marrone, 2003; Egeland & Sroufe, 1981; Erickson, Sroufe, & Egeland, 1985; Fonagy, 2001; Fonagy & Target, 1996, 1997; Green & Scholes, 2004; Greenspan & Lieberman, 1988; Karen, 1994; Ososfsky, 1988; Parkes & Stevenson-Hinde, 1991; Parkes, Stevenson-Hinde, & Marris, 1991; Pfäfflin & Adshead, 2003; Sable, 2001; Sameroff & Emde, 1989; Siegel, 2001; Simpson & Rholes, 1998; Southgate, 1990; Sroufe, 1985; Sroufe, Carlson, Levy, & Egeland, 1999; Sroufe, Egeland, Carlson, & Collins, 2005; Sroufe, Egeland, & Kreutzer, 1990;

Sroufe & Fleeson, 1986; Sroufe & Waters, 1977; Weinfield, Sroufe, & Egeland, 2000; Weinfield, Sroufe, Egeland, & Carlson, 1999; Weiss, 1982.

3. Phil Mollon (2005) has firmly championed this original Freudian model (1950 [1895]) in a way that might well have led Bowlby to re-think.

4. A scribbled handwritten footnote, which I deciphered at Clare's request and discussed with her, written when he was revising the manuscript—shortly before he died, Claire believed—read: "This is why I could not finish the book." The note related to his theory differentiating use of an object from object relating, and the way in which the world became perceived as real and external by surviving the recurrent—unconscious—phantasy of being destroyed, which, he believed, accompanied instinctual bodily activities such as lustily devouring/feeding experiences. While his chapter on this topic (1968h) was published in *Playing and Reality* (1971) after his death, precursors to the elaboration of the idea are to be found as early as 1948, and certainly in his 1963 dream, recorded when he was reviewing Jung's autobiography, *Memories, Dreams, Reflections* (1963; Winnicott, 1963a, 1964d; see Appendix C). His ideas about this were outlined in the poorly received paper he gave in New York that preceded his heart attack that year. So I was surprised Clare was so convinced that the note was recent: personally, I would have dated it rather some years earlier, at around the time he had the dream that was published only in 1989, a quarter of a century later. However, as the notion was one to which he had returned quite often during my weekly meetings with him, it was part of what had always been of help to me when working with a negative transference in my practice (Issroff, 1979).

5. Bowlby's contributions are addressed by, for example, Moore, Moretti, and Holland (1998), Levy and Orlans (1998), James (1994), Holmes (1993, 1996, 2001), Heard and Lake (1997), Sable (2001), Simpson and Rholes (1998), Robertson and Robertson (1989), Karen (1994), Diamond and Marrone (2003), and elsewhere—see Introduction.

6. At my suggestion Pumpi Harel (1986) wrote a thesis under my supervision for Sarah Lawrence College in Bronxville, New York, examining the then already extensive research about early mother–infant bonding and attunement that might have negated Winnicott's notion of primary maternal preoccupation, and she found none. The idea was extended by Jazid and Kestenberg (1983) to a later equally important normal stage they termed "maternal infatuation" when mothers become besotted with their babies and their developmental progress.

7. See, in addition to those already cited, for example, the IAN bibliography and the works of Levy and Orlans (1998), James (1994), Greenspan and Lieberman (1988, in Belsky & Nezworski, 1988), Fonagy, Target, and Steele (1997), Main (1999; Main & Solomon, 1986), Greenspan and Pollock (1991), Sameroff and Emde (1989), Marrone (1998; Diamond & Marrone, 2003), Lubetsky (2002), Schore (2001a, 2001b), Siegel (2001), and Trevarthen (1998).

8. Winnicott wrote to Anna Freud (Letter 8, 1987b, p. 11):

(a) The important thing to get across is that the world's troubles are not due to man's aggression, but are due to repressed aggression in individual man.

(b) Following this, the remedy is not education of children in ways of managing and controlling their aggression but is to provide for the maximum number of infants and children such steady and reliable conditions (of emotional environment) that they, each one of them, may come to know and to tolerate as part of themselves the whole of their aggression (primitive greedy love, destructiveness, capacity for hate, etc.).

(c) To enable human beings (infants, children or adults) to tolerate and accept their own aggression, respect for guilt and depression is needed and full recognition of reparative tendencies when they exist.

(d) It is also important to state clearly that in this matter of aggression and its origins in human development there is a great deal that is not yet known.

CHAPTER FIVE

A duty to care: reflections on the influence of Bowlby and Winnicott on the 1948 Children Act

Christopher Reeves

Towards the end of chapter 2, which was devoted to an examination of the differences between Bowlby and Winnicott over the understanding and treatment of juvenile delinquency, I drew attention to the social and political climate in Britain within which many of their ideas took shape, in particular to the introduction of the Welfare State legislation during the period of the Attlee Administration between 1945 and 1951. In this connection I alluded to the new perception of a "duty of care" on the part of the government towards its youngest citizens enshrined in the provisions of the 1948 Children Act. I suggested that the setting up of the wartime emergency evacuation scheme had been indirectly responsible for this development. These allusions to this important social and political development were necessarily brief in the context of that chapter. I now want to consider them further in the context of the contributions of Bowlby and Winnicott.

I have used the phrase "a duty to care" rather than "a duty of care" for the title of this chapter for three complementary reasons. First, this phrase better indicates what the British Government in 1948 came to regard as the dimensions of its newly assumed responsibility than what is conveyed nowadays by "a duty of care". Second,

Bowlby, Winnicott, and Winnicott's future wife, Clare Britton, all of whom played a major part in articulating and giving practical substance to this new sense of government responsibility, clearly regarded this obligation as entailing the assumption of some real, direct, quasi-parental responsibility for the welfare of children deprived of parents, not just a degree of administrative oversight linked to the acknowledgement of ultimate accountability, such as is usually implied nowadays by the phrase "a duty of care". Third, I shall be suggesting towards the end of this chapter that legislative developments in respect of the welfare of children since the 1948 Act, up to and including the legislation currently being enacted in the British Parliament, even though they can be said to take their point of departure from the assumptions about care implicit in this earlier landmark Act, nevertheless show a gradual shift in perception on the part of a government concerning the relationship that should exist between young people, their families, and the state, and the mutual rights and responsibilities of each—a shift that can best be described as moving from an active governmental "duty *to* care" towards a more neutral "duty *of* care". It is implicit in my thesis that such a shift would probably have represented an unwelcome development in the eyes of the two men who are the particular object of this study. However, I shall largely refrain from conjecturing how Bowlby and Winnicott might have reacted to current developments in child provision and thinking and concentrate instead on the context and issues of childcare they actually encountered during their professional careers.

After a brief account of the historical antecedents of the 1948 Act, I shall give a summary of the oral contributions of Bowlby, Winnicott, and Clare Britton at hearings of the government-sponsored Curtis Committee of Inquiry of 1945–46, whose eventual report lead to the 1948 legislation. Whereas in chapter 2 I focused primarily on areas of difference between Bowlby and Winnicott, here I shall mainly concentrate on what they shared in common and what perspective they jointly brought to the thinking of that Committee and, through it, to the subsequent legislation. Finally, I shall briefly survey some of subsequent legislative developments in the light of the priorities they identified for the protection and psychological wellbeing of children.

The background leading up to the Curtis Report and the 1948 Children Act

The emergency evacuation programme initially planned in 1938 and put into operation a year later was the first instance in which a British government, whether in peace or war, had become actively involved on a national scale with the social welfare of children—and that in two respects: one entailing planning for protection, the other planning for secondary provision arising out of the need to protect. Previously the government had assumed a measure of responsibility for the protection of children only where they were deemed to be "at risk" either by reason of the absence of parents—or their inability to support them—or because they had been brought before a Magistrate's Court as being delinquent or beyond parental control, and hence subject to a "Fit Person Order". In either case, central government was not directly involved, except in determining general guidelines about the nature of the care to be provided, as well as exercising some regulatory control over the bodies charged with putting this into effect.[1] For the most part, evacuated children were ordinary family-reared children, and as such their welfare would normally have been regarded as being the unquestioned responsibility of their parents, especially in matters concerning their upbringing and place of residence. Thus, in taking control through the evacuation programme the government was for the first time laying claim to a higher-order responsibility for the welfare of the nation's children.

The second respect in which the government was confronted through the evacuation programme with a new responsibility for the children's welfare was through having to deal with the social and psychological consequences of the family disruption it had involuntarily set in train. This is what I have chosen to call "secondary provision". There had been some foreshadowing of this development during the interwar years, so that the idea that central Government should be concerned at some level with the psychological as well as the physical wellbeing of children as a result of evacuation was not entirely unanticipated, even if its dimensions were. Already in the 1930s local authorities had, in piecemeal fashion, opened child guidance clinics in various parts of the country in acknowledgement of the fact that otherwise healthy children sometimes displayed psychological and developmental difficulties that were best addressed at a relatively early stage under the umbrella of preventive medical care, as a means of forestalling later family breakdown or delinquency. It was recognized that failure to make such provision might eventually result in greater financial burdens being placed on the government, albeit at a local level. However, the problems consequent on failed attempts to billet disrupted, distressed, and difficult youngsters threw into new and stark relief the probable nature and cause of many such behavioural difficulties: namely, the rupture of family ties—in particular the child's tie to its parents. Such were precisely the problems highlighted by Bowlby and Winnicott when the scheme was first being put into hasty operation. So the government was soon forced to recognize and confront the fact that for children there were inherent psychological consequences of family disruption—consequences that had to be addressed as part of its wider concern for the protection of the childhood population in time of war and the successful implementation of its evacuation policy. Moreover, meeting this need required a small army of personnel with the appropriate knowledge and skills to address these difficulties. In other words, its duty of care entailed a duty to care in an organized fashion in the area not just of the child's physical health but of its psychological welfare also. Once again, this was a quite new commitment and undertaking on the part of the government.

It is conceivable that these fresh governmental responsibilities would have remained time-bound and circumscribed to the conditions of evacuation had it not been for a number of concurrent developments taking place within British society during the war years. The first, of course, was a developing recognition among the British people, shared by its wartime coalition government, of a need to transfer to the later conditions of peacetime the sense of social cohesiveness and common purpose engendered by the particular circumstances of war. This had not happened after the First World War, with almost disastrous social and political consequences. Such sentiments gave rise to, and made possible, the introduction of many aspects of the post-war welfare state, particularly more equitable access to education and health services, as embodied in the 1944 Education Act and the 1946 National Health Service Act, respectively.

The widespread sense of the need to provide a better deal for all citizens came to encompass, perhaps almost fortuitously, that hitherto largely neglected group in society—namely, homeless or unprovided-for children—of whom there were now many more as a result of the war, and in particular as a consequence of the aerial bombardment of cities. I say "fortuitously" because by chance in the summer of 1944 a devastating case of child neglect occurred that was reported and widely commented on in the press. This provided a timely focus and impetus for a campaign already being waged by a prominent peer, Lady Allen, through pamphlets and letters to *The Times*. She urged a thorough revision of the laws relating to "boarded-out children"—the term then most frequently used to denote children not brought up by their birth parents or relatives or else by adoptive parents—in other words, those to whom we would nowadays refer as "children in care" or "looked-after children".

The scandalous case in question involved two brothers, Terence and Dennis O'Neill. Brought up in Wales, they had been "boarded out" on a remote Shropshire farm. Six months later one of the boys died due to a combination of physical maltreatment and starvation, while the other was found to be greatly emaciated and suffering from gross neglect. Such was the public outcry at their mistreatment and the failure of the authorities to monitor their placement properly that the government instituted a special inquiry into the circumstances surrounding the case. This was conducted by Sir Walter (later Lord) Monckton. At the same time, in recognition of the widespread public concern about the welfare of "boarded-out children" generally, it appointed a parallel committee of inquiry, the Curtis Committee—so called after the name of its Chair, Myra Curtis—whose task was:

> To inquire into existing methods of providing for children who from loss of parents or from any cause whatever are deprived of a normal home life with their own parents or relatives; and to consider what further measures should be taken to ensure that these children are brought up under conditions best calculated to compensate them for the lack of parental care [Curtis Report, 1946, p. 5]

In 1946 the Committee prefaced its report by referring to the then unprecedented nature and scope of its given terms of reference:

> It is of interest to note that this is the first enquiry in this country directed specifically to the care of children deprived of a normal home and covering all groups of such children. [p. 5]

Another factor contributing to the government's readiness to contemplate the prospect of assuming ongoing responsibility at national level for the welfare of parentless children in the post-war era was the persuasive belief, articulated notably by Bowlby in his *Forty-Four Juvenile Thieves* study (1946), that the evident improvements in children's physical health achieved in the interwar years as result of mass inoculation and vitamin provision could be paralleled in the sphere of child psychological and social wellbeing, if only measures were put in place by central government to deal with their most glaring causes. Longstanding among these causes, of course, were poor housing and poverty due to unemployment. However, largely thanks to Bowlby, it was increasingly recognized that to these causes had to be added family breakdown and the disruption of a child's tie to its parents. The ameliorist, crusading outlook of Bowlby—who had close friends in government circles—began to be echoed by Winnicott as a result of his wartime experience in working with hard-to-place evacuees in residential hostels. What gave their urgings extra credibility in the eyes of the government was the fact that they had been foremost among those warning in advance about some of the likely consequences of large-scale evacuation. Not only that, but Winnicott, particularly, had distinguished himself in the eyes of government—due in no small measure to Clare Britton's organizational skills—in providing an effective psychological back-up service through the Oxfordshire Evacuation Programme to redress some of the identified psychological and social consequences manifested by disturbed and distressed evacuee children. All of this suggested that a comparable preventive and curative social-psychological programme for homeless children could be implemented effectively after the war. At the very least, the government of the day was proving unusually receptive to such representations.

The Curtis Committee's deliberations

It will be evident to anyone acquainted with how legislation relating to child protection has developed in Britain that the immediate circumstances leading to the setting up of the Curtis Committee of Inquiry and its legislative sequel are by no means unusual: that is to say, like the half-dozen others that have since taken place over the last six decades, this inquiry was precipitated by a high-profile case wherein a series of professional and administrative failures, shortages of personnel, poor communication between departments, low morale, and neglectful attitudes had culminated in the tragic death of a vulnerable child. What was notable about the Curtis Committee, however, was its evident desire from the outset to inform itself about the nature and shortcomings of the system of care—such as it was—then in place, coupled with an equal determination to find new and constructive solutions in an open-minded manner without rushing to identify immediate scapegoats for current failures. Subsequent inquiries, adopting an inquisitorial rather than investigative stance, have often focused more on apportioning blame for systemic or professional failures in care structures already in place nationally. Though the Curtis Committee recognized that institutional attitudes and poor practice often played a large part in compounding the disadvantages suffered by already deprived children and did not hesitate to say so, it shared the widely held view, strongly articulated by Lady Allen in her pamphlet *Whose Children?* (Allen, 1945), that the government's failure up to that time to make the plight of homeless children a central object of its concern was a major contributory factor to the shortcomings revealed. This contrasts with the perspective adopted by most later inquiries, where the underlying assumption tended to be that the government had already established a satisfactory framework for the care of vulnerable children, thanks to the enactments of the 1948 Children Act and its successors, so that failures could be more readily blamed primarily on those responsible for implementing care policies, rather than on the government's own lack of involvement.

In large part the Curtis Committee was concerned with the need to regularize the haphazard existing arrangements for "boarding out", which at the time were shared between seven different government departments, each with its own independent system of operation and supervision. I shall not enlarge unduly on this important aspect of the Committee's work, save to remark that its final recommendations fell short of advocating the setting up either of a single new department of government solely responsible for children's welfare, or of a new social services department—the term "social services" being then practically unknown. Instead, it recommended coordinating child welfare provision for homeless children in its social and psychological aspects under the overall direction of a single government department that was already in existence—in practice, the "Home Department"—while accepting that such children's educational and medical needs should continue to be discharged by the relevant government departments, as before. Although Bowlby was not invited to express a view on this aspect of the Committee's deliberations when he appeared before it to give oral evidence, he did subsequently urge in government committees that this continued division of government responsibility, preferable though it was to the previous haphazard arrangements, was nevertheless undesirable. What was needed, he argued, was the setting up of a quite separate Children's Department of State. His views were not heeded at the time—indeed, they were resented in some Whitehall quarters. Ironically, over five decades and several inquiries later, Bowlby's suggestion is currently being implemented by the government.

Turning to the care of deprived and homeless children at a more local level, the Curtis Committee recommended the centralizing of responsibility for the oversight and care in a unitary local authority department exercised through a Children's Committee. With the 1948 Act, each local authority was to have a children's officer, "an executive officer of high standing and qualifications who would be a specialist in childcare". She—it was assumed in almost all cases this post would be filled by a woman—would have vested in her "the parental functions" on behalf of the authority (Curtis Report, 1946, para. 443). The Committee saw it as its crucial recommendation to government, stressing that the children's officer should be "the pivot" of the new system of care, and that she would be "the *person* to whom the child would look as guardian" (para. 443—the italicized emphasis is from the report itself). So while appearing at first sight to create a bureaucratic solution to the previous muddle of services for children, the Committee in fact went out of its way to underline the importance of the non-institutional aspect of the children's officer's function. Of course, it was not envisaged that the children's officer in each local authority could know each child for whom she was responsible personally. She would require a team of child care officers working under her, each with a caseload sufficiently small to allow her—again it was presumed that this would be for the most part a woman's job—"to be the friend of those particular children [in her caseload] up to the age of sixteen or eighteen" (para. 445).

This emphasis on the importance of a personal relationship of the departmental official to the individual child in care was unique to the 1948 Children Act. Not only was the specificity of the role of the children's officer unusual—she was to be concerned solely with the interests of children, not with any other aspect of community social care provision—but so, too, was the overriding emphasis on maintaining close contact with those for whom she was responsible. It is easy to dismiss these recommendations, and the subsequent legislation that gave them effect, as hopelessly unrealistic. How could the administrative burden of decision-making for all children coming into and leaving care, proposals for adoption and the vetting of prospective adopters, the monitoring of the local authority's children's homes and those of voluntary bodies, appointment of staff, financial accountability, all be combined with a personal interest in each and every child? And even if some of these tasks were delegated, how was it possible to ensure the continuity of oversight for the individual child for the duration of his care that was envisaged by the Committee?

In fact, it was not the supposedly impossible dimensions of the task that caused the eventual demise in the early 1970s of the posts of children's officer and child care officer, but organizational pressures of a different sort—in particular, the desire to make social work more of a higher-status profession, with wider scope for responsibility and career advancement. By then two further significant developments had taken place within childcare that altered the perspective of 1948 and contributed to the collapse of the power of the children's departments in local authorities. The first was that residential care, as distinct from fostering or adoption, went out of favour as an intrinsically desirable option for children in care. The second was that the aspect of retrieving children from dysfunctional families as opposed to providing children with no families at all with substitute care became the dominant focus of childcare intervention. A noticeable feature, indeed, of the Curtis Committee deliberations was its relative lack of concern with spelling out the practical and legal implications of State intervention in order to take a child into care—or to keep a child in care—against the wishes of its family. The assumption at the time was that the rights of parents and families to bring up their children were not being radically challenged by the proposed legislation. The Committee's primary concern was with homeless or abandoned children, not with contesting the claims of parents who wanted to care for their own children, albeit sometimes in less than ideal fashion. Indeed, it was made explicit that in all cases where the parents wanted to reclaim responsibility for the upbringing of a child in care, the presumption should be that this wish should be respected. Only in exceptional cases was it seen as the duty of the local authority to object to such a request through the Courts; and if it happened, the onus would be on it to demonstrate an overriding need, rather than on the family to demonstrate its fitness to look after the child.

The contrast in this respect with the underlying assumptions behind the later 1989 Children Act is significant, even though this may not at first be apparent. Although the latter was premised on the superficially similar assumption that receiving a child into care where the child had a family of its own was a last resort, not a first option, in practice the determining criteria were much more focused on qualitative factors—in particular, on how adequately the family functioned so as to ensure the best interests of the child, rather than on whether the family existed as a viable unit at all. And in reaching this qualitative judgement, the views of the Social Services Department—as it now was—were to be much more determinant than had been contemplated in the provisions of the 1948 Act. The social worker's role, in other words, became much more investigative—even, in certain circumstances, inquisitorial. Moreover, the legal framework with which decisions were to be reached was expected to be adversarial. At the same time the 1989 Act left the role and scope of local authority residential care actual provision greatly attenuated. Henceforth its task was primarily to afford respite, not long-term nurturing care. This much was evident from the official government policy document accompanying the 1989 Act, entitled *The Care of Children*, in which it was stated that "Admission to public care by virtue of a compulsory order is itself a risk to be balanced against others" and "Time is a crucial element and should be reckoned in days and months rather than years."

As to the actual care provision for young children recommended by the Curtis Committee in 1946, preference not unnaturally was given to adoption, provided it was properly regulated and not rushed into. (The Committee discouraged the widespread practice of so-called "third-party adoptions" but fell short of attempts to proscribe it altogether.) The next-most-desirable option was seen as "boarding out": that is to say, fostering under Local Authority supervision. It is interesting, and perhaps significant, that the Committee chose to retain this descriptive term in its report, especially given that the concept of "boarding out" had become negatively coloured in the public mind both by the equivocal experience of wartime evacuation and billeting and, more immediately, by the disastrous experience that had befallen the O'Neill brothers. The term "boarding out" conveys the sense of a rather impersonal, remote sort of care, while the Committee was clearly anxious to stress the desirability of its very family-centredness. Its reasons for nevertheless continuing to use the term "boarding out" in preference to fostering seem to have been three-fold: The first was the wish to emphasize that "boarded-out" children did not "belong" to those fostering them. Rather, they belonged to the family of origin, who were expected and encouraged to visit them. Second, the person whom the child was expected to regard as ultimately responsible for him or her in the absence of the parents—save in the case of adoption—was the children's officer rather than the immediate carers. It was she who was expected to be the abiding figure throughout all the years the child' was in care. And, third, the term "fostering" had hitherto been confined to informal arrangements of substitute care, where parents confided their child to a relative or neighbour. The Committee wanted to make it clear that such fostering that was "boarding out by private persons" should in future be regulated and supervised by the local authority.

Not far behind "boarding out" in desirability was placement either of a family of children in a single "family group home" or of groups of children of mixed age and sex in individual "cottage homes" that could be—and often were—linked together. These latter homes were to comprise a housemother with a husband or an assistant and between six and a dozen children. Though linked for administrative purposes, special emphasis was placed on these homes being small and independently staffed.

The Committee also considered other types of residential accommodation provision for deprived children. They were clearly in favour of the retention of the sort of therapeutic hostels that Winnicott and Clare Britton had successfully pioneered through the Oxfordshire evacuation scheme, but they were inhibited from making explicit recommendations for their continuance due to the fact that meeting the needs of "maladjusted children" had recently become the responsibility of the Department of Education through the 1944 Education Act. As approved schools, on the other hand, still remained the responsibility of the Home Office, under whose aegis the Curtis Committee had been set up, it had no hesitation in recommending their continuance. It was felt that they provided satisfactorily for the needs of antisocial children, whether or not the latter had actually been convicted of any criminal offence. So it can be seen that the Committee, while wishing to stress the importance of family-based or family-type care for the majority of homeless children, nevertheless recognized a continuing role for large and relatively more "institutional" types of provision for certain categories of youngster.

Not all the recommendations of the Curtis Committee were incorporated unmodified into the 1948 Children Act. Separate residential nurseries for the youngest children, for instance, had been recommended as a resource that should be available to each local authority, but the government decided that this should not be a universal provision. It is difficult to determine what accounted for this shift, but it is significant that the question of whether or not there should be residential nurseries for the youngest children was an issue that divided Bowlby and Winnicott, the former arguing against them, the latter in their favour. It is at least possible that Bowlby, with his closer access to government than Winnicott, won the political argument over this in the couple of years that intervened between publication of the Report and the subsequent legislation.

The evidence of Bowlby, Winnicott, and Clare Britton to the Curtis Committee

It may seem a little strange that I have summarized some of the main recommendations of the Curtis Committee before discussing the detailed testimony to the Inquiry of the figures with whom we are directly concerned. However, I have chosen to do so because the importance of the impact of Bowlby and Winnicott lay less in their specific suggestions, some of which were either not turned into recommendations or not embodied in the subsequent legislation, or else were only partially acted upon. More important was the influence they brought to bear on the general outlook of its members in determining the priorities and focus of the Committee faced with the whole dismal panorama of post-war homelessness and deprivation. One has to bear in mind that apart from their input and the experience gained from its members' own extensive visits of inquiry to residential institutions, most of the evidence available to the Committee came from the testimony of voluntary bodies, some of them long established, who were already engaged in providing for such children and had evolved their own philosophies, strategy, and physical structures to suit, many of these being institutional, outmoded, and inflexible. Given the financial constraints of a wartime economy, together with the fact that local authorities throughout the country lacked actual homes for the children for whom they were newly expected to be responsible, it would have been tempting for the Committee, and later for the government, to have allowed themselves to be strongly influenced by the conservative perspective and organizational presumptions of these bodies: in other words, even while trying to counteract some of the adverse effects of institutionalized care, out of expediency to have come up with institutional or at least predominantly bureaucratic solutions to the problem of dealing with homeless children.

All of this makes it the more remarkable that in its final report the Curtis Committee placed such sustained emphasis on the importance of the *personal* nature of the care that needed to be provided for the deprived child. And much credit for this must surely lie with Bowlby, Winnicott, and Clare Britton, who had humanized the evacuation process and were determined that its lessons should be incorporated in the new provisions. It was not simply that childcare in the new order of things was to have a human face. The task, as they saw it, for the government was nothing less than the vicarious assumption of parental responsibilities for deprived children's upbringing. This meant that plans for children had to be well considered, and that they should have a childhood-long perspective. There was no question here of the provision of care by the state being viewed by its potential providers as a necessary evil, to be endured by the hapless child in care for as short a time as possible. Adoption might continue to be the preferred option for most deprived children, but the care to be afforded to those who could not benefit from adoption was to be equal to it in quality, commitment, and continuity.

Nevertheless, for all it indebtedness to this trio of experts, it is clear that the Committee found some difficulty in reconciling many of their specific recommendations with its wider remit. For one thing, not all of their suggestions were mutually consistent. Bowlby, as we have seen, was against separate nursery provision; Winnicott and Britton were marginally in favour. Again, Bowlby did not approve of the concept of reception centres for assessing the needs of children newly arrived in care, whereas Winnicott and Britton felt that such centres were essential if appropriate and lasting plans were to be made for a child's long-term future. However, the Committee's main difficulty in assimilating their evidence and giving it practical expression derived from a fundamental difference of perspective between itself and these psychoanalytically informed experts. This was about how much childhood homelessness and deprivation were to be regarded as primarily a social, or primarily a psychological issue. All were agreed that it was a mixture of both. The difference was over the balance.

As had been said, the recent experience of the evacuation scheme had a large influence on the Committee's deliberations, but in somewhat equivocal fashion. Bowlby and Winnicott, for their part, had uncompromisingly stated that from a psychological point of view the enforced break-up of families and childhood separation from parents entailed by the evacuation scheme had to be regarded as nothing less than a social "disaster", even if an unavoidable one. Still, there was one positive outcome of the evacuation experience when looked at as an adventitious piece of social research. The Cambridge Evacuation Survey had shown that where evacuated children came from previously intact and well-functioning families, they could usually attach to their host families and adjust to the separation without too much lasting psychological damage, provided they were not too young when the move from the parents occurred—that is to say, not under five years of age. In other words, in certain conditions children—even small children—*could* survive psychologically the absence of their parents and temporally transfer their affections onto other caregivers.

Faced with the very large number of homeless children in the immediate post-war period, it was perhaps understandable then for the Committee to fasten on this relatively more optimistic possibility in the light of the Cambridge survey and consider that the homeless population as a whole might comprise a comparable range of disturbed and not-so-disturbed young people. If that were the case, it reasoned, then might not a significant proportion of homeless children, those who were relatively less disturbed, be able to settle down successfully with substitute families—that is, be "boarded out"—even while conceding that the remainder, or many of them, would require different, possibly more specialized types of residential provision, with an emphasis not so much on substitute family provision as on therapeutically remedial care? Such was the Committee's—and the government's—initial expectation. It was therefore somewhat disconcerting for the Committee to find that in the firm opinion of Bowlby and Winnicott *all* the children for whom they were having to make provision were to be considered psychologically scarred, simply by virtue of their external circumstances of being orphaned, lost, or rejected by their families of origin, regardless of other secondary emotional or behavioural disabilities. During the oral testimony hearing attended by Winnicott and Clare Britton on 17 December 1945, the Chair of the Committee was even led to comment to her fellow members in a tone of slight exasperation: "I think our witnesses feel that every child is a problem child. If that is so, if we have to accept the need for caring for children in hostels or institutions, then we must make up our minds what sort of hostels we need."

But there was a further complication hereabouts. Bowlby, who had given his oral testimony to the Committee some months earlier, had drawn a rather different corollary from the basic premise he shared with Winnicott, that all homeless children ought to be regarded as significantly disturbed. His consequential view was that the care for deprived children provided by the State must as far as possible avoid compounding the child's problems and traumas, such as would inevitably happen if there were to be a series of changes of placement or the dispersal of brothers and sisters following reception into care on the basis of supposedly more pressing psychological needs. Nothing in his opinion could outweigh the need for stability and continuity of environmental provision. So his main recommendation to the Committee was simple and stark: the immediate and near-universal provision of individualized or family unit fostering for all children from the moment they were received into care. His belief about the adverse effects of administratively determined types of provision underlay his opposition to reception centres as well as to residential nurseries. Whatever the diagnostic or other benefits these might be said to serve, they were more than offset by the lack of continuous, individualized child-centred care, which in his view would alone enable the deprived child to develop relationships with significant adults secure in the expectation that these would endure. Bowlby's stance was predictably trenchant. After all, his written testimony to the Committee had consisted of his *Forty-Four Juvenile Thieves* paper (Bowlby, 1946), with its clear portrayal of the consequences of early and frequent changes of primary caregiver. Though he was prepared to allow the practical need for some alternative forms of provision, notably "cottage homes", and grudgingly accepted that these latter, if small enough, were at least preferable to any larger-scale alternatives, he was still reluctant fully to endorse the sort of therapeutic benefits to be derived from systematic, specialized hostel-type provision such as Winnicott and Britton had evolved in Oxfordshire, and which they were to advocate as an integral part of the post-war care provision. In declining to do so, Bowlby did admit, however, that his recent wartime duties—from 1941 he had been on Army service, attached to the War Office Officer Selection Board—had largely prevented him from becoming acquainted at first hand with the development of specialist hostels.[2] And while claiming that "one move and one move only is the right move" for children coming into care (Bowlby, oral evidence to the Curtis Committee, 25 June 1945), he did not ignore the difficulties likely to be imposed on the carers if this prescription were to be adopted. Indeed, he emphasized the inevitable challenges, the bouts of disruptiveness, the prevalence of enuresis and incontinence, as well as a variety of other neurotic symptoms that carers would have to contend with. He insisted on the need for foster carers to be properly prepared and trained in advance, and the importance of their having ready access to psychological support through the Child Guidance Service for the length of a child's placement.

Bowlby's recommendations to the Committee were straightforward in theory, if rather impractical to implement, at least on the scale he was advocating. The Committee was conscious of the great dearth of potential foster carers for "boarded-out children" in the aftermath of war, even though Bowlby's stress on family-based "non-institutional" care was in accord with its overall thinking. Compared with his, the evidence provided by Winnicott and Britton[3] to the Committee was challenging in a different way. In essence they wanted the Committee to regard the government's task of providing for homeless children as being as much a therapeutic as a social one. In their joint paper "The Problem of Homeless Children" (Winnicott & Britton, 1944), presented as written evidence to the Committee, this was clearly spelt out. Their starting point was that an essential ingredient of a good home for the growing child is a sense of security built on the experience of "a father and a mother [living] together in a stable relationship into which the child can be accepted and welcomed" (p. 103). The child's capacity for trust engendered in the well-functioning family unit depended on the ability for testing out "over and over again" the parents' reliability "to remain good parents in spite of anything he may do to hurt or annoy them" (p. 103).

If this was the case for the ordinary child, the amount of testing out was bound to be that much greater for a child whose initial capacity for taking for granted the reliability of his environment had been undermined. For this reason, and based on their evacuation experience, they were not confident in the resilience of an ordinary family to provide the requisite structure within which the deprived youngster could test out the durability of the environment. The danger was not just that the fostering arrangement would break down under the strain. More insidious, because more hidden, might be the development of a superficial, false compliance on the part of the child in response to the threatened loss of his carers, masking for the time being his rebelliousness and rage, only for this to resurface with more devastating personal consequences at a later date. It was to forestall this risk that they advocated the widespread initial use of small residential homes—"hostels"—the purpose of which would be two-fold: to provide a *primary home experience* and to prepare the child for eventual fostering or adoption.

It seems at first sight paradoxical that Winnicott, especially given his insistence on the importance of the earliest relational bonds, should be found here advocating as standard a type of provision for deprived and homeless youngsters that was, at least structurally, non-familial in character. Yet it was consistent with another long-held premise of his: namely, that the containing function of the mother, or mother substitute, depended greatly on her, in turn, being safely contained within a supportive—"facilitating"—environment. The one was as important as the other. Thus the ability of the home environment for deprived youngsters successfully to cope with their disruptive behaviour without suppressing its expression through an enforced conformity—allowing for its "nuisance value", in Winnicott's words—assumed paramount importance. For this to happen, there had to be a capacity within the home environment to tolerate, without retaliation, challenge, violence, hate. He saw the small but well supported family group home as being able to provide the basic ingredients of "family home experience"—including allowance for the development of close personal relationships—while affording the desired sense of security better—because more reliably—than the average foster home. The latter, he felt, would be less able to withstand the sustained challenges that a needy child was likely to make on the substitute parents' capacity to love, care, and appropriately control him, as the price of recovery from his sense of loss and trust.

In urging this view, Winnicott did not shirk from acquainting the Committee with his own failed attempt at fostering, which, from the account he gave there, had culminated not just in his putting the foster child in question out on the doorstep after several episodes of unmanageable behaviour, but in having to undergo a follow-up visit from the local police, to whom he was required to explain why he had seen fit to leave the boy out at night alone on the streets of London in the blackout—a detail omitted from his later reference to same the incident (Winnicott, 1947/1958, pp. 199–200). It would seem as if Winnicott wanted to use this example to highlight the dangers of a simplified and sentimental attitude to the enterprise of looking after other people's children, and to warn the Committee against embracing too eagerly a policy of wholesale fostering that on the surface could appear ideally child-centred as well as politically convenient, while actually carrying great responsibilities and risks.

Winnicott's warnings were only partially heeded. As we have seen, the Committee eventually promoted "boarding out with families" as the optimum if not universal solution to homelessness and deprivation. Still, with a nod in their direction, it also advocated the alternative but parallel benefits of small group homes. Even here though, the Committee proved more receptive to Winnicott's and Clare Britton's recommendations about the need for small group homes as potential sites of "primary home provision" than to their further suggestion that these might best be diversified according to the diagnostic classification of the children to be accommodated. The

Committee's definite preference was for a mix of ages and types of children in each home, and for it to be "homely" rather than "therapeutic". In this the Committee members were inclining to the optimistic view already mentioned: namely, that most children received into care as homeless orphans would be capable of responding to a generally benign, non-punitive, child-centred regime and so would not automatically require an environment specifically designed to cater for more than ordinary impulsiveness and unmanageability. While it was anticipated that a good proportion of difficult-to-manage children would have to be catered for within the new care system, the Committee expressed the hope that the specialist hostels left over from the evacuation programme could meet this need and that the majority of emotionally disturbed—"maladjusted"—children would be absorbed into the special residential schools envisioned in the government's newly enacted education programme.

In summary, one may say that the major positive influence of Bowlby and Winnicott on the Curtis Committee's thinking was less in their specific recommendations than in their representations to its members about the overriding need to maintain a non-institutional perspective, faced with the task of planning to meet such an enormous and far-reaching social challenge. There was, however, one other indirect way in which Winnicott's influence in particular had a significant practical bearing on the Committee's subsequent recommendations. This concerns the key role to be accorded to the local authority children's officer in the new order of things. The model or prototype for such a figure was undoubtedly Clare Britton, Winnicott's wartime collaborator on the Oxfordshire evacuation programme and later to be his second wife. It is clear from her subsequent reminiscences about this period, as well as from the recently republished joint document they submitted to the Committee as part of their written evidence, that Clare Britton's role evolved considerably between 1941 and the end of the war (Kanter, 2004a, 2004b). From being at the outset a junior social worker put into the scheme by her superiors rather precipitately in order to provide practical assistance and structure to the visiting child psychiatrist—in the wake of reports reaching upwards about the rather erratic early interventions of Winnicott—she gradually came to assume overall management not just of the billeting scheme itself, but of all the child placement arrangements in Oxfordshire that were being made by many different agencies, often from other Counties seeking places to board out children in that relatively prosperous area. Not only did Clare Britton undertake the arrangements for these, she also continued personally to monitor all the children so placed. In doing so she unwittingly pioneered the profile of the future children's officer, someone with an overall grasp of the needs and resources in an area, personally committed, flexible, and able to offer practical and psychological support to all the families looking after other people's children.

Although this development in her role was due largely to Clare Britton's own skill and initiative, it could not have happened without Winnicott's readiness to support her and his ability to provide her with important and timely psychological insights. Their vital collaboration provided a model of a collegial relationship wherein their different but complementary skills were combined to produce an effective partnership in action, born of a mutual recognition that each needed the other in order for the caring enterprise to succeed. Winnicott's pattern, or reference point, for such a partnership was the well-functioning parental couple, cooperating in complementary fashion in the upbringing of their child. It was this model also that informed the working relationship of Clare Britton and Winnicott jointly with the staff running the several hostels housing the difficult-to-place evacuees who were their immediate concern within the scheme. And it became, in due course, the pattern for the working relationship envisaged by the Curtis Committee as being desirable between the child care officers and all those individual families undertaking the boarding out of children.

This principle of collegiality was a notable feature of the recommendations embodied in the 1948 Children Act. It informed the relationship envisaged between central and local government, and between the children's officer and her team of child care officers responsible for casework on the one hand, and the home staff or foster parents who undertook the active upbringing of the children in care on the other. It also underlay the principles on which it was hoped that the relationship between the local authority and the deprived child's family of origin would be based. "Cooperative endeavour" was to be the watchword, the desired cooperation stemming from the shared recognition both of the existence of complementary roles—namely, of provision and support, and of co-responsibility in ensuring "the conditions best calculated to compensate [these children] for the lack of parental care".

The positive tenor both of the Report and of the subsequent legislation may seem to be have been naively optimistic in retrospect. However, in reaching a judgement about this the present-day commentator needs to keep in mind the very different social and political climate that prevailed in Britain at the time these proposals were formulated, and the quite different assumptions then in play about the relationship between family and governmental responsibilities in regard to children. I consider some of these briefly in the final section of this chapter.

Bowlby, Winnicott, and the 1948 Children Act: some retrospective reflections

I have drawn attention in this chapter to the positive spirit in which the Curtis Committee was set up and the subsequent legislation—the 1948 Children Act—was passed, contrasting this with the dispiriting series of later reports about gross failures in children's care and the piecemeal reactive government measures to address them. After the war, the government believed that it had a responsibility to care for deprived children and that it could bring into effect measures that would make such institutional failures in care a thing of the past. Later inquiries and reports, such as the official 1973 report into the circumstances leading up to the death of Maria Colwell, seem to demonstrate a depressing truth: namely, that well-intentioned legislation could only achieve a limited amount in countering child neglect and abuse in society. As each new major case of a child's death in local authority care has come and gone, the shortcomings of social workers and other professionals have been highlighted, on the one hand prompting pleas and pressures for new legislation, and on the other giving rise to a sense of despair that even once the fresh suggested changes had been implemented, it would only be a matter of time before another shocking case came to light.

This is one reason why the Curtis Report and the 1948 Act can appear in retrospect to have been hopelessly idealistic and Bowlby and Winnicott naively collusive in this idealizing tendency. The Committee really did function on the premise that significant and lasting improvements in the quality of care could be made and sustained and that all parties, including the parents of deprived children, would be prepared willingly to cooperate in achieving this objective. Tempting though such a dismissive conclusion might be in the light of subsequent events, I think it is over-severe and unhistorical to judge it so. The legislation we have been considering, together with other child and family welfare enactments of the Attlee Administration, did achieve remarkable, if incomplete, successes. The total number of children in care came down: in 1945, according to the figures provided to the Curtis Committee, it was estimated that there were in England and Wales 124, 900 children "deprived of a normal family life" (Curtis Report, 1946, p. 27); the comparable total for children in care to the local authority in 2003 was 64,500 (Source: Office of Government Statistics). Closer examination of the statistical summary of the 1946 figures reveals that of the total, 61,200 comprised children who were either war orphans or homeless—unclaimed—evacuees. Part of the purpose of the 1948 legislation had been to ensure that in the immediate post-war era these children should be properly taken care of, in conjunction with another large cohort of deprived children: namely, those who had previously been assigned into care simply on grounds of extreme family poverty, through the antiquated provisions of the Poor Law, which were still in force up to the time of the passing of the new Act. It is clear that in the subsequent two decades both these groups of children—comprising roughly half the 1948 total of deprived children—were provided for and ceased to be a fixed part of the care system. Thus the positive outlook and proposals of the 1948 legislation seem to have been at least partially vindicated.

Nevertheless, if we take out of the 1948 total those children who had been made homeless due to war or extreme family poverty, we are left with approximately 63,700 children in care: that is to say, almost the same number as those in care nearly six decades later (64,500). It was the children comprising this further group—either delinquent, beyond parental control, seriously emotionally disturbed, psychiatrically ill, or inadequately parented—on whom Bowlby, Winnicott, and Britton concentrated their focus in evidence before the Committee. In hindsight, and judging from the comparative figures, these would appear to constitute something like an abiding core of "(to be) looked-after children". The question we have to ask, therefore, is whether the recommendations made by Bowlby and Winnicott concerning these young people had any appreciable effect in terms of future patterns of care for them.

First, let us consider the quality of the care that the Curtis Committee proposed should be provided by local authorities for such children, and which the Government duly adopted in the 1948 Act. Its aim was to ensure that a child's lack of a normal upbringing with his own parents did not constitute a disadvantage throughout childhood and beyond. To avoid this happening, particular emphasis was placed on the need for the care provided to be non-institutional in character and above all *personal* in nature. To this end the children's officer was to be regarded as a guardian acting *in loco parentis* on behalf of the state for all the children in the care of that particular locality. Was this goal achieved? Well, there was undoubtedly a wholesale humanization of residential care in the years following the Act. Family group homes replaced the large voluntary-funded institutions as the primary source of such care. Child Guidance Centres proliferated throughout the country, from 95 clinics in 1945 to 344 two decades later—almost a fourfold increase (Sampson, 1980). Likewise, both day and residential schools for maladjusted children, as they were then known, were set up by most local authorities under the provisions of the 1944 Education Act, and generous financial support was offered from central government for pioneers such as Dockar-Drysdale, Lenhoff, and David Wills to start their own therapeutic units (Bridgeland, 1971). The emphasis was undoubtedly on the long-term nurture and treatment of vulnerable youngsters, with only the old Approved Schools, with their emphasis on "training", remaining relatively immune to the prevailing therapeutic climate. Of course, to profess nurturing and therapeutic aims is not the same thing as achieving them in practice, and very few schools proved capable of attaining or sustaining the quality of therapeutic care achieved by Dockar-Drysdale at the Mulberry Bush School. But great efforts were put into the training of child care officers, particularly in casework skills and in communicating with children. The number of educational psychologists multiplied, and trainings in child psychotherapy were inaugurated (Reeves, 2003). Not the least positive achievement of these years, particularly in the light of what happened in the last quarter of the century, is that no major scandals involving the neglect or abuse of children in care occurred in the years between 1948 and 1970—that is to say, during the whole period in which the system proposed and enacted in 1948 was in operation. The succession of enquiries about failures of children in care that I have already referred to all followed the coming into being in 1971 of the new Social Service Departments—replacing the Children's Departments—the reorganization of social work training, and the introduction of the concept of "generic" social work, with its concurrent shift of emphasis from developing individual casework ability, especially in regard to children, in favour of acquiring assessment and managerial skills and a perspective of resource allocation. In short, for a period of about two decades following the 1948 Act the underlying principle of the State taking care of the child did take hold, despite inevitable shortcomings, and transmitted itself into an effective system of national childcare. "Looked-after children", to use the modern term, were seen as dependent and requiring, above all, stability and security of parenting care, the object of adult responsibility. They were not regarded principally as semi-autonomous yet vulnerable clients, one of a number of distinct "user groups" within a large care provision system. Nor was it then viewed as a principal responsibility of the state in their regard, and a primary social work task, to ensure the maintenance of their rights and their protection from potential abuse by their carers or guardians. Rightly or wrongly, these were then considered duties of a second order, the first being that of the provision of continuous care.

If Bowlby and Winnicott could take some realistic satisfaction from the fact of the engagement of the post-war State in the psychological wellbeing of deprived children, might the same be said about the types of care provided? The Curtis Committee, as we have seen, wished to promote "boarding out" as far as possible, while recognizing the practical need for a plentiful supply of small children's homes for the foreseeable future. Where Bowlby was keen to maximize the number of boarded-out children, Winnicott and Britton stressed the positive benefits of small-group—hostel—provision instead. From the various tables provided by the Curtis Committee it is possible to estimate that in 1946 only about 22% of children in care lived with families, and the remainder in children's homes, schools or voluntary institutions; nearly six decades later the proportion was more than reversed: in 2003 in England only 17% and in Wales just 6.6% of children were in residential establishments.

One might say, therefore, that Bowlby's stress on the importance of securing one-to-one relationships of deprived children to their main carers had been heeded in the years following the passing of the 1948 Act. Furthermore, a key prospect held out by the Curtis Committee was realized—namely, of a gradual diminution of non-familial forms of substitute care in proportion to the rest as the level of national prosperity increased in the 1950s. Yet I personally doubt whether Bowlby would have been altogether satisfied with these figures and this outcome. Certainly he would have approved the demise particularly of the large children's homes run by charities such as the National Children's Homes and Barnados. But what his evidence to the Committee as well as his later work for the World Health Organization make clear was that Bowlby's aim was to reduce to a minimum, if not totally remove, the need for "reception into care" in whatever form.

> It may, in two or three generations, be possible to enable all boys and girls to grow up to become men and women . . . capable of providing a stable and happy life for their children. In this way, it may be hoped both to promote mental health and to get rid of very many of the factors which at present cause children to be deprived of maternal care. [Bowlby, 1953, p. 153]

More than half a century later this hope has palpably not been realized and shows no prospect of being so. The question arises, then: was it ever a realistic target; or, rather, should Bowlby ever have had reason to think that it was? Bowlby's grounds for thinking so came, I believe, from his medical background—in particular, from his acquaintance with the efficacy of preventive medicine in eradicating endemic disease conditions during the century from 1850 to 1950. He repeatedly drew comparisons between the provision of maternal care and the provision of vitamins for a child's healthy physical development; he liked to talk about "mental hygiene"; and he railed at the wrong-headedness of governments unprepared to devote money to ensuring that families could stay together, or that the mother could afford to stay at home to look after her children, at the same time as being ready to expend vastly greater public funds on what Bowlby perceived as the direct social results of their failure to do so. All this indicated an abiding conviction on his part that if only the right policies were adopted and the right means employed, deprivation and delinquency could largely be eradicated from society, much as one-time plagues had been.

Nothing better illustrates the root difference between Bowlby and Winnicott than the former's resolute adherence to this disease model of psychological disorder. Although Winnicott sometimes employed the same analogy in his writings—for instance, in referring to psychosis as an "environmental deficiency disease" (Winnicott, 1949c/1958, p. 246)—and although he shared to some degree Bowlby's belief in the corrigibility of society as well as of persons, he never abandoned the key psychoanalytic concepts of conflict and ambivalence as intrapsychic factors. Winnicott was always looking for the effects of the interplay of conflicting tendencies of love and hate that made up the dispositions and behaviour of human beings large and small, singly and collectively. For him, the problem of deprivation was never going to go away completely because its causes were rooted in the human condition as much as in the external conditions bearing on a child. He did not embrace the pessimistic outlook of Freud, with his vision of the individual and society as locked in an unending struggle based on the vicissitudes of opposition between individual instincts and societal pressures. Hence he was not passive, or passively accepting, in regard to the social dimension of human conflict. But, much more than Bowlby, he saw the process as part of a continuous dialectic—though he would not have approved of the term—wherein at times the caring capacities of the individual or groups held sway over the drive to dominate and control, and at other times were submerged by them, rather in the manner of a rotating waterwheel or the up-and-down movement of a piston.

Winnicott's thinking about how deprivation was to be understood as a phenomenon of society—as distinct from how it should be addressed as a practical problem—was still in an embryonic stage of development throughout these years. On one occasion during this period he lectured—almost harangued—magistrates about the need to tolerate the existence of deprivation in society as a fact, something to be endured, and about the corresponding need for delinquency, as one of its primary manifestations, to be publicly met, if not with a tolerance that would be tantamount to connivance, at least with an acceptance of its necessary "nuisance value" for society (Winnicott, 1946b). At other times his gaze turned more inward, to explore how deprived behaviour affected the caring individual—including himself—and the multiple resonances of concern and rejection it was capable of setting in train (Winnicott, 1947). These reflections led him down avenues seemingly far removed from Bowlby's more straightforward path to the causes and cure of deprivation. Some of Winnicott's reflections were counterintuitive. For instance, for all that he was keen, like Bowlby, to draw attention to society's responsibility, and self-interest, in attending to the needs of the deprived child, he was also ready to assert that deprivation was an external expression, an epiphenomenon, of unconscious hatred directed towards the child: not just hatred on the part of the rejecting parent but, more provocatively, hatred on the part of a civil society, inconvenienced by the social consequences of parental hate that for whatever reason had proved disproportionate to, and incapable of being bounded by, a countervailing love felt by the would-be—should be—nurturing parent(s) towards their offspring.

Why did Winnicott indulge, and that so publicly, in the expression of these "hard sayings"? His intention, like Clare Britton's in speaking dismissively about the "rescue motive" (C. Winnicott, 1955a), seems to have been provocative yet purposeful: to try to modify the expression of outraged parental and societal hate engendered by the reciprocally hateful behaviour of deprived and rejecting children, by communicating its complex underlying dynamic. Both of them were made impatient by sentimental attitudes towards deprived children. They viewed such sentimentality as an unstable reaction formation to hate that, if unacknowledged, would only reappear in destructively vengeful ways. Winnicott's hope was that by encouraging acknowledgement of how truly awful rejected and rejecting children could be, and by allowing for tolerance of the role of the impersonal retributive principle within society, it would be possible to assuage the revenge feelings arising out of affront and injury to the sense of self sufficiently to enable other loving, caring tendencies to come into play within society. In short, caring for the deprived child was not only potentially recuperative for the individual child; it could also be reparative for his parents and for society. Yet this desirable state of affairs could only come about through the adult world recognizing not just the extent of the child's plight and pain, but also the adult caring self's own sense of distress and even disappointment in the child for engendering such distress.

Winnicott seems to have sensed that in a British society that felt itself to have been collectively assaulted by the ravages of warfare, there were the stirrings of a general concern for its most vulnerable members born in part of a complex of sentiments, comprising not just loving and nurturing feelings, but also an obscure sense of guilt for past indifference. At the time it would have been impossible to know for sure whether this change within British society was something permanent or merely a passing phase. My case is that this sense of involved public concern was, indeed, a transient phenomenon, and that in barely a generation it became transformed into a rather guilt-laden and oppressive sense of accountability for children's welfare. For reasons lying beyond the purview of this book, it could be argued—though doing so would take the discussion well beyond the scope of this chapter—that concern for the plight of vulnerable children has never been a sustained feature of British society—not, at least, to the extent of it being prepared to deal with its fundamental causes regardless of cost. More commonly, concern that mobilizes action on children's behalf is reactive rather than preventative—or, rather, preventative of the danger or damage known and recognized because it has already occurred, not of the next danger that may be lying in wait to happen. Whether this is truly the case, and if it is, then why it is so, are questions the answers to which must, at best, be conjectural. What, I believe, is instructive to observe is that for at least a brief period in the middle of the twentieth century the predominant bias in British society towards individual (self-) interest rather than communitarian good was temporarily overturned; that within this context a duty of care in regard to children became widely seen as a duty to care for the parentless in a sustained and settled way, almost regardless of the financial cost; and, finally, that Bowlby and Winnicott were able to exploit the opportunity that presented itself just then in a professionally significant way.

NOTES

1. The term "fit person" denoted a person or body deemed capable of providing (substitute) care, not the potential recipient of that care. Prior to 1948, a local authority identified by a magistrate as a "fit person" to care for a delinquent

youngster was at liberty to decline that responsibility, just as any private "fit person" was, and occasionally did so, thus leaving the young person at liberty.

2. Later, in his WHO Report *Maternal Care and Mental Health* (1951), Bowlby was to write much more approvingly of the contribution made by the sort of specialist residential care that Winnicott and Britton had pioneered in the wartime hostels.

3. In this section I have paraphrased the evidence of Bowlby, Winnicott, and Clare Britton without giving page references in each instance because the documents from which they are drawn, held in the Public Records Office at Kew (Curtis Committee, 1945–46), are not numbered by page. The oral evidence is collected in the form of a series of loose bundles of typescript, comprising verbatim transcripts of the questions, answers, and comments, of the various witnesses, ordered in chronological order of their appearance before the Curtis Committee. In an interview years later, reflecting on this period, Clare Winnicott appears to suggest that she gave evidence before the Committee on a separate occasion from Donald (Cohen, 1980/Kanter, 2004b, p. 138). However, it is clear that on 17 December 1945 the Committee interviewed them together, some of the questions on that occasion being responded to by Donald, others by Clare. It is quite likely that one or a number of members of the Committee came to visit the set-up in Oxfordshire and put further questions to Clare Britton in the course of it, but, if so, this would not have constituted a separate formal presentation of evidence, such as she implies happened; nor is there other independent evidence of such a visit having taken place. There is no doubt, however, that throughout its hearings the Committee as a whole took a lively interest in the Oxfordshire experiment.

CHAPTER SIX

Postscript: from past impact to present influence

Christopher Reeves

In chapters 2 and 5 I have kept mainly to an historical approach because I believe that the contributions of Bowlby and Winnicott in the fields of child care and child mental health have to be viewed in the context of their times and the social issues that they were confronting. To do otherwise is to risk misrepresenting, even trivializing, their work. However, in a book devoted to a demonstration of the abiding importance of these two key figures of twentieth-century British psychoanalysis, it would be remiss of me not also to consider what relevance their views might hold for contemporary childcare theory. So, we need to ask the question: are their ideas and recommendations of the 1940s and 1950s of merely historical interest, or do they have continuing relevance today?

One way of attempting to answer this question would be to draw a direct comparison between what they themselves consistently advocated and what currently obtains in British childcare legislation and practice. I have mostly resisted the temptation of speculating overmuch on what Bowlby and Winnicott themselves might have made of changes in childcare legislation in the decades subsequent to their deaths, although at various points I have alluded to changes that could be seen as a reversal of developments of which they clearly approved. In this connection I particularly pointed out how the post-

Seebohm Social Services Acts of 1971 and 1972 that ushered in the conglomerate Department of Health and Social Services that we still inherit, and introduced the era of the generic social worker, dismantled a crucial piece of the 1948 Children Act. This dismantling Winnicott would doubtless have resisted as forcibly as his widow did, since it undermined a key principle enshrined in the earlier Act: namely, that a child's social welfare and mental health needs should comprise a distinct and separate concern of state-funded social welfare. The same could perhaps be said of the gradual demise of another aspect of child welfare provision that began in roughly the same period: the progressive closure of cottage homes and family group homes as alternatives to foster care. This also, I suspect, would have been opposed by Winnicott—though not by Bowlby—as being unrealistic and doctrinaire.

However, this point only serves to underline how difficult and ultimately unrewarding it is to guess their responses to conditions and circumstances of which they could not be aware. In general, I have tried to stress the importance of the social philosophy context in understanding their contributions, not because I believe that their proposals were situation-specific and hence devoid of contemporary relevance, but because it enables us more readily to accommodate to the fact that current concerns, proposals, and legislation are themselves more situation-specific than they are usually taken to be, and as such will eventually come to be regarded as historic yet transient responses to events and fashions. Given this, the important thing is to be able to pick out patterns, or conjunctions of circumstance, that lend impetus to certain trends in childcare and define, at least for a time, the salient priorities.

However, I do not want to sound too relativistic, as if to insinuate that ultimately all ideas and proposals in this area are historically conditioned to such an extent that no abiding lessons can be drawn from the past and no truly efficacious measures can be taken to address the mental health needs of young people now and in the future. What these twin examinations into their respective ideas about delinquency and care of the deprived reveal is that the causes of childhood and adolescent delinquency cannot be reduced simply to maternal deprivation or cured by appropriate welfare provision on the model of the immunization against childhood diseases, as Bowlby sometimes seemed to imply. While it is the case that the number of young people needing substitute care dropped by half during the 1950s following implementation of the 1948 Children Act as the aftereffects of wartime deaths and dislocation worked themselves out, it is sobering to realize that the number of young people requiring care of one sort or another organized by the State for social or psychological reasons has remained surprisingly constant since then. Bowlby and Winnicott were fortunate in being able to contribute at a peculiarly optimistic and receptive period for child welfare provision in Britain. Still, the problems have proved more complex and intractable than perhaps either of them had envisaged.

What, then, does this tell us about the lasting importance or otherwise of their input? On the positive side, what they both succeeded in introducing for the first time into public recognition and debate was the importance of thinking about children as individuals, not just for broadly humanitarian reasons but because the interests of society were best served in the long term by doing so. We take it so much for granted nowadays that children are capable of feeling anxiety, distress, rejection, neglect just as readily as adults do, and that when they do, much of their suffering is due to the way adults treat them, either unwittingly or out of malice. Indeed, the abuse of children, actual or potential, is a major cause of parental and public concern. It is consequently easy to overlook that until the middle of the last century the fact that children might suffer long-term damage through casual cruelty or careless neglect was not a universal presumption or a guiding factor in providing for the needs of parentless children. Bowlby and Winnicott were foremost in bringing this awareness to general consciousness, and it represents their principal and abiding contribution to childcare legislation and practice.

However, giving substance to the principle of "treating children as individuals" is a programme fraught with potential ambiguity. What Bowlby and Winnicott meant by it was primarily to respect the individual needs of young people as dependent and immature—that is to say, to recognize the child's needs for reliable and continuous parenting, and so ensuring the rights and underlining the responsibilities of parents were intimately associated with their idea of treating children as individuals. It is here that the ambiguity arises: how to demarcate the rights of children to be treated as individuals and the rights of parents to have their parenting responsibilities protected? And how to ensure that the state, through its legislation and through the practical implementation of its guardianship role of children and parents, respectively, does not itself become either a usurper of the parental role or else a mere anodyne back-up resource when things go wrong? Put another way, how to take on a quasi-parental role where necessary, without taking over parental responsibilities when it is not? And if this is a problematic area for the state in regard to the actual parents *vis-à-vis* their child, it is even more so in connection with substitute parents, where the state has an additional role to play in selecting and validating them. In discharging this responsibility, the temptation for government to be over-intrusive and over-directive is even greater.

I believe that what has happened in childcare legislation in Britain during the last quarter of the twentieth century is a reciprocal pattern of development that has had the effect of "squeezing" the role and responsibilities previously accorded to parents and parent substitutes. On the one hand, "treating the child as an individual" has come increasingly to mean "respecting the (autonomous) rights of the child" relative to "respecting his dependency needs"—dependency here being understood primarily as the need to be cared for as immature rather than the need to be protected as vulnerable (although of course neither facet wholly excludes the other). On the other side, government has increasingly seen its responsibility towards children in society, whether or not they are "looked after", as first and foremost one of protecting their rights and persons as "fledged", if not yet fully fledged, citizens. Previously the state sought primarily to uphold parental prerogatives to protect the rights and integrity of the child; its own responsibilities in respect of the welfare of children were mediated and vicarious, at least for those children being brought up by their own parents. To see the extent of this change, one need only contemplate current government initiatives directed towards regulating children's diet with the aim of diminishing childhood obesity. At one time such efforts would have been targeted on the parents, with the aim of enlisting their support through persuasion or practical inducements. Nowadays not only is advice aimed primarily at young people themselves, but so, too, are the government's actual directives. This is just one example of countless ways in which the authority over the child's physical and mental wellbeing traditionally vested in parents, and the family has become gradually transferred to the state. Winnicott's "outside world" is less "protective membrane" or shield for the family, more a medium or surround in which both parents and children are held.

The issues here are complex, multi-faceted. Undoubtedly changes in family patterns, the decline of the two-parent nuclear family that Bowlby and Winnicott took as standard half a century ago, together with much increased economic and social mobility, have contributed to altering the structure of inter-generational relationships and caused a flattening out of traditional intrafamilial authority patterns. Young people are likely to acquire knowledge and technical skills during their schooldays that often exceed what parents themselves acquired as school-children, and even in some cases what they have later acquired as adults. Not surprisingly, therefore, parents are often no longer seen by their children as automatic "founts of practical knowledge". Moreover, open media access to information, advice, and opinion means that they are less likely to be seen as primary "founts of wisdom" either.

There can be no question of returning to a world in which parents were accorded untrammelled authority and responsibility, whether direct or delegated, for the upbringing of children and where government's role was essentially facilitative. The "outside world" intervenes in the family to a much greater extent than was the case when Winnicott and Bowlby wrote and broadcast about children and families during and shortly after the Second World War. And an inevitable consequence of this development would seem to be an enhancement of the autonomous status of children, so that "treating the child as an individual" is bound to imply nowadays a greater degree of regard for the integrity of the child, his "unit status", compared with recognizing and respecting his dependency needs as stressed in their different ways by Bowlby and Winnicott.

And yet, notwithstanding these new realities, there remains the perennial need for nurturing, containment, continuity of care if children are to experience positively the enhanced autonomy that now appears as their birthright. Here Winnicott's writings in particular continue, I believe, to have much to contribute. I am thinking especially of his stress on the need in the child for triangularity in relationships, not only within the family, but in the relationship of the child to his family and the outside world. The danger of government assuming an increasingly directive role in the lives and upbringing of children where previously parents had held sway is that it risks forsaking another important, albeit external role: that of being both a foil and a back-up to the family unit. Winnicott was fond of emphasizing how the growing child needed to test, even transgress, parental norms on the way to achieving a personal identity. Here society with its norms and constraints acted as an outer limit to the young person's challenges. For Winnicott antisocial behaviour did, literally, mean behaviour that was "anti"—directed against the social order, not so much to repudiate it but, rather, to experience its reality and durability, its containing, controlling function, after parental norms had been transgressed. Where, as now, the state is increasingly drawn into representing the first obstacle of challenge for the young person, the parent's personal sense of responsibility and authority *independent of the state* having been effectively emasculated, the state's norms will be challenged from the outset without there being recourse to an outer protective layer of order, regulation, control to meet the young person's challenge. In such circumstances, challenging young individuals are liable to become "asocial" rather than "antisocial"—a far worse predicament, both for themselves and for society—or else, out of fear of a loss of boundaries, become unduly conformist and falsely compliant, having lost their capacity for creativity and invention.

What, then, might be the implications of this? I would suggest that there is a need for three principal changes if the concerns and warnings or Bowlby and Winnicott are to be heeded:

1. recognition and support from government for continuity and consistency of early infant and childhood care, ensuring, if possible, that the mother becomes the primary focus of that care-giving, at least through the first five years of life;
2. enhancement of the authority and independence of parents and parental substitutes as primarily responsible for determining and meeting the best interests of the child;
3. for "looked-after children", the need to ensure that they are cared for, including the provision of containment and protection from themselves as much as from others, in a way comparable to what they might desirably have experienced, had they been brought up within an intact and well functioning family home.

The 2004 Children Bill shows welcome evidence of the desire of legislators to heed more closely the needs and concerns of children by adopting a more child-centred rather than organizational and bureaucratic approach, as was the case with some antecedent government enactments relating to the welfare of children. The appointment of a Children's Commissioner would doubtless have been a prospect welcomed by both men. Yet, more than paying attention to the voice of children is required to redress the balance in childcare theory and practice back towards genuine caring for children, rather than more generalized caring about them.

APPENDIX A

Masud Khan and Bowlby

Masud Khan's version of how he came to meet John Bowlby and thus accepted for training as a psychoanalytic candidate should be treated with a great deal of suspicion and circumspection (Hopkins, 2004). Bowlby was never an admirer of Khan's. Khan "lived in the interface between fact and fiction, truth and metaphor, reality and fantasy" (Judy Cooper, quoted by Boynton, 2002/2003). Robert Stoller, Khan's friend to whom he entrusted his diaries and work books, wrote in a letter composed immediately after Khan's death, "any obituary [I would have written] would be unacceptable. I would have stomped up and down in my anger at Masud's lying ... his total fabrication of the clinical material in the last book" (Boynton, 2002/2003).

This applies also to parts of Khan's Work Books and clinical material. Masud said to me: "Truth? Who needs truth? That's for literature." Khan's depiction of this alleged meeting is highly out of character for John Bowlby, and his acceptance as a candidate should not be blamed on Bowlby any more than the responsibility for Khan's flagrant professional—and personal—misconduct be mis-attributed to Winnicott. Winnicott's explicit attitude was recorded by John Davis, who recollects "asking him once naively why the GMC were more likely to order a doctor to be struck off the medical register for committing adultery with a patient (or a patient's mother!) than, for instance, for removing the wrong leg when carrying out an amputation. 'It is because,' he said quite lightly, 'doctors can only help their patients if they love them: and the patient and those who care for her must know for certain that such love is safe—not exploitative of dependency: otherwise, they couldn't accept it'" (J. Davis, 1993, p. 97).

APPENDIX B

George Lyward

George Lyward was as original and eccentric an educator–therapist as Winnicott a paediatrician–psychoanalyst. Turning down the headmastership of one of England's most prestigious public schools, he ran, instead, a community for gifted misfits in a rambling old house set in large grounds in Kent countryside near Tenterden. Many of the boys were ill. Some of his unorthodox but effective methods are described in *Mr Lyward's Answer* (Burn, 1953).

John Bowlby suggested I visit there, along with identifying other unconventional educational establishments. At that stage I did not know that he had himself been a teacher in a residential school, but in retrospect I acknowledge my debt to Bowlby who was responsible for ensuring that I did not overlook the immense importance of school life in the practice of child psychiatry. Both Bowlby and Winnicott, as well as Sutherland and Derek Miller, accepted and practised the extension of psychoanalytic thinking to include a critical analysis of society as playing a weighty role in the construction of influences on an individual and his family's inner world. Lyward (1958), like Winnicott, would deliver himself of sage but cryptic comments and questions: "Consider the function of the full stop" might occupy a morning's discussion; or "The answer to the management of delinquent behaviour lies in time and space", reminiscent in its *koanic* qualities of Winnicott's "We must remember the creativity of salivation" (Issroff, 1993).

The Planned Environment Therapy Trust (PETT) Archives are a valuable resource of materials pertaining to this important field of interest to both Winnicott and Bowlby.

APPENDIX C

Winnicott's critically significant dream

In 1963, while reviewing Jung's autobiography, Winnicott developed "a splitting headache", went to sleep where he was on the floor, and dreamt a dream (1963a) which he described in three parts:

1. There was absolute destruction, and Winnicott was part of the world and of all people, and therefore he was being destroyed. (For him "the important thing in the early stages was the way in which in the dream the pure destruction got free from all the mollifications, such as object relating, cruelty, sensuality, sado-masochism, etc.")
2. Then there was absolute destruction, and he was the destructive agent. Winnicott perceived this as a problem for the ego, how to integrate these two aspects of destruction?
3. The third part now started, and in the dream he awakened. As he awakened, he knew he had dreamt that he was both part of what was being destroyed and the agent of this absolute destruction. He decided that he had solved the problem of how to integrate the two aspects of destruction by using the difference between the waking and the sleeping states. Because here he was awake, in the dream, and he knew he had dreamed of being destroyed and of being the destroying agent. There was no dissociation, so his three "I"s were altogether in touch with each other—he remembered dreaming the first and second parts.

Although the dream work done had made tremendous demands on him, he felt it to be immensely satisfactory. As he began to wake up, he worked on his splitting headache and realized he had these three essential selves, "I[3] could remember dreaming the I[2] and I[1]."

Winnicott was acutely aware in the third part of the dream that destructiveness belongs to relating to objects that are outside the subjective world or the area of omnipotence—essentially, the world of imagination and of dreaming.

APPENDIX D

Reality and fantasy

The healthy child becomes capable of the full dream of genital sexuality. In the remembered dream there can be found all the kinds dream work that were carefully worked out by Freud. In the remembered and unending dream the full consequences of the instinctual experience must be met. The boy who takes his father's place cannot avoid dealing with:

- The idea of the death of the father and therefore of his own death.
- The idea of castration by the father or castration of the father.
- The idea of being left with full responsibility for the satisfaction of the mother.
- The idea of a compromise with the father along homosexual lines.
- In the girl's dream she cannot avoid dealing with:
- The idea of the death of the mother and therefore of her own death.
- The idea of robbing the mother of her husband, of his penis, of her children, and so the idea of her own sterility.
- The idea of being at the mercy of the father's sexuality.
- The idea of a compromise with the mother along homosexual lines.

When parents actually exist, and also a home setting and the continuance of familiar things, the solution comes through the sorting out of what is called reality and fantasy. Seeing the parents together makes the dream of their separation, or the death of one of them, tolerable. The primal scene (parents together sexually) is the basis of individual stability since it makes possible the whole dream of taking the place of one partner. This does not discount the fact that the primal scene, the actual witnessing of intercourse, can put the maximum strain in a child and can (by happening quite apart from the child's needs) be traumatic, so that as a result of being forced to witness it as child starts to develop illness. Both statements are needed, showing the value and also the danger of the primal scene. Parents who are otherwise satisfactory may easily fail in child care by being unable to distinguish clearly between the child's dream and fact. (Winnicott, 1988b, pp. 58–59).

APPENDIX E

Politics and preventive psychiatry

Although at the time I was in no way conscious of any connection, when recalling these stimulating and fascinating discussions initiated by Bowlby, I became aware of their enduring influence on my "road less travelled" professional life. Accordingly, I would like here to pay tribute to the enduring influence of John Bowlby's seminar about the possible social role of a child and family psychiatrist by giving one illustration that led to formal constructive developments: conceivably in time these ideas, which were deliberately drawn up as widely as possible, could have further positive consequences in a number of conflict-ridden highly complex situations. While at a personal level I may feel deeply pessimistic, nonetheless, I believe that one cannot choose to go on living without behaving optimistically.

A conference on "Conflict Resolution: Building Tolerance for Diversity" was held in 1994 under the auspices of the World Federa-tion of Mental Health, the Washington Institute for the Victims of Trauma, and the patronage of the Grand Mufti of Egypt, organized by the El Azayam Hospital, the World Federation of Islamic Psychiatrists, the Egyptian Ministries of Health, Religion, Education, Security and Tourism, and the Foreign Service of Egypt, the Egyptian Psychiatric Federation, the Cairo High Institute of Social Work, and other Egyptian organizations, the American Cultural Centre in Cairo, the Israeli Foreign Ministry, and the Palestinian Red Crescent Association. Dr Fathi Arafat and Dr Judith Issroff co-chaired ground-breaking discussions held at the Palestinian Red Crescent Hospital that did enable some joint work and many further meetings to occur.

Participants were delegates from not only Egypt, Israel, and Palestinian territories, but also Saudi Arabia, Jordan, Lebanon, Kuwait, Qatar, Pakistan, and, in addition, diplomats, police, and scholars attended, as did Winston Nagan, an ex-South African International Human Rights legal expert, selected Conflict Resolution specialists with fieldwork experience from the United States and Australia, a Basque Spanish historian from Gernika-Goggeratuz, a peace and conflict management organization, and a psychiatrist from Northern Ireland.

Attempts were made to establish local and regional working parties of mental health and lay people

- to work towards the goals of non-violent transformation of conflict,
- to create bridges between diverse peoples of trust, of shared concerns and caring,
- to find ways to re-educate and
- to mitigate and mend the effects of trauma, to prevent its snowballing and transgenerational transmission,
- to focus on human rights and watch over ourselves and each other locally and regionally, and use them as a negotiating tool, in short, to implement the above resolutions and recommendations.

Projects were handed over to Palestinian UNDP head, Mr Qliebo, for implementation. At the subsequent conference of the World Federation of Islamic Psychiatrists I was afforded the opportunity of presenting a paper addressing the subject of "Islam and Peace of Mind" [*El Islam Walsalam Elnafsi*].

Recommendations regarding the contribution which mental health and conflict resolution professionals can make to establishing and maintaining a momentum towards peaceful relations in the different fields of life

The following list of recommendations was drawn up, translated into Arabic, unanimously carried and adopted in the seat of the Grand Mufti, the Dar El Ifta in Cairo, on 5 February 1994, by the interdisciplinary and multinational participants of the Third Joint Conference on "Conflict Resolution: Building Tolerance for Diversity".

Dr Judith Issroff, together with Prof. Winston Nagan, Prof. of Law, University of Florida, Human Rights legalist and ex-Chair of Amnesty International, USA, drafted the recommendations at the request of Dr Abu Gamal El Azayam.

Whereas: Human survival begins with non-violence;

Whereas: preventive mental health seeks positively to promote health and welfare of all human beings;

Whereas: The Human Right to peace is the right and obligation of all states and peoples and ultimately individuals;

Recognizing that tolerance at all levels of social organization, international, regional, national, and internal, is essential for the establishment of mutual respect and the recognition of all peoples and groups;

Recognizing that there is some critical point at which the number of traumatized people in any particular society cannot be contained by the number of relatively secure people, and, accordingly,

Recognizing that programs to promote welfare and overall psycho–somato–spiritual health are essential;

Recognizing that states, communities and families tend to be repressive within themselves, rendering communities or individuals invisible and voiceless;

Recognizing that in the co-operative pursuit of the common goal of peace and social justice for all, non-governmental groups, representatives of the civil society, and professional groups specialized in health care, religious leadership, educational, business and intellectual leadership can further the cause of conflict containment and transformation;

Recognizing that, in this particular regional conflict at least, currently a momentum is underway in the direction of peace and that interdisciplinary and international meetings such as this meeting have a role to play in helping to find ways to mitigate the effects of traumatization and to facilitate the continuation of the peace process in non-partisan practical ways;

Recognizing that religion offers solace and ways for communities to come together to reflect and pray within the context of their traditions and that this can be a source for positively influencing an agenda for peace and reconstruction;

Recognizing that the post-cold war era poses both challenges and opportunities for modification of the entire global power process and that this presents a special responsibility for bringing international standards as represented in the promise of the United Nations charter directly to bear on communities involved in conflict situations and for the promotion of the norms of non-discrimination affecting decision-making regarding groups and individuals;

Recognizing also that peace, tolerance and respect for diversity can be furthered by the following recommendations:

We Recommend:

1. that we attempt to increase and facilitate *face to face encounters* in the entire region at all levels, governmental, community, ethnic, religious, professional, business, sporting, and so on;
2. the creation of *educational* programs including:
   - education for dispute and conflict resolution; and trauma training, viz., effects of trauma; symptom recognition; rehabilitation;
   - special programs like making use of gifted, creative, dropout and disadvantaged children;

- promoting in the educational system awareness that diverse points of view must be tolerated and respected;
- that different people perceive the same events differently;
- the teaching of comparative religion and cultures to enhance cross-cultural understanding; and recognize that religion and the sacred books carry common messages for peace and human dignity;
- work toward the generation of signs and symbols that humanize enemies and identify the common humanity, along with drawing attention to behaviours which distance and de-humanize the other;
- programs for identifying and dealing with violence-prone elements and individuals in the communities; that such programs be set up together with training and future monitoring of the social pathology of violence;
- the use of mass media to promote public information, awareness and participation in dialogue, and techniques of conflict resolution;

3. that an inter-group monitoring system on inter-group mediation be set up with all deliberate speed;
4. that the history of our respective communities be subjected to a complete process of re-thinking and re-appraisal so as to factor in the selective and alternative versions of the divided past, the transitional present, and a future of peace, hope and understanding in all communities;
5. that dialogues about fundamental moral values including ethical precepts; and interfaith dialogues be conducted in a search for a clarification of a common interest that all share in their recognition of the necessity of tolerance for diversity, peace, dignity, and common values;
6. that support groups for mental health professionals in all regional countries be set up. These should include those who work with victims and their families, all those who work in crisis situations, and also those who work with the crisis intervention personnel. These groups should meet periodically and should form a commission amongst themselves to enable them to exchange views, expertise, and to gain support internationally.
   7. that every effort be made to deal with the treatment of the traumatized, to enable them to heal, and to promote psycho–somato–spiritual health starting with preventive measures like peri-natal and infant and mother and family health care programs; and implementation of all basic human rights and codes, including the ethical conduct for professional groups and associations; including the business community;

8. that centres be set up regionally and internationally to promote the post-graduate and inter-disciplinary study of conflict analysis and resolution;
9. that a Sub-committee be set up to facilitate ongoing meetings at regional and international levels, to find means of funding, and to disseminate information of activities of various regional bodies which might be useful also in other areas;
10. the setting up of a multi-cultural conflict resolution commission, and that an ad hoc committee be set up to look at ways of implementing these recommendations.

I ASC-ASULHAH

I ASC-ASULHAH *The Israeli Association for Social Care, Change and Solution of Conflicts,* a non-profit-making non-governmental organization, was set up in Israel specifically to implement the recommendations made in Dar El Iftah, Cairo, February, 1994, at the JPCR Conference on "Conflict Resolution: Building Tolerance for Diversity".

Aims:
1. To facilitate the implementation of the Recommendations regarding the contribution which mental health and conflict resolution professionals can make to establish and maintain a momentum towards peaceful relations in the different fields of life, at all possible levels. These recommendations are a broad and ambitious plan for Non-Violent Conflict Containment, Transformation and Resolution, Peaceful Relations, and the promotion of Psycho-Social Health.
2. To this end, as a non-profit-making organization I ASC-ASULHAH aimed
   – to network and co-operate widely both within Israel and abroad with all organizations with similar and related aims;
   – to study this and related relevant fields, conduct research, publish information, findings and work in relevant fields, as necessary; & to make use of the media,
   – to raise necessary funds, run an office, in order to acquire, collate, assess and disseminate relevant information, and to this end, acquire and maintain whatever resources and equipment was necessary for the furtherance of these aims.
   – to liaise with or set up resource centres, training courses, support groups, study courses, practical consultations and interventions in all walks of life, at all levels of personal, interpersonal, familial, group and societal interaction, including local, regional

and international activities and cooperative support of organizations with similar goals;
- to intervene in all manner of professional ways;
- to attempt where requested or where advisable to initiate actions to intervene in order to try to help resolve conflicts;
- to work wherever possible with existing organizations, to support, encourage and co-operate with them, not to compete re funding, but to broaden, deepen and render as efficient as possible the ongoing work which fell within the brief of the Cairo recommendations;
- to work in small and large ways as practicable and to plan and work thus towards furtherance of the Recommendations and Resolutions agreed at the aforementioned International Congress.

Among many other activities, 18 project proposals were drawn up: these included professional training, dealing with parenting and ordinary expectable life course crises, conflict and trauma management, violence-reduction, anti-substance abuse and research programmes. They were handed over to the Palestinian UNDP representative in Al Quds/Jerusalem, Mr Qliebo, by Prof. As'ad Masri and myself.

* * *

I wonder what John Bowlby would have said about the unforeseen influence of his seminars? In the aftermath of these experiences, I am sorry that we could not discuss them in person.

REFERENCES AND BIBLIOGRAPHY

Selected bibliography

Re Winnicott, I have been accumulating a personal bibliography of works about and making use of Winnicott, but they multiply exponentially in an array of fields to the extent that it is not possible to read everything. I recommend those in the Bibliography and single out the work of Bonaminio, 2001; Clancier and Kalmanovitch, 1984; Cox, 2001; De Astis, 2001, re Tustin; Eigen, 1985, 1986, 1989, 1991, 1993, 1995, 1996, 1998, 2004; Forrester, 1997; Fromm and Smith (and their contributing authors), 1989; Giovacchini, 1990; Green, 1978, 1999, 2000; Grolnik, 1990; Grotstein, 1989; Hamilton, 1982, 1996a, 1996b; Hernandez and Giannakoulas, 2001; Hopkins, 2002; Jallinsky, 1997; Kahr, 1996a, 1996b, 2001a, 2001b, 2002, 2003; Khan, Davis, and Davis, 1974; King, 2004; Little, 1990; Ogden, 1985, 1986, 1989, 1999, 2001; Padel, 2001a, 2001b; Pena, 2001a, 2001b; Raphael-Leff, 2001; Schacht, 1972, 2001; Smith, 1989a, 1989b; and Tonnesmann, 1995. There are also his biographers: Abram, 1996; Caldwell, 2005; Clare Winnicott, 1978; Davis and Wallbridge, 1983; Davis, 1995; Goldman, 1993a, 1993b; Jacobs, 1995; Kahr, 1996b; Kanter, 2004a, 2004b; Milner, 2001; Newman, 1988, 1995; Phillips, 1988; Rodman, 1990, 2003; among others.

Re Bowlby, aside from citations here, see those by: Alexander, 1992; Allen, 2000; Belsky, 2002; Bradshaw, Schore, Brown, Poole, and Moss, 2005; Brave and Ferid, 1990; Coates, 2004; Cortina and Marrone, 2003; Diamond and Marrone, 2003; Eagle, 1995, 1997; Fonagy, 2001; Fonagy, Target, and Steele, 1997; Greenspan and Lieberman, 1988; Greenspan and Pollock, 1991a, 1991b, 1991c, 1991d; Grossman and Grossman, in press; Grossman, Grossman, and Waters, 2005; Hamilton, 1987a, 1987b; Harris, 2004a, 2004b; Heard and Lake, 1997; Holmes, 1993, 1997, 2000; Hopkins, 1990; IAN bibliography; James, 1994; Levy and Orlans, 1998; Lubetsky, 2002; Main and Solomon, 1986; Main, 1999; Marrone, 1998; Parkes, Stevenson-Hinde, and Marris, 1991; Sameroff and Emde, 1989; Schore, 2001a, 2001b, 2003a, 2003b, 2005; Siegel, 2001; Slade, 2000; Trevarthen, 1998.

Abram, J. (1996). *The Language of Winnicott: A Dictionary of Winnicott's Use of Words*. London: Karnac.
Abram, J. (Ed.) (2000). *André Green at The Squiggle Foundation*. Winnicott Studies Monograph Series. London: Karnac, for The Squiggle Foundation.
Abram, J. (in preparation). *The Collected Works of Winnicott*. London: Routledge.
Ackermann, R. (1976). *The Philosophy of Karl Popper*. Amherst, MA: University of Massachusetts Press.
Acquarone, S. (2004). *Infant–Parent Psychotherapy: A Handbook*. London: Karnac.
Adler, S. (1959). Darwin's illness. *Nature, 10* (10 October): 1102–1103.
Ainsworth, M. D. S. (1962). The effects of maternal deprivation: A review of findings and controversy in the context of research strategy. In: *Deprivation of Maternal Care: A Reassessment of Effects*. Public Health Papers No.14. Geneva: World Health Organization.
Ainsworth, M. D. S. (1967). *Infancy in Uganda: Infant Care and the Growth of Love*. Baltimore, MD: Johns Hopkins University Press.
Ainsworth, M. D. S. (1969). Object relations, dependency and attachment: A theoretical review of the infant–mother relationship. *Child Development*, 40: 969–1025.
Ainsworth, M. D. S. (1985a). Attachments across the life-span. *Bulletin of the New York Academy of Medicine*, 61: 792–812.
Ainsworth, M. D. S. (1985b). Patterns of mother–infant attachment: Antecedents and effects on development. *Bulletin of the New York Academy of Medicine*, 61: 771–791.
Ainsworth, M. D. S. (1990). Appreciation of John Bowlby. *Tavistock*

Gazette, 29 (Autumn). Reprinted in: *Journal of the Institute for Self-Analysis*, 4 (1): 12–14 [Special Issue, *On Attachment: Commemorating the Work of John Bowlby*].

Ainsworth, M., Blehar, M. C., Waters, E., & Wall, S. (1978). *Patterns of Attachment*. Hillsdale, NJ: Lawrence Erlbaum.

Alexander, P. D. (1992). Application of attachment theory to the study of sexual abuse. *Journal of Consulting and Clinical Psychology*, 10: 185–195.

Allen, J. G. (2000). *Traumatic Attachments*. New York: Wiley.

Allen, Lady M. (1945). *Whose Children?* London: Favill Press.

Alvarez, A. (1996). The clinician's debt to Winnicott. *Journal of Child Psychotherapy*, 22 (3): 377–382.

Amado, G. (1995). Why psychoanalytical knowledge helps us to understand organizations: A discussion with Elliott Jaques. *Human Relations*, 48 (4): 351–357.

Amado, G., & Ambrose, A. (Eds.) (1998). *The Transitional Approach to Change: The Harold Bridger Transitional Series, Vol. 2*. London: Karnac.

Antonovsky, A. (1988). *Unravelling the Mystery of Health: How People Manage Stress and Stay Well*. San Francisco, CA, & London: Jossey-Bass, Joint Social and Behavioural Science Series and Health Series.

Arden, M. (2004). The development of Charles Rycroft's thought. In: J. Pearson (Ed.), *Analyst of the Imagination: The Life and Work of Charles Rycroft* (pp. 57–72). London: Karnac.

Aron, L. (1991). John Bowlby: In memoriam. *Psychoanalytic Dialogues*, 1: 241.

Axline, V. (1947). *Play Therapy*. New York: Ballantine, 1967.

Axline, V. (1955). Play therapy procedures and results. *American Journal of Orthopsychiatry*, 25: 618–626.

Axline, V. (1967). *Dibs: In Search of Self*. New York: Ballantine.

Bacal, H. A. (1989). Winnicott and self psychology: Remarkable reflections. In: D. W. Detrick & S. P. Detrick (Eds.), *Self Psychology: Comparisons and Contrasts*. Hillsdale, NJ: Analytic Press.

Balbernie, R. (1966). *Residential Work with Children*. Oxford: Pergamon.

Balbernie, R. (1971). The impossible task? In: C. Fees (Ed.), *Residential Experience* (pp. 5–17). Birmingham: Association of Workers for Maladjusted Children, 1990.

Balint, M. (1952). *Primary Love and Psychoanalytic Technique*. London: Hogarth Press. Reprinted London: Karnac, 1985.

Balint, M. (1959). *Thrills and Regression*. London: Hogarth Press. Reprinted London: Karnac, 1987.

Balint, M. (1968). *The Basic Fault: Therapeutic Aspects of Regression*. London: Tavistock. Reprinted London: Karnac, 1979.

Beebe, B., & Lachmann, F. (1998). Mother–infant mutual influence and precursors of psychic structure. In: A. Holdberg (Ed.), *Progress in Self Psychology, Vol. 3. Frontiers in Self Psychology* (pp. 3–25). Hillsdale, NJ: Analytic Press.

Belsky, J. (2002). Developmental origins of attachment styles. *Attachment and Human Development, 6* (2): 166–170.

Belsky, J., & Nezworski, T. (Eds.) (1988). *Clinical Implications of Attachment*. Hillside, NJ: Lawrence Erlbaum.

Bertolini, M., Giannakoulas, A., & Hernandez, M., with Molino, A. (Eds.) (2001). *Squiggles and Spaces: Revisiting the Work of D. W. Winnicott, Vol. 1*. London & Philadelphia, PA: Whurr.

Bettelheim, B. (1950). *Love Is Not Enough*. Glencoe, IL: Free Press of Glencoe.

Bettelheim, B. (1967). *The Empty Fortress*. New York: Free Press; London: Collier-Macmillan.

Bettelheim, B. (1983). *Freud and Man's Soul*. New York: Alfred A. Knopf.

Biebel, D. (1999). *Psychoanalysis and Science*. Retrieved from http://www.aperturas.org

Bollas, C. (1985). *The Shadow of the Object*. London: Free Association Books.

Bonaminio, V. (2001). Through Winnicott to Winnicott. In: M. Bertolini, A. Giannakoulas, & M. Hernandez, with A. Molino (Eds.), *Squiggles and Spaces: Revisiting the Work of D. W. Winnicott, Vol. 1* (pp. 88–98). London & Philadelphia, PA: Whurr.

Bonaminio, V., & Di Renzo, M. (2005). Creativity, playing, dreaming: Overlapping circles in the work of Marion Milner and D. W. Winnicott. In: L. Caldwell (Ed.), *Art, Creativity, Living* (pp. 97–112). London: Karnac.

Bourne, H. (2004). The innocence of Charles Rycroft. In: J. Pearson (Ed.), *Analyst of the Imagination: The Life and Work of Charles Rycroft* (pp. 164–191). London: Karnac.

Bowlby, J. (1940). The influence of early environment in the development of neurosis and neurotic character. *International Journal of Psycho-Analysis, 21*: 154–178.

Bowlby, J. (1944). Forty-four juvenile thieves: Their characters and home life. *International Journal of Psycho-Analysis, 25*: 19–53. Reprinted as: *Forty-Four Juvenile Thieves: Their Characters and Home Life*. London: Bailliere, Tindall & Cox, 1946.

Bowlby, J. (1946). *Forty-Four Juvenile Thieves: Their Characters and Home Life*. London: Bailliere, Tindall & Cox.

Bowlby, J. (1951). *Maternal Care and Mental Health*. WHO Monograph Series, Number 2. Geneva: World Health Organization.

Bowlby, J. (1953). *Child Care and the Growth of Love.* Harmondsworth, Middlesex: Penguin.
Bowlby, J. (1957). An ethological approach to research in child development. *British Journal of Medical Psychology, 30* (4): 230–240.
Bowlby, J. (1958a). *Can I Leave My Baby?* London: National Association for Mental Health.
Bowlby, J. (1958b). The nature of the child's tie to his mother. *International Journal of Psycho-Analysis, 39*: 350–373.
Bowlby, J. (1959). Separation anxiety. *International Journal of Psycho-Analysis, 41*: 89–113.
Bowlby, J. (1960a). *Discussions on Child Development*, ed. by J. M. Tanner & B. Inhelder. London: Tavistock.
Bowlby, J. (1960b). Grief and mourning in infancy. *Psychoanalytic Study of the Child, 15*: 3–39.
Bowlby, J. (1966). *Maternal Care and Mental Health.* New York: Schocken.
Bowlby, J. (1970a). *Attachment and Loss, Vol. 1: Attachment.* London: Hogarth Press and The Institute of Psycho-Analysis; New York: Basic Books, 1977.
Bowlby, J. (1970b). *Attachment and Loss. Vol. 2: Separation Anxiety.* London: Hogarth Press and The Institute of Psycho-Analysis; New York: Basic Books, 1977.
Bowlby, J. (1973). *Attachment and Loss, Vol. 2: Separation Anxiety.* London: Hogarth Press and The Institute of Psycho-Analysis.
Bowlby, J. (1977). *Separation, Anxiety and Anger.* Philadelphia, PA: Perseus Books.
Bowlby, J. (1979). *The Making and Breaking of Affectional Bonds.* London: Tavistock.
Bowlby, J. (1980). *Attachment and Loss, Vol. 3: Loss, Sadness and Depression.* London: Hogarth Press and The Institute of Psycho-Analysis.
Bowlby, J. (1981). *A Secure Base: Clinical Applications of Attachment Theory.* London: Routledge, 1988.
Bowlby, J. (1988a). Attachment, communication and the therapeutic process. In: *A Secure Base: Clinical Applications of Attachment Theory* (pp. 137–157). London: Routledge.
Bowlby, J. (1988b). Commentary: Where science and humanism meet. *Group Analysis, 21* (1): 81–82.
Bowlby, J. (1988c). Developmental psychiatry comes of age. *American Journal of Psychiatry, 145*: 1–10.
Bowlby, J. (1991a). Postscript. In: C. M. Parkes, J. Stevenson-Hinde, & P. Marris (Eds.), *Attachment Across the Life Cycle* (pp. 293–297). London & New York: Routledge.

Bowlby, J. (1991b). The role of the psychotherapist's personal resources in the treatment situation. *Bulletin of the British Psychoanalytical Society*, 27 (11): 26–30.

Bowlby, J. (1992). *Charles Darwin: A New Biography*. London: Hutchinson.

Bowlby, J. (2004). *Fifty Years of Attachment Theory: The Donald Winnicott Memorial Lecture*. London: Karnac, on behalf of the Winnicott Clinic of Psychotherapy.

Bowlby, J., with Ainsworth, M. D, Andrey, R. G., Harlow, R. G., Lebovici, S., Mead, M., Prugh, D. G, & Wootton, B. (1966). *Deprivation of Maternal Care: A Reassessment of Its Effects*. New York: Schocken.

Bowlby, J., Figlio, K., & Young, R. (1986). An interview with John Bowlby on the origins and reception of his work. *Free Associations*, 6: 36–64.

Bowlby, J., Miller, E., & Winnicott, D. W. (1939). Evacuation of small children (letter). *British Medical Journal* (16 December). Reprinted in: D. W. Winnicott, *Deprivation and Delinquency*, ed. C. Winnicott, R. Shepherd, & M. Davis. London: Tavistock; New York: Methuen, 1984.

Boynton, R. (2002/2003). The return of the repressed: The strange case of Masud Khan. *Boston Review* (December/January). Retrieved from http://bostonreview.net/

Bradley, S. J. (2000). *Affect Regulation and the Development of Psychopathology*. New York: Guilford Press.

Bradshaw, G. A., Schore, A. N., Brown, J. L., Poole, J. H., & Moss, C. J. (2005). Elephant breakdown. Social trauma: Early disruption of attachment can affect the physiology, behavior and culture of animals and humans over generations. *Nature, 433*: 807.

Brave, A., & Ferid, H. (1990). John Bowlby and feminism. *Journal of the Institute for Self-Analysis*, 4 (1): 30–35 [Special Issue, *On Attachment: Commemorating the Work of John Bowlby*].

Brazelton, T. B., & Cramer, B. G. (1991). *The Earliest Relationship: Parents, Infants, and the Drama of Early Attachment*. London: Karnac.

Bretherton, I. (1987). New perspectives on attachment relationships: Security, communication and internal working models. In: J. D. Osofsky (Ed.), *Handbook of Infant Development* (pp. 1061–1100). New York: Wiley.

Bretherton, I. (1991). The roots and growing points of attachment theory. In: C. M. Parkes, J. Stevenson-Hinde, & P. Marris (Eds.), *Attachment Across the Life Cycle*. London & New York: Routledge.

Bretherton, I. (1992). The origins of attachment theory: John Bowlby and Mary Ainsworth. *Developmental Psychology, 28*: 759–775.

Bridgeland, M. (1971). *Pioneer Work with Maladjusted Children*. London: Staples Press.

Bridgeland, M. (1987). Love was never enough. In: C. Fees, (Ed.), *Residen-*

tial Experience. Birmingham: Association of Workers for Maladjusted Children.

Bridger, H. (1985). Northfield revisited. In: M. Pines (Ed.), *Bion and Group Psychotherapy*. London: Routledge.

Burn, M. (1953). *Mr. Lyward's Answer*. London: Holt, Rinehart, Hamish Hamilton.

Bütz, M. R. (Ed.) (1998). *Clinical Chaos: A Therapist's Guide to Nonlinear Dynamics and Therapeutic Change* (pp. 154–159). Ann Arbor, MI: Brunner/Mazel.

Byng-Hall, J. (1991). Address at John Bowlby Memorial Service. *Infant Mental Health Journal*, 12: 267–268.

Caldwell, L. (Ed.) (2005). *Sex and Sexuality: Winnicottian Perspectives*. Winnicott Studies Monograph Series. London: Karnac, for The Squiggle Foundation.

Call, J. D., Galenson, E., & Tyson, R. J. (Eds.) (1983). *Frontiers of Infant Psychiatry, Vols. 1 & 2*. New York: Basic Books.

Cameron, K. (1996). Winnicott and Lacan: Selfhood versus subjecthood. In: V. Richards, with G. Wilke (Eds.), *The Person Who Is Me: Contemporary Perspectives on the True and False Self* (pp. 37–46). Winnicott Studies Monograph Series. London: Karnac, for The Squiggle Foundation.

Casement, P. J. (1985). *Learning from the Patient*. London & New York: Tavistock.

Casement, P. J. (1990). *Further Learning from the Patient: The Analytic Space and Process*. London & Hove: Brunner-Routledge.

Casement, P. J. (1991). *Learning from the Patient* (combined edition). New York: Guilford Press.

Casement, P. J. (2002a). *Learning from Our Mistakes: Beyond Dogma in Psychoanalysis and Psychotherapy*. Hove: Brunner-Routledge.

Casement, P. J. (2002b). Learning from life. *Psychoanalytic Inquiry*, 22: 519–533.

Castro, C. (1996). A first approach to clinical work: Taken by the hand of Winnicott. In: V. Richards, with G. Wilke (Eds.), *The Person Who Is Me: Contemporary Perspectives on the True and False Self* (pp. 62–70). Winnicott Studies Monograph Series. London: Karnac, for The Squiggle Foundation.

Clancier, A., & Kalmanovitch, J. (1984). *Winnicott and Paradox: From Birth to Creation*, trans. (from French) by A. Sheridan. London: Tavistock, 1987.

Coates, S. (2004). John Bowlby and Margaret Mahler: Their lives and theories. *Journal of the American Psychoanalytic Association*, 52 (2): 571–601.

Cohen, A. (1980). Child care in Oxfordshire [interview with Clare Winnicott]. In: J. Kanter (Ed.), *Face to Face with Children: The Life and Work of Clare Winnicott* (pp. 127–141). London: Karnac 2004.

Cooper, J. (1993). *Speak of Me As I Am: The Life and Work of Masud Khan.* London: Karnac.

Cooper, P. J., & Murray, L. (1998). Postnatal depression. *British Medical Journal, 316*: 1884–1886.

Cortina, M. (2003). Defensive processes, emotions and internal working models: A perspective from attachment theory and contemporary models of the mind. In: M. Cortina & M. Marrone (Eds.), *Attachment Theory and the Psychoanalytic Process* (pp. 271–306). London & Philadelphia, PA: Whurr.

Cortina, M., & Marrone, M. (2003). Attachment theory, transference and the psychoanalytic process. In: M. Cortina & M. Marrone (Eds.), *Attachment Theory and the Psychoanalytic Process* (pp. 42–61). London & Philadelphia, PA: Whurr.

Cox, M. (2001). On the capacity for being inside enough. In: B. Kahr (Ed.), *Forensic Psychotherapy and Psychopathology: Winnicottian Perspectives* (pp. 111–124). London: Karnac.

Cox, M., & Thielgaard, A. (1987). *Mutative Metaphors in Psychotherapy: The Aeolian Mode.* London: Tavistock.

Cox, M., & Thielgaard, A. (1994). *Shakespeare as Prompter: The Amending Imagination and the Therapeutic Process.* London: Jessica Kingsley.

Cramer, B., & Stern, D. N. (1988). Evaluation of changes in mother–infant brief psychotherapy: A single case study. *Infant Mental Health Journal, 9*: 20–45.

Crapanzano, V. (2004). Vincent Crapanzano. In: A. Molino (Ed.), *Culture, Subject, Psyche: Dialogues in Psychoanalysis and Anthropology* (pp. 63–79). London & Philadelphia, PA: Whurr.

Crittenden, P. M. (1988). Relationships at risk. In: J. Belsky & T. Nezworski (Eds.), *Clinical Implications of Attachment* (pp. 136–174). Hillsdale, NJ: Lawrence Erlbaum.

Curtis Committee (1945–46). *Care of Children Committee (Curtis Committee): Transcripts of Oral Evidence.* Home Office Division Records MH102/145B/C/D/E. Public Records Office, Kew, London.

Curtis Report (1946). *Report of the Care of Children Committee.* Cmnd 6922. London: HMSO.

Darwin, C. (1859). *On the Origin of Species by Means of Natural Selection.* Harmondsworth, Middlesex: Penguin, 1968.

Darwin, C. (1871). *The Descent of Man.* London: John Murray.

Davis, J. (1993). Winnicott as physician: A review of Winnicott's first book: *Clinical Notes on Disorders of Childhood* (London, Heinemann,

1931). *Winnicott Studies: The Journal of the Squiggle Foundation, 7*: 95–97.

Davis, M. E. V. (1985). Some thoughts on Winnicott and Freud. *Bulletin of the British Association of Psychotherapists, 16*: 57–71.

Davis, M. E. V. (1987). The writing of D. W. Winnicott. *International Review of Psycho-Analysis, 14*: 491–501.

Davis, M. E. V. (1990). Play and symbolism in Lowenfeld and Winnicott. *Free Associations, 23*, 2 (3): 395–422.

Davis, M. E. V. (1992). Destruction as an achievement in the work of Winnicott. *Winnicott Studies: The Journal of the Squiggle Foundation, 7*: 85–92.

Davis, M. E. V. (1993). Winnicott and the spatula game. *Winnicott Studies: The Journal of the Squiggle Foundation, 8*: 57–67.

Davis, M. E. V. (1995). Winnicott and object relations. *Winnicott Studies: The Journal of the Squiggle Foundation, 10*: 33–46.

Davis, M. E. V., & Wallbridge, D. (1983). *Boundary and Space: An Introduction to the Work of D. W. Winnicott*. Harmondsworth, Middlesex: Penguin.

Daws, D. (1996). The spatula, the electric socket and the spoon. *Journal of Child Psychotherapy, 22* (3): 392–393.

De Astis, G. (2001). The influence of Winnicott on the evolution of Francis Tustin's thinking. In: M. Bertolini, A. Giannakoulas, & M. Hernandez, with A. Molino (Eds.), *Squiggles and Spaces: Revisiting the Work of D. W. Winnicott, Vol. 2* (pp. 190–195). London & Philadelphia, PA: Whurr.

DeMause, L. (Ed.) (1975). *The History of Childhood*. New York: Harper Torchbooks.

DeMause, L. (1982). *The Evolution of Childrearing: The Foundations of Psychohistory*. New York: Creative Roots.

DeMause, L. (2001a). The evolution of childrearing. *Journal of Psychohistory, 28* (4): 362–451.

DeMause, L. (2001b). The childhood origins of terrorism. New York: Harper Torchbooks, 2003.

DeMause, L. (2002). *Psychohistory: Childrearing and the Emotional Life of Nations: The History of Childhood*. New York: Harper Torchbooks.

Deri, S. (1984). *Symbolization and Creativity*. New York: International Universities Press.

De Vore, I. (1965). *Primate Behaviour: Field Studies of Monkeys and Apes*. New York: Holt, Rinehart & Winston.

Diamond, N., & Marrone, M. (2003). *Attachment and Intersubjectivity*. London & Philadelphia, PA: Whurr.

Dicks, H. V. (1950). Personality traits and National Socialist ideology: A wartime study of German prisoners of war. *Human Relations, 3*.

Dicks, H. V. (1969). *The Tavistock Clinic and Institute*. London: Tavistock.

Dockar-Drysdale, B. (1953). Some aspects of damage and restitution. In: *Therapy and Consultation in Child Care*. London: Free Association Books, 1993.

Dockar-Drysdale, B. (1958). The residential treatment of frozen children. In: *Therapy and Consultation in Child Care*. London: Free Association Books, 1993.

Dockar-Drysdale, B. (1968). Possibility of regression in a structured environment. In: *Therapy in Child Care* (pp. 78–79). London: Longmans, Green.

Dockar-Drysdale, B. (1980). Therapy and the first year of life. In: C. Fees (Ed.), *Residential Experience* (pp. 37–46). Birmingham: Association of Workers for Maladjusted Children, 1990.

Dockar-Drysdale, B. (1991). *The Provision of Primary Experience: Winnicottian Work with Children and Adolescents*. Northvale, NJ, & London: Jason Aronson.

Dockar-Drysdale, B. (1993). *Therapy and Consultation in Child Care*. London: Free Association Books.

Durbin, E. F. M., & Bowlby, J. (1939). *Personal Aggressiveness and War*. London: Routledge & Kegan Paul.

Eagle, M. (1995). The developmental perspectives of attachment and psychoanalytic theory. In: S. Goldberg et al. (Eds.), *Attachment Theory: Social, Developmental, and Clinical Perspectives* (pp. 113–150). New York & London: Analytic Press.

Eagle, M. (1997). Attachment and psychoanalysis. *British Journal of Medical Psychology*, 58: 281–291.

Egeland, B., & Sroufe, L. A. (1981). Attachment and early maltreatment. *Child Development*, 52: 44–52.

Eibl-Eibesfeldt, I. (1971). *Love and Hate: On the Natural History of Basic Behaviour Patterns*, trans. (from German) by G. Strachen. New York: Holt, Rinehart & Winston.

Eibl-Eibesfeldt, I. (1989). *Human Ethology*. New York: Aldine de Gruyter.

Eigen, M. (1985). Aspects of omnipotence. *Psychoanalytic Review*, 72: 149–159.

Eigen, M. (1986). *The Psychotic Core*. Northvale, NJ, & London: Jason Aronson.

Eigen, M. (1989). Aspects of omniscience. In: M. G. Fromm & B. L. Smith (Eds.), *The Facilitating Environment* (pp. 604–628). Madison, CT: International Universities Press.

Eigen, M. (1991). Winnicott's area of freedom: The uncompromiseable. In: N. Schwartz-Salant & M. Stein (Eds.), *Liminality and Transitional Phenomena* (pp. 67-88). Wilmette, IL: Chiron.

Eigen, M. (1993). *The Electrified Tightrope*. Northvale, NJ: Jason Aronson.
Eigen, M. (1995). *Reshaping the Self: Reflections on Renewal Through Therapy*. Madison, CT: Psychosocial Press.
Eigen, M. (1996). *Psychic Deadness*. Northvale, NJ: Jason Aronson.
Eigen, M. (1998). *The Psychoanalytic Mystic*. London & New York: Free Associations Press.
Eigen, M. (2004). *The Sensitive Self*. Middletown, CT: Wesleyan University Press.
Eliot, T. S. (1942). Little Gidding [*Four Quartets*]. In: *T. S. Eliot: The Complete Poems and Plays* (pp. 172–198). London: Faber & Faber, 1969.
Erickson, M. F., Sroufe, L. A., & Egeland, B. (1985). The relationship between quality of attachment and behavior problems in preschool in a high-risk sample, *Monographs of the Society for Research in Child Development*, 50 (1–2): 147–166.
Esman, A. H. (1990). Three books by and about Winnicott. *International Journal of Psycho-Analysis*, 71: 695.
Fairbairn, W. R. D. (1952). *Psychological Studies of the Personality*. London: Routledge & Kegan Paul.
Farhi, N. (1996). The Squiggle Foundation. *Journal of Child Psychotherapy*, 22 (3): 404–406.
Fees, C. (1995). "Record of Chris Beedell interview with the Dockar-Drysdales", 13 September. (T)CF155. Planned Environment Therapy Trust Archive and Study Centre, Toddington.
Fees, C. (1998). "Interview with Josephine Lomax-Simpson by Craig Fees", 15 July. (T)CF260. Planned Environment Therapy Trust Archive and Study Centre, Toddington.
Fees, C. (1999). "Harold Bridger, therapeutic community pioneer, talking about Donald Winnicott in the 1999 Maxwell Jones Lecture." (T)CF325. Planned Environment Therapy Trust Archive and Study Centre, Toddington.
Fees, C. (2002). "Harold Bridger talking about Donald Winnicott", 12 February. (T)CF372. Planned Environment Therapy Trust Archive and Study Centre, Toddington.
Ferenczi, S. (1924). Thalassa: A theory of genitality. *Psychoanalytic Quarterly*, 2 (1933): 361–403. Reprinted as *Thalassa: A Theory of Genitality*. London: Karnac, 1989.
Ferenczi, S. (1955). *Final Contributions to the Problems and Methods of Psycho-Analysis*. London: Hogarth Press. London: Karnac, 1989.
Fielding, J. (1988). Prove true, imagination: Keats, Coleridge and Winnicott. *Winnicott Studies: The Journal of the Squiggle Foundation*, 3: 4–12 [Special Issue, *A Celebration of the Life and Work of Marion Milner*].

Flavell, J. H. (1963). *The Developmental Psychology of Jean Piaget.* Princeton, NJ: Van Nostrand.

Follett, M. P. (1924). *Creative Experience*: New York: Longmans, Green.

Fonagy, P. (1999). "Pathological Attachments and Therapeutic Action." Presented to the Developmental and Psychoanalytic Discussion Group, American Psychoanalytic Association Meeting, Washington, DC, 13 May. Retrieved from http://psychematters.com/papers/fonagy3.htm

Fonagy, P. (2000). "The Psychoanalysis of Violence." Presented to the Dallas Society for Psychoanalytic Psychotherapy, March 15. Retrieved from http://psychematters.com/papers/fonagy4.htm

Fonagy, P. (2001). *Attachment Theory and Psychoanalysis.* New York: Other Press.

Fonagy, P., Moran, G. S., & Target, M. (1993). Aggression and the psychological self. *International Journal of Psycho-Analysis, 74*: 471–485.

Fonagy, P., & Target, M. (1995). Towards understanding violence: The use of the body and the role of the father. *International Journal of Psycho-Analysis, 76*: 487–502.

Fonagy, P., & Target, M. (1996). Playing with reality: I. Theory of mind and the normal development of psychic reality. *International Journal of Psycho-Analysis, 77*: 217–233.

Fonagy, P., & Target, M. (1997). Attachment and reflective function: Their role in self-organization. *Development and Psychopathology, 9*: 679–700.

Fonagy, P., Target, M., & Steele, M. (1997). Morality, disruptive behaviour, borderline personality disorder, crime, and their relationships to security of attachment. In: C. Atkinson & K. J. Zucker (Eds.), *Attachment and Psychopathology* (pp. 223–274). New York: Guilford Press.

Fordham, M. (1972). Commemorative Meeting for Donald W. Winnicott, January 19th, 1992. *Scientific Bulletin of the British Psychoanalytical Society and The Institute of Psycho-Analysis, 57*: 23.

Forrester, J. (1997). On holding as metaphor: Winnicott and the figure of St Christopher. In: V. Richards, with G. Wilke (Eds.), *Fathers, Families and the Outside World* (pp. 41–58). Winnicott Studies Monograph Series. London: Karnac, for The Squiggle Foundation.

Fraiburg, S. (1980). *Clinical Studies in Infant Mental Health: The First Year of Life.* London: Tavistock.

Fraser, J. G. (1890). *The Golden Bough.* Oxford: Oxford University Press, 1994.

Freud, A. (1945). *The Ego and the Mechanisms of Defence.* New York: International Universities Press.

Freud, A. (1960). Discussion of John Bowlby's paper. *Psychoanalytic Study of the Child, 15*: 53–62.

Freud, S. (1901a). *On Dreams*. S.E., 5.
Freud, S. (1916–17). *Introductory Lectures on Psycho-Analysis* [Part II, Dreams: Lecture X, Symbolism in dreams; Lecture XI, The dream work]. S.E., 15.
Freud, S. (1939a [1937–39]). *Moses and Monotheism*. S.E., 23.
Freud, S. (1950 [1895]). A project for a scientific psychology. S.E., 1.
Fromm, M. G. (1989). Winnicott's work in relation to classical psychoanalysis and ego psychology. In: M. G. Fromm & B. L. Smith (Eds.), *The Facilitating Environment: Clinical Applications of Winnicott's Theory* (pp. 3–26). Madison, CT: International Universities Press.
Fromm, M. G., & Smith, B. L. (Eds.) (1989). *The Facilitating Environment: Clinical Applications of Winnicott's Theory*. Madison, CT: International Universities Press.
Gaddini, R. (1990). Regression and its uses in treatment: An elaboration of the thinking of Winnicott. In: P. L. Giovacchini (Ed.), *Tactics and Techniques in Psychoanalytic Therapy, Vol. 3: The Implications of Winnicott's Contributions*. Northvale, NJ, & London: Jason Aronson.
Gaddini, R. (2004). Thinking about Winnicott and the origins of the Self. *Psychoanalysis and History*, 6 (2): 225–235.
Garmezy, N. (1992). The case for the single case in research. *New Directions for Methodology of Social and Behavioural Sciences*, 13: 5–17.
Giannakoulas, A. (2005). Childhood sexual theories and childhood sexuality: The primal scene and parental sexuality. In: L. Caldwell (Ed.), *Sex and Sexuality: Winnicottian Perspectives* (pp. 55–68). London: Karnac.
Gillespie, C. H. C. (1960). *The Edge of Objectivity: An Essay on the History of Scientific Ideas*. Princeton, NJ: Princeton University Press.
Gillespie, W. (1972). Commemorative Meeting for Donald W. Winnicott, January 19th, 1992. *Scientific Bulletin of the British Psychoanalytic Society and The Institute of Psycho-Analysis*, 57: 2.
Giovacchini, P. L. (Ed.) (1990). *Tactics and Techniques in Psychoanalytic Therapy, Vol. 3: The Implications of Winnicott's Contributions*. Northvale, NJ, & London: Jason Aronson.
Gleick, J. (1987). *Chaos: Making a New Science*. New York: Viking.
Godley, W. (2001a). Saving Masud Khan. *London Review of Books*, 22 February.
Godley, W. (2001b). My lost hours on the couch. *The Times*, 23 February.
Godley, W. (2004). Commentary on A.-M. Sandler, "Institutional Responses to Boundary Violations: The Case of Masud Khan." *International Journal of Psycho-Analysis*, 85 (1): 42–44.
Goldfarb, W. (1943). Effects of early institutional care on adolescent personality. *Journal of Experimental Education*, 12: 106–129.

Goldfarb, W. (1945). Psychological privation in infancy and subsequent adjustment. *American Journal of Orthopsychiatry, 15:* 247–255.
Goldman, D. (Ed.) (1993a). *In One's Bones: The Clinical Genius of Winnicott.* Northvale, NJ, & London: Jason Aronson.
Goldman, D. (1993b). *In Search of the Real: The Origins and Originality of D. W. Winnicott.* Northvale, NJ, & London: Jason Aronson.
Goldstein, J., Freud, A., & Solnit, A. (1973). *Beyond the Best Interests of the Child.* New York: Free Press.
Goldstein, J., Freud, A., & Solnit, A. (1979). *Before the Best Interests of the Child.* New York: Free Press.
Goswami, A. (1995). *The Self-Aware Universe: How Consciousness Creates the Material World.* New York: Jeremy P. Tarcher.
Green, A. (1978). Potential space in psychoanalysis: The object in the setting. In: G. Kohon (Ed.), *The Dead Mother: The Work of André Green* (pp. 205–221). London: Routledge & The Institute of Psycho-Analysis, 1999.
Green, A. (1997). The intuition of the negative in *Playing and Reality*. *International Journal of Psycho-Analysis, 78:* 1071–1084. Reprinted and revised in: In: J. Abram (Ed.), *André Green at The Squiggle Foundation* (pp. 85–106). Winnicott Studies Monograph Series. London: Karnac, for The Squiggle Foundation, 2000.
Green, A. (1999). *The Work of the Negative.* London: Free Association Books.
Green, A. (2000). The posthumous Winnicott: On *Human Nature*. In: J. Abram (Ed.), *André Green at The Squiggle Foundation* (pp. 69–84). Winnicott Studies Monograph Series. London: Karnac, for The Squiggle Foundation.
Green, A. (2005). *Play and Reflection in Winnicott's Writings.* London: Karnac.
Green, M., & Scholes, M. (Eds.) (2004). *Attachment and Human Survival.* London: Karnac.
Greenberg, M., Cichetti, D., & Cummings, E. M. (Eds.) (1990). *Attachment in the Pre-School Years: Theory, Research, and Intervention.* Chicago, IL: University of Chicago Press.
Greenspan, S. J., & Lieberman, A. F. (1988). A clinical approach to attachment. In: J. Belsky & T. Nezworski (Eds.), *Clinical Implications of Attachment* (pp. 387–424). Hilldale, NJ: Lawrence Erlbaum.
Greenspan, S., & Pollock, G. (Eds.) (1991a). *The Course of Life. Vol. 1: Infancy.* Madison, CT: International Universities Press.
Greenspan, S., & Pollock, G. (Eds.) (1991b). *The Course of Life. Vol. 2: Early Childhood.* Madison, CT: International Universities Press.

Greenspan, S., & Pollock, G. (Eds.) (1991c). *The Course of Life. Vol. 3: Middle and Late Childhood*. Madison, CT: International Universities Press.

Greenspan, S. & Pollock, G. (Eds.) (1991d). *The Course of Life. Vol. 4: Adolescence*. Madison, CT: International Universities Press.

Gribben, J. (1984). *In Search of Schrödinger's Cat: Quantum Physics and Reality*. London: Wildwood House, Corgi; Lexington, KY: Black Swan Books.

Gribben, J. (1998). *In Search of SUSY: Supersymmetry, String and the Theory of Everything*. Harmondsworth, Middlesex: Penguin.

Groarke, S. (2003). A life's work: On Rodman's *Winnicott*. *Free Associations*, 10 (4, No. 56): 472–497.

Grolnik, S. A. (1990). *The Work and Play of Winnicott*. Northvale, NJ, & London: Jason Aronson.

Grolnik, S. A., Barkin, L., & Münsterberger, W. (Eds.) (1978). *Between Reality and Fantasy: Transitional Objects and Phenomena*. New York & London: Jason Aronson.

Grosskurth, P. (1986). *Melanie Klein: Her World and Her Work*. London: Hodder & Stoughton.

Grossman, K., & Grossman, K. E. (in press). Early care and the roots of attachment and partnership representations in the Bielefeld and Regensburg longitudinal studies. In: K. Grossman, K. Grossman, & E. Waters (Eds.), *The Power of Longitudinal Attachment Research*. New York: Guildford Press. Paper retrieved from http://www.brown.edu/Departments/Human_Development_Center/Roundtable/Grossman1

Grossman, K. E., Grossman, K., & Waters, E. (2005). *Attachment from Infancy to Adulthood: The Major Longitudinal Studies*. New York: Guilford Press.

Grotstein, J. S. (1989). Winnicott's importance in psychoanalysis. In: M. G. Fromm & B. L. Smith (Eds.), *The Facilitating Environment: Clinical Applications of Winnicott's Theory* (pp. 130–158). Madison, CT: International Universities Press.

Hall, E. S. (1959). *The Silent Language*. New York: Doubleday.

Hamilton, V. (1982). *Narcissus and Oedipus: The Children of Psycho-Analysis*. London: Routledge & Kegan Paul.

Hamilton, V. (1985). John Bowlby: An ethological basis for psychoanalysis. In: J. Reppen (Ed.), *Beyond Freud: A Study of Modern Psychoanalytic Theorists* (pp. 1–28). New York: Analytic Press.

Hamilton, V. (1987a). Bowlby's "yearning and searching phase of mourning" as seen in adult psychotherapy. *Psychoanalytic Psychotherapy*, 2 (3): 251–262.

Hamilton, V. (1987b). Some problems in the clinical application of attachment theory. *Psychoanalytic Psychotherapy, 3* (1): 67–83.
Hamilton, V. (1988). The concept of mourning and its roots in infancy. *Psychoanalytic Psychotherapy, 3* (3): 191–209.
Hamilton, V. (1995). Personal reminiscences of John Bowlby. *Tavistock Gazette*, Autumn.
Hamilton, V. (1996a). On the otherness of being: Winnicott's ideas on "object usage" and "the experience of externality". *Journal of Child Psychotherapy, 22* (3): 383–391.
Hamilton, V. (1996b). *The Analyst's Preconscious*. New York & London: Analytic Press.
Harel, P. (1986). "An Assessment of D. W. Winnicott's Contributions in Relation to Current Research in the Field of Infant Development and Infant Psychiatry and Care." Unpublished thesis, Sarah Lawrence College, Bronxville, New York.
Harlow, H. F. (1958). The nature of love. *The American Psychologist, 3*: 673–685.
Harlow, H. F., & Harlow, M. K. (1966). Learning to love. *American Scientist, 54*: 244–272.
Harris, T. (2004a). Discussion of the Special Issue: Chef or chemist? Practicing psychotherapy within the attachment paradigm. *Attachment and Human Development, 6* (June, No. 2).
Harris, T. (2004b). Attachment-related psychodynamics: Another shake to the kaleidoscope. *Attachment and Human Development, 6* (September, No. 2).
Harwood, R. L., Miller, J. G., & Irizarry, N. L. (1995). *Culture and Attachment Perceptions of the Child in Context*. New York & London: Guilford Press.
Heard, D., & Lake, B. (1997). *The Challenge of Attachment for Care-Giving*. London: Routledge.
Hermann, I. (1943). *L'Instinct filial*. Paris: Denowl, 1972.
Hernandez, M., & Giannakoulas, A. (2001). On the construction of potential space. In: M. Bertolini, A. Giannakoulas, & M. Hernandez, with A. Molino (Eds.), *Squiggles and Spaces: Revisiting the Work of D. W. Winnicott, Vol. 1* (pp. 146–163). London & Philadelphia, PA: Whurr.
Hinde, R. A. (1966). *Animal Behaviour: A Synthesis of Ethology and Comparative Psychology*. London: McGraw-Hill.
Holbrook, D. (2002). D. W. Winnicott. In: B. Kahr (Ed.) (2002). *The Legacy of Winnicott: Essays on Infant and Child Mental Health* (pp. 146–150). London: Karnac.
Holmes, J. (1993). *John Bowlby and Attachment Theory*. London: Routledge.
Holmes, J. (1996). *Attachment, Intimacy, Autonomy: Using Attachment*

Theory in Adult Psychotherapy. Northvale, NJ, & London: Jason Aronson.

Holmes, J. (1997). Bowlby, Fairbairn, and Sutherland: The Scottish connection in psychotherapy. *Free Associations, 6* (3, No. 39): 351–378.

Holmes, J. (2001). *The Search for the Secure Base: Attachment Theory and Psychotherapy*. Hove & Philadelphia, PA: Brunner-Routledge.

Home Office (1945–46). *Care of Children Committee (Curtis Committee): Transcripts of Oral Evidence*. Public Records Office, Kew.

Home Office (1946). *Report of the Care of Children Committee (Curtis Report)*. Cmd. 6636. London: HMSO.

Hopkins, J. (1987). Failure of the holding relationship: Some effects of physical rejection on the child's attachment and on his inner experience. *Journal of Child Psychotherapy, 13*: 5–17.

Hopkins, J. (1990). The observed infant of attachment theory. *British Journal of Psychotherapy, 6* (4): 460–470. Reprinted in: *Journal of the Institute for Self-Analysis, 4* (1): 12–29 [Special Issue, *On Attachment: Commemorating the Work of John Bowlby*].

Hopkins, J. (1996). The dangers and deprivations of too-good mothering. *Journal of Child Psychotherapy, 22* (3): 407–422.

Hopkins, J. (2002). From baby games to let's pretend: The achievement of playing. In: B. Kahr (Ed.), *The Legacy of Winnicott: Essays on Infant and Child Mental Health* (pp. 91–99). London: Karnac.

Hopkins, L. B. (2000). D. W. Winnicott's analysis of Masud Khan: A preliminary study of failures of object usage. *Contemporary Psychoanalysis, 34* (1): 4–57.

Hopkins, L. B. (2004). How Masud Khan fell into psychoanalysis. *American Imago: Studies in Psychoanalysis and Culture, 61* (4): 483–494.

Hopkins, L. B. (in press). *Blessings and Humiliations: A Biography of Masud Khan*. New York: Other Press.

Hughes, J. M. (1989). *Reshaping the Psycho-Analytic Domain: The Work of Melanie Klein, W. R. D. Fairbairn and D. W. Winnicott*. Los Angeles, CA, & London: University of California Press.

Hunter, V. (1991). John Bowlby: An interview. *Psychoanalytic Review, 78*: 159–175.

Huxley, J. (1968). *The Courtship Habits of the Great Crested Grebe*. London: Grossman.

Isaacs, S. S. (1930). *Intellectual Growth in Young Children*. London: Routledge & Kegan Paul, 1944, 1948; New York: Shocken Books, 1966, 1972.

Isaacs, S. S. (1933). *Social Development of Young Children*. London: Routledge & Kegan Paul.

Isaacs, S. S. (1972). D.W.W. 1896–1971, at Commemorative Meeting for

Donald W. Winnicott, January 19th, 1992. *Scientific Bulletin of the British Psychoanalytic Society and The Institute of Psycho-Analysis,* 57: 29.

Issroff, J. (1974). A group training program dealing with the problems of senior staff in custodial institutions. *Mental Health & Society,* 1: 98–109.

Issroff, J. (1975). Adolescence and creativity. In: S. Meyerson (Ed.), *Adolescence: The Crises of Adjustment: A Tavistock Approach* (pp. 143–164). London: Allen & Unwin.

Issroff, J. (1979). From existing to living: The narrative of a transformation. *Bulletin of the British Psychoanalytical Society,* 6 (June): 1–21.

Issroff, J. (1980). "Affect Contagion Phenomena: Ongoing Effects Subsequent to Massive Traumatization: A Study of a Large Group Discussion of the Holocaust in a "Survivor Syndrome" Workshop and Further Implications". Paper presented to First Gathering of Children of Survivors of the Holocaust, City University, New York, Summer, 1980; to Second International Congress on Organized Persecution of Children, Hamburg, October, 1993; and as "Affect and Image Contagion Phenomena and the Contextualization of Vicarious Traumatization: Identification, Significance for Therapists, Society, and Notes on Healing Counter-influences" presented as Plenary Address Pre-formation of African Society for Traumatic Stress Studies, at Centre for Study of Violence and Trauma and International Society for Traumatic Stress Studies Conference in Johannesburg, January, 1999.

Issroff, J. (1983). A reaction to reading *Boundary and Space: An Introduction to the Work of D. W. Winnicott* by Madeleine Davis and David Wallbridge. *International Review of Psycho-Analysis,* 10: 231–235.

Issroff, J. (1992). "An Evaluation of the Implications of Donald W. Winnicott's Contribution in Understanding and Working with Groups". Presented to Israel Group Analytic Society, Ramat Gan, (Autumn) and Jerusalem (February 1994).

Issroff, J. (1993). Kitchen therapy: Remembering "the creativity of salivation" and advocating cooking as an aid in psychoanalytic child psychotherapy with latency-age children. *Winnicott Studies: The Journal of The Squiggle Foundation,* 7: 42–51.

Issroff, J. (1994a). Building for democracy: An end to violence, prevention and mitigation of trauma. How? And what next? *The Jerusalem Times,* 25 May.

Issroff, J. (1994b). "'Potential Space' and 'Holding': Winnicott's Approach to Psychoanalytic Intervention." Paper presented to the Norwegian Association of Psychotherapists, Oslo.

Issroff, J. (1995a). D. W. Winnicott's ability to facilitate "turning points".

Voices: Journal of the American Association for Psychotherapy (Spring) [Special issue, *Turning Points*].

Issroff, J. (1995b). "Reflections about 'Understanding' Violence and Its Effects on Others." Paper presented at the International Federation of University Women's Conference, Yokohama, September. Published as: Strategies for counteracting violence. In: A. Holden-Rönning & E. M. Horkin (Eds.), *Women's Future: Survival or Progress?* (pp. 179–200). Geneva: International Federation of University Women, 1997.

Issroff, J. (1997). Phänomene der Affekt-Kontamination. Fortdauernde Auswirkungen massiver Traumatisierung: Untersuchung einer Grossgruppendiskussion über den Holocaust in einem Workshop zum "Survivor-Syndrom". *Gruppenpsychotherapie Gruppendynamik*, 33: 83.

Issroff, J. (1998a). Therapists' dilemmas in triage situations: Weeping in a downpour, howling in the heart of bellowing thunder . . . attending to the needs of caregivers. In: B. Efraime, Jr., P. Riedesser, J. Waiter, H. Adam, & P. Steudtner (Eds.), *Children, War and Persecution: Rebuilding Hope* (pp. 88–93). Maputo, Mozambique: Rebuilding Hope.

Issroff, J. (1998b). Women and the Middle East Peace Process. In: A. Holden-Rönning (Ed.), *Women and Peace: Selected Papers from the 25th IFUW Triennial Conference, Yokohama, 1995*. Geneva: International Federation of University Women.

Issroff, J. (1999a). "Affect and Image Contagion Phenomena and the Contextualization of Vicarious Traumatization: Identification, Significance for Therapists, Society, and Notes on Healing Counter-Influences." Paper presented at the Centre for the Study of Violence and Trauma and International Society for Traumatic Stress Studies Conference pre-formation of African Society for Traumatic Stress Studies, Johannesburg, January. Pamphlet. Johannesburg: CSVR.

Issroff, J. (1999b). Therapists' dilemmas in triage situations: Weeping in a downpour, howling in the heart of bellowing thunder . . . working with refugees. In: A. Rönning (Ed.), *Women's Future: Women's World*. Geneva: IFUW.

Issroff J. (2001). Reflections on *Playing and Reality*. In: M. Bertolini, A. Giannakoulas, & M. Hernandez, with A. Molino (Eds.), *Squiggles and Spaces: Revisiting the Work of D. W. Winnicott, Vol. 1* (pp. 59–70). London & Philadelphia, PA: Whurr.

Issroff, J. (2002a). Michelangelo's Moses re-visited—reflections through post-Freudian theoretical lenses on the roots of creativity. *Free Associations*, 9 (2, No. 50): 271–281.

Issroff, J. (2002b). "M.M.R. Khan." [Poem.] In: J. Raphael-Leff (Ed.), *Beyond The Couch* (pp. 252–253). Colchester: University of Essex Press.

Issroff, J. (2004). Time for psychoanalysts to speak up: A reaction to reading *Violence or Dialogue? Psychoanalytic Insights on Terror and Terrorism*, ed. S. Varvin & V. D. Volkan. *Free Associations, 11* (2, No. 58): 242–269.

Issroff, J. (in press). *Review of Fifty Years of Attachment Theory: The Donald Winnicott Memorial Lecture by Sir Richard Bowlby.* London: Karnac, on behalf of The Winnicott Clinic of Psychotherapy.

Issroff, J. (in preparation-a). In search of Alice Winnicott. In: *Something Short of Everything About Donald Woods Winnicott.* London & New York: Free Association Press.

Issroff, J. (in preparation-b). Winnicott: A Cubist collage portrait. In: *Something Short of Everything About Donald Woods Winnicott.*

Issroff, J. (in preparation-c). *Something Short of Everything About Donald Woods Winnicott.* London & New York: Free Association Press.

Jackson, J. (1996). An experimental investigation of Winnicott's set situation: A study of South African white, black and institutionalized infants aged 7 to 9 months old. *Journal of Child Psychotherapy, 22* (3): 343–361.

Jacobs, M. (1995). *D. W. Winnicott.* London, Thousand Oaks, CA, & New Delhi: Sage.

Jacobson, E. (1954). The self and the object world: Vicissitudes of the infantile cathexes and their influence on ideational and affective development. *Psychoanalytic Study of the Child, 9*: 75–127.

Jacobson, E. (1965). *The Self and the Object World.* Journal of the American Psychoanalytic Society Monograph Series, No. 2. New York: International Universities Press.

Jallinsky, S. (1997). Donald W. Winnicott: The illusionist of psychoanalysis. In: R. Zac de Goldstein, L. Valenti de Greif, & S. Jallinsky (Eds.), *Winnicott's Space. Encounters, No. 1* (pp. 41–50). Buenos Aires: Asociacion Psicoanalítica Argentina.

James, B. (1994). *Handbook for Treatment of Attachment Trauma Problems in Children.* London: Jessica Kingsley; New York: Free Press.

James, M. (1982). D. W. Winnicott: Review of *Boundary and Space: An Introduction to the Work of D. W. Winnicott* by Madeleine Davis & David Wallbridge, 1981. *International Journal of Psycho-Analysis, 56* (4): 493–497.

Janis, I. L. (1972). *Victims of Groupthink: A Psychological Study of Foreign Policy Decisions and Fiascos.* Boston, MA: Houghton Mifflin.

Jazid, G. A., & Kestenberg, J. (1983). Entrancement of the mother with her young baby and implications for the older sibling. *Dynamic Psychotherapy, 1*: 37–51.

Jung, C. G. (1963). *Memories, Dreams, Reflections*, ed. A. Jaffe, trans. R. Winston & C. Winston. London: Collins & Routledge.

Kahr, B. (1996a). Donald Winnicott and the foundations of child psychotherapy. *Journal of Child Psychotherapy*, 22 (3): 327–342.

Kahr, B. (1996b). *D. W. Winnicott: A Biographical Portrait*. London: Karnac.

Kahr, B. (Ed.) (2001a). Introduction. In: *Forensic Psychotherapy and Psychopathology: Winnicottian Perspectives*. London: Karnac.

Kahr, B. (2001b). Winnicott's contribution to the study of dangerousness. In: *Forensic Psychotherapy and Psychopathology: Winnicottian Perspectives*. London: Karnac.

Kahr, B. (2002). Donald Woods Winnicott: The cartographer of infancy. In: B. Kahr (Ed.), *The Legacy of Winnicott: Essays on Infant and Child Mental Health* (pp. 1–12). London: Karnac.

Kahr, B. (Ed.) (2003). *The Legacy of Winnicott: Essays on Infant and Child Mental Health*. London: Karnac.

Kahr, B. (2004a). Introduction. In: *Fifty Years of Attachment Theory: The Donald Winnicott Memorial Lecture*. London: Karnac, on behalf of the Winnicott Clinic of Psychotherapy.

Kahr, B. (2004b). Introduction to John Bowlby and Donald Winnicott: Collegial comrades in child mental health. In: *Fifty Years of Attachment Theory: The Donald Winnicott Memorial Lecture* (pp. 3–10). London: Karnac, on behalf of the Winnicott Clinic of Psychotherapy.

Kanter, J. (2004a). Clare Winnicott: Her life and legacy. In: J. Kanter (Ed.), *Face to Face with Children: The Life and Work of Clare Winnicott* (pp. 1–94). London: Karnac.

Kanter, J. (2004b). *Face to Face with Children: The Life and Work of Clare Winnicott*. London: Karnac.

Kanter, J. (2004c). 'Let's Never Ask Him What to Do." Claire Britton's transformative impact on Donald Winnicott. *American Imago: Studies in Psychoanalysis and Culture*, 61 (4): 457–482.

Karen, R. (1994). *Becoming Attached: First Relationships and How They Shape Our Capacity to Love*. Oxford: Oxford University Press.

Kennell, J. H., & Klaus, M. H. (1983). Early events, later effects on the infant. In: J. D. Call, E. Galenson, & R. Tyson (Eds.), *Frontiers of Infant Psychiatry* (pp. 7–16). New York: Basic Books.

Kestenberg, J., & Buelte, A. (1977). Prevention, infant therapy, and the treatment of adults. 1: Toward understanding mutuality. *International Journal of Psycho-Analytic Psychotherapy*, 6: 339–396.

Khan, M. M. R. (1986). Introduction. In: D. W. Winnicott, *Holding and Interpretation: Fragment of an Analysis*. London: Hogarth Press & The Institute of Psycho-Analysis. Reprinted London: Karnac, 1989.

Khan, M. M. R, Davis, J., & Davis, M. E. V. (1974). The beginning and fruition of the self: An essay on D. W. Winnicott. In: J. A. Davis & J. Dutting (Eds.), *The Scientific Foundations of Paediatrics*. London: Heinemann Medical.

King, M., & Trowell, J. (1992). *Children's Welfare and the Law: The Limits of Legal Intervention*. London: Sage.

King, P. (2004). Recollections of Donald Winnicott and John Bowlby. In: *Fifty Years of Attachment Theory: The Donald Winnicott Memorial Lecture* (pp. 31–38). London: Karnac, for the Winnicott Clinic of Psychotherapy.

King, P., Rayner, E., Menzies-Lyth, I., & Bowlby, U. (1991) John Bowlby (1907–1990) Memorial Meeting. *Bulletin of the British Psychoanalytical Society, 27* (11): 16–33.

King, P., & Steiner, R. (1991). *The Freud–Klein Controversies 1941–1945*. London: Routledge.

Klaus, M. H., & Kennell, J. H. (1976a). Human maternal and paternal behaviour. In: *Maternal–Infant Bonding: The Impact of Early Separation or Loss on Family Development* (chap. 3). St. Louis, MO: Mosby.

Klaus, M. H., & Kennell, J. H. (1976b). *Maternal–Infant Bonding: The Impact of Early Separation or Loss on Family Development*. Saint Louis, MO: Mosby.

Kosko, B. (1993). *Fuzzy Thinking: The New Science of Fuzzy Logic*. New York: Hyperion.

Kretchmar, M. D., & Jacobvitz, D. B. (2002). Observing mother–child relationships across generations: Boundary patterns, attachment, and the transmission of caregiving. *Family Process, 41* (3): 351–374.

Kristeva, J. (2002). *The Portable Kristeva. Updated Edition: European Perspectives*, ed. K. Oliver. New York: Columbia University Press.

Kristeva, J. (2003). Remarks from podium. Conference on Psychoanalysis and Gender, the Psychoanalysis Unit, University College London, 14–15 June.

Lacan, J. (1977). *Écrits: A Selection*. New York: W. W. Norton.

Lacan, J. (1979). *The Four Fundamental Concepts of Psycho-Analysis*. London: Penguin.

Laing, R. D. (1960). *The Divided Self: A Study of Sanity and Madness*, London: Tavistock; Harmondsworth, Middlesex: Penguin.

Laing, R. D. (1967). *The Bird of Paradise and the Politics of Experience*. Harmondsworth, Middlesex: Penguin.

Laing, R. D., Phillipson, H., & Lee, A. R. (1966). *Interpersonal Perception: A Theory and a Method of Research*. London: Tavistock; New York: Harper & Row, 1972.

Langer, S. K. (1953). *Feeling and Form*. New York: Scribner.

Laschinger, B., Purnell, C., Schwartz, J., White, K., & Wingfield, R. (2004). Sexuality and attachment from a clinical point of view. *Attachment and Human Development, 6* (June, No. 2).

Levy, T. M., & Orlans, M. (1998). *Attachment, Trauma, and Healing: Understanding and Treating Attachment Disorder in Children and Families.* Washington, DC: CWLA Press.

Lichtenberg, J. D. (1989). *Psychoanalysis and Motivation.* Hillsdale, NJ: Analytic Press.

Liedloff, J. (1977). *The Continuum Concept: Allowing Human Nature to Work Successfully.* Reading, MA: Addison-Wesley.

Liedloff, J. (1986). *The Continuum Concept: In Search of Happiness Lost.* New York & London: Arkana; Reading, MA: Perseus.

Lifton, R. J. (1979). *The Broken Connection: On Death and the Continuity of Life.* New York: Simon & Schuster.

Lifton, R. J. (1993). *The Protean Self: Human Resilience in an Age of Fragmentation.* New York: Basic Books.

Liotti, G. (1992). Disorganized/disoriented attachment in the etiology of dissociative disorders. *Dissociation, 5:* 196–204.

Little, M. I. (1985). Winnicott working in areas where psychotic anxieties predominate: A personal record. *Free Associations, 3:* 9–42.

Little, M. I. (1987). On the value of regression to dependence. *Free Associations, 10:* 7–22.

Little, M. I. (1990). *Psychotic Anxieties and Containment: A Personal Record of an Analysis with Winnicott.* Northvale, NJ, & London: Jason Aronson.

Lorenz, K., Huxley, J., & Wilson, M. K. (1952). *King Solomon's Ring: New Light on Animal Ways.* New York & London: Routledge, 2002.

Lorenz, K., & Wilson, M. K. (2002). *On Aggression.* New York & London: Routledge.

Lubetsky, O. (2002). The impact of premature birth on fear of personal death and attachment styles in adolescence. *Death Studies, 26* (7): 523–543.

Lustgarten de Canteros, N. (1997). Winnicott and clinical practice in psychosomatic narcissistic hypersensitivity and its vicissitudes. In: R. Zac de Goldstein, L. Valenti de Greif, & S. Jallinsky (Eds.), *Winnicott's Space. Encounters, No. 1* (pp. 61–70). Buenos Aires: Asociacion Psicoanalítica Argentina.

Lyward, G. A. (1958). The school as a therapeutic community. In: *Psychiatry in a Changing Society.* London: Tavistock.

MacCurdy, J. T. (1928). *Common Principles in Psychology and Physiology.* New York & Cambridge: Macmillan.

Mahler, M. S. (1975). *The Psychological Birth of the Human Infant: Symbiosis and Individuation.* New York: Basic Books.

Main, M. (1999). Adult attachment rating and classification systems. In: M. Main (Ed.), *A Typology of Human Attachment Organization Assessed in Discourse, Drawings and Interviews*. New York, New Haven, CT, & London: Cambridge University Press.

Main, M., & Hesse, M. (1990). Parent's unresolved traumatic experiences are related to infant disorganised attachment status: Is frightened or frightening parental behaviour the linking mechanism? In: M. T. Greenberg, D. Cichetti, & E. M. Cummings (Eds.), *Attachment in the Pre-School Years: Theory, Research and Intervention*. Chicago, IL: University of Chicago Press.

Main, M., & Solomon, J. (1986). Discovery of new insecure-disorganized/disoriented attachment pattern. In: M. Yogman & T. B. Brazelton (Eds.), *Affective Development in Infancy* (pp. 95–124). Norwood, NJ: Ablex.

Main, M., & Weston, D. (1981). The quality of the toddler's relationship to mother and to father: Related to conflict behaviour and readiness to establish new relationships. *Child Development, 52*: 932–940.

Main, T. (1983). The concept of the therapeutic community. In: M. Pines (Ed.), *The Evolution of Group Analysis*. London: Routledge.

Main, T. (1989). *The Ailment and Other Psychoanalytic Essays*. London: Free Association Books.

Malan, D. (1990). Contribution to reminiscences and reflections about John Bowlby. *The Tavistock Gazette, 29*: 13–16.

Maratos, J. (1986). Bowlby and Kohut: Where science and humanism meet. *Group Analysis, 19* (4): 303–309.

Marrone, M. (1998). *Attachment and Interaction* (with a contribution by N. Diamond and a Foreword by M. Pines). London & Philadelphia, PA: Jessica Kingsley.

Marrone, M., & Cortina, M. (2003). Introduction: Reclaiming Bowlby's contribution to psychoanalysis. In: M. Cortina & M. Marrone (Eds.), *Attachment Theory and the Psychoanalytic Process* (pp. 1–24). London & Philadelphia, PA: Whurr.

Martin, F. E. (1991). John Bowlby, 1907–1991: A tribute and personal appreciation. *Melanie Klein and Object Relations, 9*: 63–69.

Maslow, A. (1970). Religious aspects of peak-experiences. In: *Personality and Religion*. New York: Harper & Row.

McDougall, J. (2003). *Donald Winnicott the Man: Reflections and Recollections. The Donald Winnicott Memorial Lecture*. London: Karnac, for The Winnicott Clinic of Psychotherapy.

McDougall, W. (1923). *An Outline of Psychology*. London: Methuen.

Meloy, J. R. (1997). *Violent Attachments*. Northvale, NJ, & London: Jason Aronson.

Middlemore, M. (1941). *The Nursing Couple*. London: Hamish Hamilton.
Milgram, S. (1974). *Obedience to Authority: An Experimental View*. New York: Harper & Row.
Mill, J. S. (c. 1840). Autobiography (posthumous). *Part I: Childhood*. New York: Collier & Son, 1909–14; New York: Bartleby, Harvard Classics, Vol. 25, Part 1, 2001. Retrieved from www.bartleby.com/25/1/
Miller, D. H. (1969). *The Age Between: Adolescents in a Disturbed Society*. London: Hutchinson.
Miller, D. H. (1973). *Growth to Freedom: Adolescence: Psychology, Psychopathology, Psychotherapy*. New York & London: Jason Aronson.
Miller, D. H. (1983). *The Age Between: Adolescents and Therapy*. New York & London: Jason Aronson.
Milner, M. (1969). *The Hands of the Living God: An Account of a Psychoanalytic Treatment*. London: Hogarth Press & The Institute of Psycho-Analysis.
Milner, M. (1972). Commemorative Meeting for Donald W. Winnicott, January 19th, 1992. *Scientific Bulletin of the British Psychoanalytical Society and The Institute of Psycho-Analysis, 57*: 5.
Milner, M. (1978). D. W. Winnicott and the two-way journey. In: S. A. Grolnik, L. Barkin, & W. Müensterberger (Eds.), *Between Reality and Fantasy: Transitional Objects and Phenomena* (pp. 35–42). New York & London: Jason Aronson.
Milner, M. (2001). On Winnicott. In: M. Bertolini, A. Giannakoulas, & M. Hernandez, with A. Molino (Eds.), *Squiggles and Spaces: Revisiting the Work of D. W. Winnicott, Vol. 1* (pp. 265–268). London & Philadelphia, PA: Whurr.
Mitchell, J. (1999). Deconstructing difference: Gender, splitting, and transitional space. In: *John Bowlby: In Memoriam: A Symposium on Gender. Psychoanalytic Dialogues, 1* (3).
Mitchell, S. A. (1999). Attachment theory and the psychoanalytic tradition: Reflections on human relationality. *Psychoanalytic Dialogues, 9* (1): 85–107.
Mitchell, S. A., & Aron, L. (Eds.) (1999). *Relational Psychoanalysis: The Emergence of a Tradition*. Hillsdale, NJ: Analytic Press.
Molino, A. (2001). Preface. In: M. Bertolini, A. Giannakoulas, & M. Hernandez, with A. Molino (Eds.), *Squiggles and Spaces: Revisiting the Work of D. W. Winnicott, Vol. 2* (p. x). London & Philadelphia, PA: Whurr.
Molino, A. (Ed.) (2004). *Culture, Subject, Psyche: Dialogues in Psychoanalysis and Anthropology* (pp. 63–79). London & Philadelphia, PA: Whurr.
Mollon, P. (2001). *Releasing the Self: The Healing Legacy of Heinz Kohut*. London & Philadelphia, PA: Whurr.

Mollon, P. (2004). *EMDR and the Energy Therapies: Psychoanalytic Perspectives*. London: Karnac.
Monckton, Sir W. (1945). *Report on the Circumstances which Led to the Boarding Out of Dennis and Terence O'Neill at Bank Farm, Ministerly, and the Steps Taken to Supervise Their Welfare*. Cmd. 636. London: HMSO.
Money-Kyrle, R. (1978). *The Collected Papers of Roger Money-Kyrle*. Strath Tay, Perthshire: Clunie Press.
Moore, K., Moretti, M. M., & Holland, R. (1998). A new perspective for youth care programs: Using attachment theory to guide interventions for troubled youth. *Residential Treatment for Children & Youth, 15* (3): 1–24.
Morris, D. (1967). *The Naked Ape*. London & New York: Jonathan Cape.
Morris, D. (1970). *The Human Zoo*. London & New York: Jonathan Cape.
Morris, D. (1978). *Manwatching*. St. Albans: Triad/Panther Books.
Murray, L. (1989). Winnicott and the developmental psychology of infancy. *British Journal of Psychotherapy, 5* (3): 333–348.
Murray, L. (1991). Intersubjectivity, object relations theory, and empirical evidence from mother–infant interactions. *Infant Mental Health Journal, 12*: 219–232.
Murray, L. (1992). The impact of postnatal depression on child development. *Child Psychology and Psychiatry, 33*: 543–561.
Murray, L., & Cooper, P. J. (1997a). Effects of postnatal depression on infant development. *Archives Diseases of Childhood, 77*: 99–101.
Murray, L., & Cooper, P. J. (1997b). The impact of psychological treatments of post-partum depression on maternal mood and infant development. In: L. Murray & P. J. Cooper (Eds.), *Postpartum Depression and Child Development* (pp. 201–220). New York: Guilford Press, 1998.
Neill, A. S. (1962). *Summerhill: A Radical Approach to Education*, with a Foreword by Erich Fromm. London: Gollancz.
Newcombe, N., & Lerner, J. (1982). Britain between the wars: The historical context of Bowlby's theory of attachment. *Psychiatry, 45* (1): 1–12.
Newman, A. (1988). The breakdown that was: Winnicott and the fear of breakdown. *Winnicott Studies: The Journal of the Squiggle Foundation, 3*: 36–47.
Newman, A. (1995). *Non-Compliance in Winnicott's Words: A Companion to the Work of D. W. Winnicott*. London: Free Association Books.
NICHD (2005). *Child Care and Child Development*, ed. by The NICHD Early Child Care Research Network. London: Guilford Press.
Nicolis, G., & Prigogine, I. (1989). *Understanding Complexity*. New York: Freeman.
Oakeshott, E. (1972). Commemorative Meeting for Donald W. Winnicott,

January 19th, 1992. *Scientific Bulletin of the British Psychoanalytical Society and The Institute of Psycho-Analysis, 57*: 21.

Ogden, T. H. (1985). On potential space. *International Journal of Psycho-Analysis, 66*: 129–141.

Ogden, T. H. (1986). *The Matrix of the Mind: Object Relations and the Psychoanalytic Dialogue*. Northvale, NJ, & London: Jason Aronson.

Ogden, T. H. (1989). *The Primitive Edge of Experience*. Northvale, NJ, & London: Jason Aronson.

Ogden, T. H. (1994). *Subjects of Analysis*. London: Karnac.

Ogden, T. (1999). "The music of what happens" in poetry and psychoanalysis. *International Journal of Psycho-Analysis, 80*: 979–994.

Ogden, T. H. (2001). Reading Winnicott. *Psychoanalytic Quarterly, 70:* 299–323.

Oliver, K. (Ed.) (2002). *The Portable Kristeva: European Perspectives* (revised edition). New York: Columbia University Press.

Orbach, S. (2002). The body as transitional object. In: B. Kahr (Ed.), *The Legacy of Winnicott: Essays on Infant and Child Mental Health* (pp. 124–134). London: Karnac.

Osofsky, J. (Ed.) (1987). *Handbook of Infant Development* (2nd edition). New York: Wiley.

Osofsky, J. (1988). Attachment theory and research in the psychoanalytic process. *Psychoanalytic Psychology, 5*: 159–177.

Osofsky, J., & Fitzgerald, H. E. (Eds.) (2000). *WAIMH Handbook of Infant Mental Health*. World Association for Infant Mental Health. New York: John Wiley & Sons.

Padel, J. (2001a). Nothing so practical as a good theory. In: M. Bertolini, A. Giannakoulas, & M. Hernandez, with A. Molino (Eds.), *Squiggles and Spaces: Revisiting the Work of D. W. Winnicott, Vol. 1* (pp. 3–17). London & Philadelphia, PA: Whurr.

Padel, J. (2001b). Winnicott's thinking. In: M. Bertolini, A. Giannakoulas, & M. Hernandez, with A. Molino (Eds.), *Squiggles and Spaces: Revisiting the Work of D. W. Winnicott, Vol. 1* (p. 269). London & Philadelphia, PA: Whurr.

Pally, R. (1998). Emotional processing: The mind–body connection. *International Journal of Psycho-Analysis, 79*: 349–362.

Panksepp, J. (1999). Emotions as viewed by psychoanalysis and neuroscience: An exercise in consilience. *Neuro-Psychoanalysis, 1*: 15–37.

Parkes, C. M. (1972). *Bereavement: Studies of Grief in Adult Life*. New York: International Universities Press.

Parkes, C. M., & Stevenson-Hinde, J. (Eds.) (1991). *The Place of Attachment in Human Behaviour*. New York: Basic Books.

Parkes, C. M, Stevenson-Hinde, J., & Marris, P. (Eds.) (1991). *Attachment Across the Life Cycle*. London & New York: Routledge.

Parsons, M. (1999). The logic of play in psychoanalysis. *International Journal of Psycho-Analysis, 80*: 871–884.

Pearlman, L. A., & Saakvitne, K. W. (1995). *Trauma and the Therapist: Countertransference and Vicarious Traumatization in Psychotherapy with Incest Survivors*. New York & London: W. W. Norton.

Pearson, J. (2004). Glimpses of a life. In: J. Pearson (Ed.), *Analyst of the Imagination: The Life and Work of Charles Rycroft*. London: Karnac.

Pena, S. (2001a). My formative experience as a psychoanalyst of children and adolescents. Retrieved from http://www.etatsgeneraux-psychanalyse.net/archives/texte173.html

Pena, S. (2001b). The presence of Winnicott in me. In: M. Bertolini, A. Giannakoulas, & M. Hernandez, with A. Molino (Eds.), *Squiggles and Spaces: Revisiting the Work of D. W. Winnicott, Vol. 1* (pp. 236–241). London & Philadelphia, PA: Whurr.

Pfäfflin, F., & Adshead, G. (Eds.) (2003). *A Matter of Security: The Application of Attachment Theory to Forensic Psychiatry and Psychotherapy*. London: Jessica Kingsley.

Phillips, A. (1988). *Winnicott*. Fontana Modern Masters. London: Harper Collins.

Pontalis, J. B. (1981). *Frontiers in Psychoanalysis: Between the Dream and Psychic Pain*. New York: International Universities Press.

Popper, K. (1963). *Conjectures and Refutations: The Growth of Scientific Knowledge*. London: Routledge.

Popper, K. (1965). *The Logic of Scientific Discovery*. New York: Basic Books.

Popper, K. (1972). *Objective Knowledge: An Evolutionary Approach*. Oxford: Clarendon Press.

Prechtl, H., & Beintera, D. (1964). The neurological examination of the full-term newborn infant. In: *Clinics in Developmental Medicine, 2*. London: Prentice Hall.

Pribram, K. H. (1971). *Languages of the Brain*. New York: Prentice-Hall.

Quine, W. V. (1936). Truth by convention. In: O. H. Lee (Ed.), *Philosophical Essays for A. N. Whitehead*. New York: Longmans. Revised version in: W. V. Quine, *The Ways of Paradox*. New York: Random House, 1966; Cambridge, MA: Harvard University Press, 1976 (revised edition, 2004).

Raphael-Leff, J. (2000). *"Spilt Milk": Perinatal Loss and Breakdown*. London: Institute of Psycho-Analysis.

Raphael-Leff, J. (2001). Primary maternal persecution. In: B. Kahr (Ed.), *Forensic Psychotherapy and Psychopathology: Winnicottian Perspectives* (pp. 27–42). London: Karnac.

Rayner, E. (1990). *The Independent Mind in British Psychoanalysis* (pp. 263–265). London: Free Association Books.
Rees, C. (1995). The dialectic between holding and interpreting in Winnicott's psychotherapy. *Psychoanalytic Psychotherapy in South Africa, 3*: 13–30.
Reeves, C. (1983). Maladjustment: Psycho-dynamic theory and the role of therapeutic education in a residential setting. *Maladjustment and Therapeutic Education, 1* (2): 25–31.
Reeves, C. (1990). Therapeutic education in a residential setting: The contribution of psycho-dynamic theory. In: C. Fees (Ed.), *Residential Experience* (pp. 71–78). Birmingham: Association of Workers for Maladjusted Children.
Reeves, C. (1996). Transition and transience: Winnicott on leaving and dying. *Journal of Child Psychotherapy, 22* (3): 444–455.
Reeves, C. (2001). Minding the child: The legacy of Dockar-Drysdale. *Emotional and Behavioural Difficulties, 6*: 213–235.
Reeves, C. (2002). A necessary conjunction: Dockar-Drysdale and Winnicott. *Journal of Child Psychotherapy, 28* (1): 3–27.
Reeves, C. (2003). Creative space: A Winnicottian perspective on child psychotherapy. *Insikten, 12* (4): 22–29.
Reeves, C. (2004). On being "intrinsical": A Winnicott enigma? *American Imago: Studies in Psychoanalysis and Culture 61* (4): 427–455.
Rice, A. K. (1968). *Cotswold Community and School. Working Note Number 1* (mimeographed). Tavistock Institute, February.
Richards, V., with Wilke, G. (Eds.) (1996). *The Person Who Is Me: Contemporary Perspectives on the True and False Self.* Winnicott Studies Monograph Series. London: Karnac, for The Squiggle Foundation.
Ricks, M. H. (1985). The social transmission of parental behavior: Attachment across generations. In: I. Bretherton & E. Waters (Eds.), *Growing Points in Attachment Theory and Research. Monographs of the Society for Research in Child Development, 50* (Serial No. 209): 211–227.
Riviere, J. (1936). On the genesis of psychical conflict in earliest infancy. In: A. Hughes (Ed.), *The Inner World and Joan Riviere: Collected Papers 1920–1958.* London: Karnac, 1991.
Roazen, P. (2001). Charles Rycroft and the theme of ablation. *British Journal of Psychotherapy, 18*: 269–277.
Roazen, P. (2002). A meeting with Donald in 1965. In: B. Kahr (Ed.), *The Legacy of Winnicott: Essays on Infant and Child Mental Health* (pp. 23–35). London: Karnac.
Roazen, P. (2004). Charles Rycroft and ablation. In: J. Pearson (Ed.), *Analyst of the Imagination: The Life and Work of Charles Rycroft* (pp. 24–56). London: Karnac.

Robertson, J. (1953). *A Two-Year-Old Goes to Hospital* [Film]. University Park, PA: Penn State Audio-Visual Services.
Robertson, J. (1962). *Hospitals and Children: A Parent's Eye View.* New York: Gollancz.
Robertson, J., & Robertson, J. (1989). *Separation and the Very Young.* London: Free Association Books.
Rodman, F. R. (1990). Insistence on being himself. In: P. L. Giovacchini (Ed.), *Tactics and Techniques in Psychoanalytic Therapy, Vol. 3: The Implications of Winnicott's Contributions* (pp. 21–40). Northvale, NJ, & London: Jason Aronson.
Rodman, F. R. (2003). *Winnicott: Life and Work.* Cambridge MA: Perseus.
Romano, E. (1997). Time for encounter, regression and creativity in Winnicott. In: R. Zac de Goldstein, L. Valenti de Greif, & S. Jallinsky (Eds.), *Winnicott's Space. Encounters, No. 1* (pp. 25–40). Buenos Aires: Asociacion Psicoanalítica Argentina.
Rose, M. (1990a). The Peper Harow treatment approach. In: C. Fees (Ed.), *Residential Experience* (pp. 79–90). Birmingham: Association of Workers for Maladjusted Children.
Rose, M. (1990b). *Healing Hurt Minds: The Peper Harow Experience.* London & New York: Tavistock/Routledge.
Rothschild, B. (2000). *The Body Remembers: The Psychophysiology of Trauma and Trauma Treatment.* New York & London: W. W. Norton.
Roussillon, R. (1977). Paradoxe et continuite chez Winnicott. *Bulletin de Psychologie, 34:* 35.
Rudnytsky, P. (1991). *The Psychoanalytic Vocation: Rank, Winnicott, and the Legacy of Freud.* New Haven, CT, & London: Yale University Press.
Rudnytsky, P. (Ed.) (1993). *Transitional Objects and Potential Spaces: Literary Uses of D. W. Winnicott.* New York: Columbia University Press.
Rustin, M. (1997). The generation of psychoanalytic knowledge: Sociological and clinical perspectives. Part 1: Give me a consulting room . . . . *British Journal of Psychotherapy, 13* (4): 527–541 [Summer BPS Annual Lecture 1996].
Rustin, M. (2003). Research in the consulting room. *Journal of Child Psychotherapy, 29* (2): 137–145.
Rustin, M. (2004). Michael Rustin. In: A. Molino (Ed.), *Culture, Subject, Psyche: Dialogues in Psychoanalysis and Anthropology* (pp. 116–136). London & Philadelphia, PA: Whurr.
Rutter, M. (1972). *Maternal Deprivation Reassessed.* Harmondsworth, Middlesex: Penguin.
Rycroft, C. (1985). On ablation of the parental images, *or* the illusion of

having created oneself. In: P. Fuller (Ed.), *Psychoanalysis and Beyond* (pp. 214–232). London: Chatto & Windus.
Rycroft, C. (1991). *Viewpoints*. London: Chatto & Windus; London: Hogarth Press.
Rycroft, C. (1992). *Rycroft on Analysis and Creativity*. New York: New York University Press.
Rycroft, C. (2004). Reminiscences of a survivor: Psycho-analysis 1937–1993. In: J. Pearson (Ed.), *Analyst of the Imagination: The Life and Work of Charles Rycroft* (pp. 241–247). London: Karnac.
Sable, P. (2001). *Attachment and Adult Psychotherapy*. Northvale, NJ, & London: Jason Aronson.
Sameroff, A. J., & Emde, R. N. (Eds.) (1989). *Relationship Disturbances in Early Childhood*. New York: Basic Books.
Sampson, O. (1980). *Child Guidance: Its History, Provenance and Future*. BPS Occasional Paper. Leicester: British Psychological Society.
Samuels, L. (1996). A historical analysis of Winnicott's "The Use of an Object". *Winnicott Studies: The Journal of The Squiggle Foundation, 11* (Spring): 41–50.
Sandler, A.-M. (2004). Institutional responses to boundary violations: The case of Masud Khan. *International Journal of Psycho-Analysis, 85* (1): 38–41.
Savage Scharff, J. (1994). *The Autonomous Self: The Work of John D. Sutherland*. New York: Jason Aronson.
Schacht, L. (1972). Psychoanalytic facilitation into the "Subject-Uses-Subject" phase of maturation. *International Journal of Child Psychotherapy, 1* (4): 71–88.
Schacht, L. (1988). Winnicott's position in regard to the Self with special reference to childhood. *Psycho-Analysis, 15* (4): 511–529.
Schacht, L. (2001). Between the capacity and the necessity to be alone. In: M. Bertolini, A. Giannakoulas, & M. Hernandez, with A. Molino (Eds.), *Squiggles and Spaces: Revisiting the Work of D. W. Winnicott, Vol. 1* (pp. 112–125). London & Philadelphia, PA: Whurr.
Schaffer, H. R., & Emerson, P. E. (1964). The Development of Social Attachments in Infancy. *Monographs of the Society for Research in Child Development, 29* (3, Serial No.94).
Schaller, G. B. (1971). *The Year of the Gorilla*. London: Ballantine Books.
Schmidt-Neven, R. (1994). *Exploring Parenthood: A Psychodynamic Approach for a Changing Society*. Melbourne: ACER.
Schoenewulf, G. (1990). Hate in the countertransference: D. W. Winnicott and the orphan boy (1947); and Philip (1953). In: *Turning Points in Analytic Therapy: From Winnicott to Kernberg* (pp. 1–20). Northvale, NJ, & London: Jason Aronson.

Schore, A. N. (1994). *Affect Regulation and the Origin of the Self: The Neurobiology of Emotional Development.* Hillsdale, NJ, & Hove: Lawrence Erlbaum.

Schore, A. N. (2001a). Effects of a secure attachment relationship on right brain development, affect regulation, and infant mental health. *Infant Mental Health Journal,* 22 (1–2): 7–66 [Special Issue, *Contributions from the Decade of the Brain to Infant Mental Health*].

Schore, A. N. (2001b). The effects of early relational trauma on right brain development, affect regulation, and infant mental health. *Infant Mental Health Journal,* 22 (1–2): 201–269 [Special Issue, *Contributions from the Decade of the Brain to Infant Mental Health*].

Schore, A. N. (2003a). *Affect Dysregulation and Disorders of the Self.* New York & London: W. W. Norton.

Schore, A. N. (2003b). *Affect Regulation and the Repair of the Self.* New York & London: W. W. Norton.

Schore, A. N. (2004a). *Affect Dysregulation and Disorders of the Self: The Neurobiology of Emotional Development, Vols. 1 & 2.* New York: W. W. Norton.

Schore, A. N. (2004b). *Affect Regulation and the Origin of the Self: The Neurobiology of Emotional Development.* New York: W. W. Norton.

Schore, A. N. (2005). Attachment trauma and the developing right brain. In: *Dissociation and the Dissociative Disorders: DSM-V and Beyond* (chap. 9). Arlington, VA: American Psychiatric Association Publishing House.

Schur, M. (1960). Discussion of John Bowlby's paper. *Psychoanalytic Study of the Child,* 15: 63–84.

Segal, H. (1973). *An Introduction to the Work of Melanie Klein.* London: Hogarth Press.

Senn, M. J. E. (1977). "Interview with Dr. John Bowlby." Unpublished, National Library of Medicine, Bethesda, MD.

Sharpe, E. F. (1937). *Dream Analysis: A Practical Handbook in Psychoanalysis.* London: Hogarth Press & The Institute of Psycho-Analysis.

Shaw, O. L. (1969). *Prisons of the Mind.* London: Allen & Unwin.

Siebzehner, A. V. (1997). Psychoanalysis of a child, a Winnicottian look. In: R. Zac de Goldstein, L. Valenti de Greif, & S. Jallinsky (Eds.), *Winnicott's Space. Encounters, No. 1* (pp. 103–108). Buenos Aires: Asociacion Psicoanalítica Argentina.

Siegel, D. J. (2001). Toward an interpersonal neurobiology of the developing mind: Attachment relationships, "mindsight," and neural integration. *Infant Mental Health Journal,* 22 (1–2): 67–94 [Special Issue, *Contributions from the Decade of the Brain to Infant Mental Health*].

Simpson, J. A., & Rholes, W. S. (Eds.) (1998). *Attachment Theory and Close Relationships*. New York & London: Guilford Press.

Sinason, V. (Ed.) (2002). *Attachment Trauma: Working with Dissociative Identity Disorder and Multiplicity*. Hove: Brunner-Routledge.

Slade, A. (2000). The development and organization of attachment: Implications for psychoanalysis. *Journal of the American Psychoanalytic Association, 48*: 1117–1174.

Smith, B. L. (1989a). Winnicott and the British Schools. In: M. G. Fromm & B. L. Smith (Eds.), *The Facilitating Environment: Clinical Applications of Winnicott's Theory* (pp. 27–51). Madison, CT: International Universities Press.

Smith, B. L. (1989b). Winnicott and self psychology. In: M. G. Fromm & B. L. Smith (Eds.), *The Facilitating Environment: Clinical Applications of Winnicott's Theory* (pp. 52–87). Madison, CT: International Universities Press.

Smuts, A. (1977). "Interview with Dr. J. Bowlby." Archives of Tavistock Joint Library, London.

Sofer, C. (1961). *The Organization from Within: A Comparative Study of Social Institutions Based on a Sociotherapeutic Approach*. London: Tavistock.

Sofer, C. (1973). *Organizations in Theory and Practice*. London: Heinemann.

Solms, M. (1997). *The Neuropsychology of Dreams: A Clinico-Anatomical Study*. Mahwah, NJ: Lawrence Erlbaum.

Southern, D. (1990). An appreciation of John Bowlby. *Tavistock Gazette, 29* (Autumn). Reprinted in: *Journal of the Institute for Self-Analysis, 4* (1): 14–15 [Special Issue, *On Attachment: Commemorating the Work of John Bowlby*].

Southgate, J. (1990). Remembrances of John Bowlby, who died on September 2nd 1990. *Journal of the Institute for Self Analysis, 4* (1): 4–11 [Special Issue, *On Attachment: Commemorating the Work of John Bowlby*].

Spitz, R. (1945). Hospitalism: An inquiry into the genesis of psychiatric conditions in early childhood, I. *Psychoanalytic Study of the Child, 1*: 53–74.

Spitz, R. (1946). Anaclitic depression: An inquiry into the genesis of psychiatric conditions in early childhood, II. *Psychoanalytic Study of the Child, 2*: 313–342.

Spitz, R. (1960). Discussion of Dr. John Bowlby's paper. *Psychoanalytic Study of the Child, 15*: 85–94.

Spruiell, V. (1993). Deterministic chaos and the sciences of complexity: Psychoanalysis in the midst of a general scientific revolution. *Journal of the American Psychoanalytic Association, 41*: 3–44.

Spurling, L. (1991). Winnicott and the mother's face. *Winnicott Studies: The Journal of the Squiggle Foundation*, 6: 60.
Spurling, L. (1996). Winnicott and transference: The knife-edge of belief. *Winnicott Studies: The Journal of The Squiggle Foundation*, 11: 51–61.
Sroufe, L. A. (1985). Attachment classification from the perspective of infant–caregiver relationships and infant temperament. *Child Development*, 56: 1–14.
Sroufe, L. A., Carlson, E., Levy, A., & Egeland, B. (1999). Implications of attachment theory for developmental psychopathology. *Development and Psychopathology*, 11: 1–13.
Sroufe, L. A., Egeland, B., Carlson, E., & Collins, A. W. (2005). *The Development of the Person: The Minnesota Study of Parents and Children from Birth to Maturity*. London: Guilford Press.
Sroufe, L. A., Egeland, B., & Kreutzer, T. (1990). The fate of early experience following developmental change: Longitudinal approaches to individual adaptation in childhood. *Child Development*, 61: 1363–1373.
Sroufe, L. A., & Fleeson, J. (1986). *Attachment and the Construction of Relationships* (pp. 51–57). In: W. Hartup & Z. Rubin (Eds.), *Relationships and Development*. Hillsdale, NJ: Lawrence Erlbaum.
Sroufe, L. A., & Waters, E. (1977). Attachment as an organizational construct. *Child Development*, 48: 1184–1199.
Steele, H. (2002). State of the art: Attachment. *The Psychologist*, 15 (10): 518–522.
Steele, H., & Steele, M. (1998). Attachment and psychoanalysis: Time for a reunion. *Social Development*, 7 (1): 92–119.
Stern, D. N. (1985). *The Interpersonal World of the Infant: A View From Psychoanalysis and Developmental Psychology*. New York: Basic Books.
Stern, D. N. (1995). *The Motherhood Constellation: A Unified View of Parent–Infant Psychotherapy*. New York: Basic Books.
Stern, D. N. (1998). *The Maternal Constellation*. New York: Basic Books.
Stern, D. N. (2002). Words and wordlessness in the psychoanalytic situation. *Journal of the American Psychoanalytic Association*, 50 (1): 221–248.
Stern, D. N., Sanders, L. W., Nahum, J. P., Harrison, A. M., Lyons-Roth, K., Morgan, A. C., Bruschweiler-Stern, N., & Tronkick, E. Z. (1998). Non-interpretive mechanisms in psychoanalytic psychotherapy: The "something more" than interpretation. *International Journal of Psycho-Analysis*, 79: 903–921.
Sutherland, J. (1980). The British Object Relations theorists: Balint, Winnicott, Fairbairn, Guntrip. *Journal of the American Psychoanalytic Association*, 28: 829–860.
Sutherland, J. (1983). *A Philosophy for the Caring Professions*. Aberdeen: Aberdeen University Press.

Sutherland, J. (1990). John Bowlby: Some personal reminiscences. *The Tavistock Gazette, 29* (Autumn): 13–16.
Tagore, R. (1931). The Child. In: *Selected Poetry of Rabindranath Tagore (1861-1941)*. Toronto: University of Toronto Press, 2005. Retrieved from http://eir.library.utoronto.ca/rpo/display/poet389.html
Target, M., & Fonagy, P. (1996). Playing with reality, II: The development of psychic reality from a theoretical perspective. *International Journal of Psycho-Analysis, 77*: 459–479.
Taylor Robinson, H. (2005). Adult eros in D. W. Winnicott. In: L. Caldwell (Ed.), *Sex and Sexuality: Winnicottian Perspectives* (pp. 83–104). London: Karnac.
Teilhard de Chardin, P. (1964). *The Phenomenon of Man*. London: Collins.
Thomson Salo, F. (2001). The interface with infant research: The continuing gains for psychoanalysis. *Psychoanalysis Downunder: The Online Journal of the Australian Psychoanalytical Society*. Retrieved from http://www.psychoanalysisdownunder.com/PADPapers/interface_ft.htm
Tinbergen, N. (1951). *The Study of Instinct*. Oxford: Clarendon Press
Tinbergen, N. (1958). *Curious Naturalists*. London: Country Life.
Tinbergen, N., & Tinbergen, E. A. (1972). *Early Childhood Autism: An Ethological Approach*. Berlin: Parey.
Tizard, J. P. (1971). "Memorial for a Friend: Funeral Oration: Donald Woods Winnicott." Folder 8. Planned Environment Therapy Trust Archive and Study Centre, Toddington.
Tizard, J. P. (1987). Introduction. In: D. W. Winnicott, *Babies and Their Mothers*. London: Free Association Books.
Tonnesmann, M. (1995). Early emotional development: Ferenczi to Winnicott. *Bulletin of the British Psychoanalytical Society, 30* (2): 14–19.
Trevarthen, C. (1998). The concept and foundations of infant intersubjectivity. In: S. Braten (Ed.), *Intersubjective Communication and Emotion in Early Ontogeny*. Cambridge: Cambridge University Press.
Trevarthen, C. (2001). Intrinsic motives for companionship in understanding: Their origin, development, and significance for infant mental health. *Infant Mental Health Journal, 22* (1–2): 95–131 [Special Issue, *Contributions from the Decade of the Brain to Infant Mental Health*].
Trist, E. L., & Murray, H. (1999). The foundation and development of the Tavistock Institute: Historical overview. In: *The Social Engagement of Social Science: A Tavistock Anthology*. Retrieved from www.moderntimesworkplace.com/good_reading/archives/ericsess/tavis2/tavis2.html
Trist, E. L., & Sofer, C. (1957). *Explorations in Group Relations: A Residential Conference Held in September 1957 by The University of Leicester and*

Tavistock Institute of Human Relations. Leicester: University of Leicester Press.

Trowell, J. (1990). Dr. John Bowlby. *The Tavistock Gazette, 29* (Autumn): 13–26.

Turner, J. (2004). A brief history of illusion: Milner, Winnicott, Rycroft. In: J. Pearson (Ed.), *Analyst of the Imagination: The Life and Work of Charles Rycroft*. London: Karnac.

Tustin, F. (1972). *Autism and Childhood Psychosis*. London: Hogarth Press.

Tutté, J. C. (2004). The concept of psychical trauma. *International Journal of Psycho-Analysis, 85*: 897–921.

Tuttman, S. (1981). The significance of Edith Jacobson's *Object and Self* in contemporary object relations theory. In: S. Tuttman, C. Kaye, & M. Zimmerman (Eds.), *Object and Self, a Developmental Approach: Essays in Honor of Edith Jacobson* (pp. 81–102). New York: International Universities Press.

Usuelli, A. K. (1992). The significance of illusion in the work of Freud and Winnicott: A controversial issue. *International Review of Psycho-Analysis, 19* (2): 179–187.

Valent, P. (1998). *From Survival to Fulfilment: A Framework for the Life-Trauma Dialectic*. Philadelphia & London: Brunner/Mazel.

Valent, P. (1999). *Trauma and Fulfilment Therapy: A Wholist Framework*. Philadelphia & London: Brunner/Mazel.

Valenti de Greif, L. M. (1997). Donald W. Winnicott: Illusion, paradox and metaphor in psychoanalytic practice. In: R. Zac de Goldstein, L. Valenti de Greif, & S. Jallinsky (Eds.), *Winnicott's Space. Encounters, No. 1* (pp. 51–60). Buenos Aires: Asociacion Psicoanalítica Argentina.

van Dijken, S. (1998). *John Bowlby: His Early Life*. London: Free Association Books.

von Frisch, K. (1967). *The Dance Language and Orientation of Bees*. Boston, MA, & London: Harvard University Press.

Weinfield, N. S., Sroufe, L. A., & Egeland, B. (2000). Attachment from infancy to early adulthood in a high-risk sample: Continuity, discontinuity and their correlates. *Child Development, 71* (3): 695–700.

Weinfield, N. S., Sroufe, L. A., Egeland, B., & Carlson, E. A. (1999). The nature of individual differences in infant–caregiver attachment. In: J. Cassidy & P. Shaver (Eds.), *Handbook of Attachment Theory and Research* (pp. 68–88). New York: Guilford Press.

Weiss, R. S. (1982). Attachment in adult life. In: C. M. Parkes & J. Stevenson-Hinde (Eds.), *The Place of Attachment in Human Behaviour* (pp. 171–184). New York: Basic Books.

White, K. (Ed.) (2004). *Touch: Attachment and the Body*. London: Karnac.

Wilbur, K. (2001). *A Theory of Everything: An Integral Vision for Business, Politics, Science and Spirituality*. Dublin: Gateway.

Williams, R., & White, R. (1996). *Child and Adolescent Services: Safeguards for Young Minds, Young People and Protective Legislation*. ("The HAS Report": NHS Health Advisory Service.) London: Gaskell.

Willoughby, R. (2004). *Masud Khan: The Myth and the Reality*. London: Free Association Books.

Wills, D. (1941). *The Hawkspur Experiment: An Informal Account of the Training of Wayward Adolescents*. London: Allen & Unwin.

Wilson, P. (1996). The anti-social tendency. *Journal of Child Psychotherapy*, 22 (3): 394–397.

Winnicott, C. (1955). Casework techniques in the child care services. In: J. Kanter (Ed.), *Face to Face with Children: The Life and Work of Clare Winnicott* (pp. 145–165). London: Karnac, 2004.

Winnicott, C. (1955–56). The "rescue motive" in social work. In: J. Kanter (Ed.), *Face to Face with Children: The Life and Work of Clare Winnicott* (pp. 213–215). London: Karnac, 2004.

Winnicott, C. (1978). D.W.W.: A reflection. In: S. A. Grolnik & L. Barkin (Eds.), *Between Reality and Fantasy: Transitional Objects and Phenomena*. New York & London: Jason Aronson. Reprinted in: D. W. Winnicott, *Psychoanalytic Explorations*, ed. C. Winnicott, R. Shepherd, & M. Davis (pp. 1–20). London: Karnac, 1989. Also in: P. L. Giovacchini (Ed.), *Tactics and Techniques in Psychoanalytic Therapy, Vol. 3: The Implications of Winnicott's Contributions* (pp. 3–20). Northvale, NJ, & London: Jason Aronson, 1990. Also in: J. Kanter (Ed.), *Face to Face with Children: The Life and Work of Clare Winnicott* (pp. 237–253). London: Karnac, 2004.

Winnicott, C. (1982). D. W. Winnicott: His life and work. In: J. Kanter (Ed.), *Face to Face with Children: The Life and Work of Clare Winnicott* (pp. 254–277). London: Karnac, 2004.

Winnicott, C. (1984). Introduction. In: D. W. Winnicott, *Deprivation and Delinquency*, ed. C. Winnicott, R. Shepherd, & M. Davis (pp. 1–4). London: Tavistock; New York: Methuen, 1984.

Winnicott, C., & Neve, M. (1991). Appendix: Clare Winnicott talks to Michael Neve (transcribed by P. Rudnytsky). In: P. Rudnytsky, *The Psychoanalytic Vocation: Rank, Winnicott, and the Legacy of Freud*. New Haven, CT, & London: Yale University Press. Reprinted in: The Free Associations Interview. *Free Associations*, 2 (3, No. 26): 167–184.

Winnicott, D. W. (1931). *Clinical Notes on Disorders of Childhood*. London: Heinemann.

Winnicott, D. W. (1935). The manic defence. In: *Collected Papers: Through Paediatrics to Psycho-Analysis* (pp. 129–144). London: Tavistock, 1958.

Reprinted as: *Through Paediatrics to Psycho-Analysis*. London: Hogarth Press, 1975; London: Karnac, 1992.

Winnicott, D. W. (1940). Children in the war. *New Era in Home and School, 21* (9): 229. Reprinted in: *The Child and the Outside World* (pp. 69–74). London: Tavistock, 1957. Also in: *Deprivation and Delinquency*, ed. C. Winnicott, R. Shepherd, & M. Davis (pp. 25–30). London: Tavistock; New York: Methuen, 1984.

Winnicott, D. W. (1941a). The observation of infants in a set situation. In: *Collected Papers: Through Paediatrics to Psycho-Analysis* (pp. 52–69). London: Tavistock, 1958. Reprinted as: *Through Paediatrics to Psycho-Analysis*. London: Hogarth Press, 1975; London: Karnac, 1992.

Winnicott, D. W. (1941b). Review of *The Cambridge Evacuation Survey*, ed. S. Isaacs. In: *Deprivation and Delinquency*, ed. C. Winnicott, R. Shepherd, & M. Davis (pp. 22–24). London: Tavistock; New York: Methuen, 1984.

Winnicott, D. W. (1942). Child department consultations. In: *Collected Papers: Through Paediatrics to Psycho-Analysis* (pp. 70–84). London: Tavistock, 1958. Reprinted as: *Through Paediatrics to Psycho-Analysis*. London: Hogarth Press, 1975; London: Karnac, 1992.

Winnicott, D. W. (1943). 1. Prefrontal leucotomy. Letter to the editor, *The Lancet*, 10 April. Reprinted in: *Psychoanalytic Explorations* (pp. 542–543), ed. C. Winnicott, R. Shepherd, & M. Davis. London: Karnac, 1989.

Winnicott, D. W. (1945a). The evacuated child. (B.B.C. Broadcast.). In: *The Child and the Outside World* (pp. 83–87). London: Tavistock. Also in: *Deprivation and Delinquency*, ed. C. Winnicott, R. Shepherd, & M. Davis (pp. 39–43). London: Tavistock; New York: Methuen, 1984.

Winnicott, D. W. (1945b). *Getting to Know Your Baby*. London: Heinemann.

Winnicott, D. W. (1945c). Primitive emotional development. *International Journal of Psycho-Analysis, 26*: 137–142. Reprinted in: *Collected Papers: Through Paediatrics to Psycho-Analysis* (pp. 145–156). London: Tavistock, 1958. Reprinted as: *Through Paediatrics to Psycho-Analysis*. London: Hogarth Press, 1975; London: Karnac, 1992.

Winnicott, D. W. (1946a). Letter to Lord Beveridge. In: *The Spontaneous Gesture: Selected Letters of D. W. Winnicott*, ed. F. R. Rodman. Cambridge, MA: Harvard University Press, 1987.

Winnicott, D. W. (1946b). Some psychological aspects of juvenile delinquency. In: *Deprivation and Delinquency*, ed. C. Winnicott, R. Shepherd, & M. Davis (pp. 113–119). London: Tavistock; New York: Methuen, 1984.

Winnicott, D. W. (1947). Hate in the countertransference. In: *Collected Papers: Through Paediatrics to Psycho-Analysis* (pp. 194–203). London: Tavistock, 1958. Reprinted as: *Through Paediatrics to Psycho-Analysis*. London: Hogarth Press, 1975; London: Karnac, 1992.

Winnicott, D. W. (1948a). Children's hostels in war and peace. In: *Deprivation and Delinquency*, ed. C. Winnicott, R. Shepherd, & M. Davis. London: Tavistock; New York: Methuen, 1984.

Winnicott, D. W. (1948b). Reparation in respect of mother's organized defence against depression. In: *Collected Papers: Through Paediatrics to Psycho-Analysis* (pp. 91–96). London: Tavistock, 1958. Reprinted as: *Through Paediatrics to Psycho-Analysis*. London: Hogarth Press, 1975; London: Karnac, 1992.

Winnicott, D. W. (1949a). Birth memories, birth trauma, and anxiety. In: *Collected Papers: Through Paediatrics to Psycho-Analysis* (pp. 174–193). London: Tavistock, 1958. Reprinted as: *Through Paediatrics to Psycho-Analysis*. London: Hogarth Press, 1975; London: Karnac, 1992.

Winnicott, D. W. (1949b). Leucotomy. *British Medical Students' Journal*, 3. Reprinted in: *Psychoanalytic Explorations* (pp. 543–547), ed. C. Winnicott, R. Shepherd, & M. Davis. London: Karnac, 1989.

Winnicott, D. W. (1949c). Mind and its relation to the psyche–soma. In: *Collected Papers: Through Paediatrics to Psycho-Analysis* (pp. 243–254). London: Tavistock, 1958. Reprinted as: *Through Paediatrics to Psycho-Analysis*. London: Hogarth Press, 1975; London: Karnac, 1992.

Winnicott, D. W. (1949d). *The Ordinary Devoted Mother and Her Baby*. London: Private Publication.

Winnicott, D. W. (1950). Some thoughts on the meaning of the word "democracy". *Human Relations, Vol. 1*. Reprinted in: *Home Is Where We Start From: Essays by a Psychoanalyst* (pp. 239–259), ed. C. Winnicott, R. Shepherd, & M. Davis. London: Penguin, 1986.

Winnicott, D. W. (1951a). Critical notice of *On Not Being Able to Paint* by Marion Milner. Reprinted in: *Psychoanalytic Explorations*, ed. C. Winnicott, R. Shepherd, & M. Davis (pp. 390–392). London: Karnac, 1989. Also in: L. Caldwell (Ed.), *Art, Creativity, Living* (pp. 117–120). London: Karnac, 2000.

Winnicott, D. W. (1951b). Notes on the general implications of leucotomy. Reprinted in: *Psychoanalytic Explorations*, ed. C. Winnicott, R. Shepherd, & M. Davis (pp. 548–554). London: Karnac, 1989.

Winnicott, D. W. (1951c).Transitional objects and transitional phenomena. In: *Collected Papers: Through Paediatrics to Psycho-Analysis* (pp. 229–242). London: Tavistock, 1958. Reprinted as: *Through Paediatrics to Psycho-Analysis*. London: Hogarth Press, 1975; London: Karnac, 1992.

Winnicott, D. W. (1952). Psychoses and child care. *British Journal of Medical Psychology*, 26 (1953). Reprinted in: *Collected Papers: Through Paediatrics to Psycho-Analysis* (pp. 219–228). London: Tavistock, 1958. Reprinted as: *Through Paediatrics to Psycho-Analysis*. London: Hogarth Press, 1975; London: Karnac, 1992.

Winnicott, D. W. (1953a). Review (written with M. Masud R. Khan) of *Psychoanalytic Studies of the Personality* by W. R. D. Fairbairn. In: *Psychoanalytic Explorations*, ed. C. Winnicott, R. Shepherd, & M. Davis (pp. 413–422). London: Karnac, 1989.

Winnicott, D. W. (1953b). Review of *Maternal Care and Mental Health. British Journal of Medical Psychology* by J. Bowlby. In: *Psychoanalytic Explorations*, ed. C. Winnicott, R. Shepherd, & M. Davis (pp. 423–426). London: Karnac, 1989.

Winnicott, D. W. (1953c). Symptom tolerance in paediatrics. In: *Collected Papers: Through Paediatrics to Psycho-Analysis* (pp. 101–117). London: Tavistock, 1958. Reprinted as: *Through Paediatrics to Psycho-Analysis*. London: Hogarth Press, 1975; London: Karnac, 1992.

Winnicott, D. W. (1954a). Letter to John Bowlby. In: *The Spontaneous Gesture: Selected Letters of D. W. Winnicott*, ed. F. R. Rodman (pp. 65–66). Cambridge, MA : Harvard University Press, 1987.

Winnicott, D. W. (1954b). Play in the analytic situation. In: *Psychoanalytic Explorations* (pp. 28–29), ed. C. Winnicott, R. Shepherd, & M. Davis. London: Karnac, 1989.

Winnicott, D. W. (1955). Private practice. In: *Psychoanalytic Explorations* (pp. 291–298), ed. C. Winnicott, R. Shepherd, & M. Davis. London: Karnac, 1989.

Winnicott, D. W. (1956a). The antisocial tendency. In: *Collected Papers: Through Paediatrics to Psychoanalysis* (pp. 306–315). London: Tavistock, 1958. Reprinted as: *Through Paediatrics to Psycho-Analysis*. London: Hogarth Press, 1975; London: Karnac, 1992. Also in: *Deprivation and Delinquency*, ed. C. Winnicott, R. Shepherd, & M. Davis (pp. 120–131). London: Tavistock; New York: Methuen, 1984.

Winnicott, D. W. (1956b). Primary maternal preoccupation. In: *Collected Papers: Through Paediatrics to Psychoanalysis* (pp. 300–305). London: Tavistock, 1958. Reprinted as: *Through Paediatrics to Psycho-Analysis*. London: Hogarth Press, 1975; London: Karnac, 1992.

Winnicott, D. W. (1957a). *The Child and the Family: First Relationships*. London: Tavistock.

Winnicott, D. W. (1957b). *The Child and The Outside World: Studies in Developing Relationships*. London: Tavistock.

Winnicott, D. W. (1957c). *Mother and Child*. New York: Basic Books.

Winnicott, D. W. (1958). *Collected Papers: Through Paediatrics to Psycho-*

Analysis. London: Tavistock. Reprinted as: *Through Paediatrics to Psycho-Analysis*. London: Hogarth Press, 1975; London: Karnac, 1992.

Winnicott, D. W. (1959a). Classification: Is there a psycho-analytic contribution to psychiatric classification? [Postscript dated 1964]. In: *The Maturational Processes and the Facilitating Environment* (pp. 124–139). London: Hogarth Press & The Institute of Psycho-Analysis, 1965. Reprinted London: Karnac, 1990.

Winnicott, D. W. (1959b). Discussion of "Grief and Mourning in Infancy", by John Bowlby. In: *Psychoanalytic Explorations*, ed. C. Winnicott, R. Shepherd, & M. Davis (pp. 426–432). London: Karnac, 1989.

Winnicott, D. W. (1960a). Comments on "The Concept of the Superego", by Joseph Sandler. In: *Psychoanalytic Explorations*, ed. C. Winnicott, R. Shepherd, & M. Davis (pp. 465–473). London: Karnac, 1989.

Winnicott, D. W. (1960b). Ego distortion in terms of true and false self. In: *The Maturational Processes and the Facilitating Environment* (pp. 140–152). London: Hogarth Press & The Institute of Psycho-Analysis, 1965. Reprinted, London: Karnac, 1990.

Winnicott, D. W. (1960c). String: A technique of communication. In: *The Maturational Processes and the Facilitating Environment* (pp. 153–157). London: Hogarth Press, 1965. Reprinted London: Karnac, 1984.

Winnicott, D. W. (1961a). Psychoanalysis and science: Friends or relations? In: *Home Is Where We Start From: Essays by a Psychoanalyst* (pp. 13–18), ed. C. Winnicott, R. Shepherd, & M. Davis. London: Penguin, 1986.

Winnicott, D. W. (1961b). Psycho-neurosis in childhood. In: *Psychoanalytic Explorations* (pp. 64–72), ed. C. Winnicott, R. Shepherd, & M. Davis. London: Karnac, 1989.

Winnicott, D. W. (1962). The beginnings of a formulation of an appreciation and criticism of Klein's envy statement. In: *Psychoanalytic Explorations*, ed. C. Winnicott, R. Shepherd, & M. Davis (pp. 447–464). London: Karnac, 1989.

Winnicott, D. W. (1963a). D.W.W.'s dream related to reviewing Jung. In: *Psychoanalytic Explorations*, ed. C. Winnicott, R. Shepherd, & M. Davis (pp. 228–230). London: Karnac, 1989.

Winnicott, D. W. (1963b). Fear of breakdown. In: *The Maturational Processes and the Facilitating Environment* (pp. 87–95). London: Hogarth Press & The Institute of Psycho-Analysis, 1965. Reprinted London: Karnac, 1990.

Winnicott, D. W. (1963c). Psychiatric disorder in terms of infantile maturational processes. In: *The Maturational Processes and the Facilitating Environment* (pp. 230–241). London: Hogarth Press & The Institute of Psycho-Analysis, 1965. Reprinted London: Karnac, 1990.

Winnicott, D. W. (1964a). *The Child, The Family and The Outside World*. London: Penguin.
Winnicott, D. W. (1964b). Deductions drawn from a psycho-therapeutic interview with an adolescent. *Psychoanalytic Explorations*, ed. C. Winnicott, R. Shepherd, & M. Davis (pp. 325-340). London: Karnac, 1989.
Winnicott, D. W. (1964c). Psycho-somatic illness in its positive and negative aspects. *International Journal of Psycho-Analysis, 47* (1966): 510. Reprinted in: *Psychoanalytic Explorations*, ed. C. Winnicott, R. Shepherd, & M. Davis (pp. 103–114). London: Karnac, 1989.
Winnicott, D. W. (1964d). Review of *Memories, Dreams, Reflections* by C. G. Jung. *International Journal of Psycho-Analysis, 45*. Reprinted in: *Psychoanalytic Explorations*, ed. C. Winnicott, R. Shepherd, & M. Davis (pp. 482–492). London: Karnac, 1989.
Winnicott, D. W. (1965a). A child psychiatry case illustrating delayed reaction to loss. In: M. Schur (Ed.), *Drives, Affects, Behavior: Essays in Memory of Marie Bonaparte, Vol. 2*. New York: International Universities Press. Reprinted in: *Psychoanalytic Explorations*, ed. C. Winnicott, R. Shepherd, & M. Davis (pp. 341–368). London: Karnac, 1989.
Winnicott, D. W. (1965b). Comments on "On the Concept of the Superego" by Joseph Sandler. In: *Psychoanalytic Explorations*, ed. C. Winnicott, R. Shepherd, & M. Davis (pp. 465–473). London: Karnac, 1989.
Winnicott, D. W. (1965c). *The Family and Individual Development*. London: Tavistock.
Winnicott, D. W. (1965d). *The Maturational Processes and the Facilitating Environment: Studies in the Theory of Emotional Development*. London: Hogarth Press & Institute of Psycho-Analysis. Reprinted London: Karnac, 1990.
Winnicott, D. W. (1965e). The price of disregarding psychoanalytic research. In: *Home Is Where We Start From: Essays by a Psychoanalyst* (pp. 172–182), ed. C. Winnicott, R. Shepherd, & M. Davis. London: Penguin, 1986.
Winnicott, D. W. (1965f). Review of *Childhood and Society* by Erik H. Erikson. *New Society*. 30 September. Reprinted in: *Psychoanalytic Explorations*, ed. C. Winnicott, R. Shepherd, & M. Davis (pp. 493–494). London: Karnac, 1989.
Winnicott, D. W. (1966a). The absence of a sense of guilt. In: D. W. Winnicott, *Deprivation and Delinquency*, ed. C. Winnicott, R. Shepherd, & M. Davis (pp. 106–112). London: Tavistock, ; New York: Methuen, 1984.
Winnicott, D. W. (1966b). Letter from Donald Winnicott to Josephine

Lomax-Simpson, 18th April 1966. Folder 6, Josephine Lomax-Simpson. Planned Environment Therapy Trust Archive and Study Centre, Toddington.

Winnicott, D. W. (1967a). Addendum to "The Location of Cultural Experience." In: *Psychoanalytic Explorations*, ed. C. Winnicott, R. Shepherd, & M. Davis (pp. 200–202). London: Karnac, 1989.

Winnicott, D. W. (1967b). Mirror-role of mother and family in child development. In: P. Lomas (Ed.), *The Predicament of the Family*. London: Hogarth Press. Reprinted in: D. W. Winnicott, *Playing and Reality* (pp. 111–118). London: Tavistock, 1971.

Winnicott, D. W. (1967c). Postscript: D.W.W. on D.W.W. In: *Psychoanalytic Explorations*, ed. C. Winnicott, R. Shepherd, & M. Davis (pp. 569–582). London: Karnac, 1989.

Winnicott, D. W. (1968a). Comments on my paper "The Use of an Object". In: *Psychoanalytic Explorations*, ed. C. Winnicott, R. Shepherd, & M. Davis (pp. 238–240). London: Karnac, 1989.

Winnicott, D. W. (1968b). Delinquency as a sign of hope. *The Prison Service Journal, 7* (27): 2–9. Reprinted in: *Home Is Where We Start From: Essays by a Psychoanalyst* (pp. 90–100), ed. C. Winnicott, R. Shepherd, & M. Davis. London: Penguin, 1986.

Winnicott, D. W. (1968c). Foreword. In: B. Dockar-Drysdale, *Therapy in Child Care*. London: Longmans, Green. Also in: B. Dockar-Drysdale, *Therapy and Consultation in Child Care*. London: Free Association Press, 1993.

Winnicott, D. W. (1968d). Interpretation in psychoanalysis. In: *Psychoanalytic Explorations*, ed. C. Winnicott, R. Shepherd, & M. Davis (pp. 207–212). London: Karnac, 1989.

Winnicott, D. W. (1968e). Playing: Its theoretical status in the clinical situation. *International Journal of Psycho-Analysis, 49*: 591. In: *Psychoanalytic Explorations*, ed. C. Winnicott, R. Shepherd, & M. Davis (pp. 28–29). London: Karnac, 1989.

Winnicott, D. W. (1968f). Playing and culture. In: *Psychoanalytic Explorations*, ed. C. Winnicott, R. Shepherd, & M. Davis (pp. 203–206). London: Karnac, 1989.

Winnicott, D. W. (1968g). Roots of aggression. In: *Psychoanalytic Explorations*, ed. C. Winnicott, R. Shepherd, & M. Davis (pp. 458–461). London: Karnac, 1989.

Winnicott, D. W. (1968h). The use of an object and relating through identifications. *International Journal of Psycho-Analysis, 50*. Reprinted in: *Playing and Reality* (pp. 86–94). London: Tavistock, 1971. Also in: *Psychoanalytic Explorations*, ed. C. Winnicott, R. Shepherd, & M. Davis (pp. 218–227). London: Karnac, 1989.

Winnicott, D. W. (1969a). Additional note on psycho-somatic disorder. In: *Psychoanalytic Explorations*, ed. C. Winnicott, R. Shepherd, & M. Davis (pp. 115–118). London: Karnac, 1989.

Winnicott, D. W. (1969b). Berlin Walls. In: *Home Is Where We Start From: Essays by a Psychoanalyst* (pp. 221–227), ed. C. Winnicott, R. Shepherd, & M. Davis. London: Penguin, 1986.

Winnicott, D. W. (1969c). James Strachey: Obituary. *International Journal of Psycho-Analysis, 50*. Reprinted in: *Psychoanalytic Explorations*, ed. C. Winnicott, R. Shepherd, & M. Davis (pp. 506–510). London: Karnac, 1989.

Winnicott, D. W. (1969d). Letter to R. Tod. In: *The Spontaneous Gesture: Selected Letters of D. W. Winnicott* (pp. 196–197), ed. F. R. Rodman. Cambridge, MA: Harvard University Press, 1987.

Winnicott, D. W. (1969e). The mother–infant experience of mutuality. In: *Psychoanalytic Explorations*, ed. C. Winnicott, R. Shepherd, & M. Davis (pp. 251–260). London: Karnac, 1989.

Winnicott, D. W. (1969f). The use of an object in the context of *Moses and Monotheism*. In: *Psychoanalytic Explorations* (pp. 240–246), ed. C. Winnicott, R. Shepherd, & M. Davis. London: Karnac, 1989.

Winnicott, D. W. (1970a). The place of the monarchy. In: *Home Is Where We Start From: Essays by a Psychoanalyst* (pp. 260–268), ed. C. Winnicott, R. Shepherd, & M. Davis. London: Penguin, 1986.

Winnicott, D. W. (1970b). The mother–infant experience of mutuality. In: E. J. Anthony & T. Benedek (Eds.), *Parenthood: Its Psychology and Psychopathology*. Boston: Little Brown; London: Churchill. Reprinted in: *Psychoanalytic Explorations* (pp. 251–260), ed. C. Winnicott, R. Shepherd, & M. Davis. London: Karnac, 1989.

Winnicott, D. W. (1970c). Residential care as therapy. In: *Deprivation and Delinquency*, ed. C. Winnicott, R. Shepherd, & M. Davis (pp. 220–228). London: Tavistock; New York: Methuen, 1984.

Winnicott, D. W. (1970d). "Residential Care as Therapy." David Wills Lecture to the Association of Workers for Maladjusted Children. Highdene Association Archives, photocopy. Planned Environment Therapy Trust Archive and Study Centre, Toddington.

Winnicott, D. W. (1971a). Playing: Creative activity and the search for the self. In: *Playing and Reality* (pp. 53–62). London: Tavistock. Reprinted Hove: Brunner-Routledge, 2001

Winnicott, D. W. (1971b). Playing: A theoretical statement. In: *Playing and Reality* (pp. 38–52). London: Tavistock. Reprinted Hove: Brunner-Routledge, 2001.

Winnicott, D. W. (1971c). *Playing and Reality*. London: Tavistock.

Winnicott, D. W. (1971d). *Therapeutic Consultations in Child Psychiatry*. London: Hogarth Press & Institute of Psycho-Analysis.

Winnicott, D. W. (1977). *The Piggle: An Account of the Psychoanalytic Treatment of a Little Girl*. London: Hogarth Press & The Institute of Psycho-Analysis.

Winnicott, D. W. (1984). *Deprivation and Delinquency*, ed. C. Winnicott, R. Shepherd, & M. Davis. London: Tavistock; New York: Methuen.

Winnicott, D. W. (1986a). *Holding and Interpretation: Fragment of an Analysis*. London: Hogarth Press & The Institute of Psycho-Analysis. Reprinted London: Karnac, 1989.

Winnicott, D. W. (1986b). *Home Is Where We Start From: Essays by a Psychoanalyst*, ed. C. Winnicott, R. Shepherd, & M. Davis. London: Penguin.

Winnicott, D. W. (1986c). This feminism. In: *Home Is Where We Start From: Essays by a Psychoanalyst* (pp. 183–194), ed. C. Winnicott, R. Shepherd, & M. Davis. London: Penguin.

Winnicott, D. W. (1987a). *Babies and Their Mothers*. Reading, MA: Addison Wesley; London: Free Association Books,1988.

Winnicott, D. W. (1987b). *The Spontaneous Gesture: Selected Letters of D. W. Winnicott*, ed. F. Rodman. Cambridge, MA: Harvard University Press.

Winnicott, D. W. (1988a). *Babies and Their Mothers*. London: Free Association Books.

Winnicott, D. W. (1988b). *Human Nature*. London: Free Association Press.

Winnicott, D. W. (1989a). *Psychoanalytic Explorations*, ed. C. Winnicott, R. Shepherd, & M. Davis. London: Karnac.

Winnicott, D. W. (1989b). Notes on play. (Undated.) In: *Psychoanalytic Explorations*, ed. C. Winnicott, R. Shepherd, & M. Davis (pp. 59–63). London: Karnac, 1989.

Winnicott, D. W. (1989c). On the split-off male and female elements to be found in men and women. In: *Psychoanalytic Explorations*, ed. C. Winnicott, R. Shepherd, & M. Davis (pp. 168–192). London: Karnac, 1989.

Winnicott, D. W. (1989d). On "the use of an object". In: *Psychoanalytic Explorations*, ed. C. Winnicott, R. Shepherd, & M. Davis (pp. 217–246). London: Karnac, 1989.

Winnicott, D. W. (1993). *Talking to Parents*, ed. C. Winnicott, C. Bollas, R. Shepherd, & M. Davis. Wokingham, NY: Addison Wesley; London: Karnac.

Winnicott, D. W. (2003). Preface to Renata Gaddini's Italian translation of *The Family and Individual Development*. *Psychoanalysis and History*, 5 (1): 49–52.

Winnicott, D. W., Bowlby, J., & Miller, E. (1939). Evacuation of small children. (Letter.) *British Medical Journal*. Reprinted in: D. W. Winnicott, *Deprivation and Delinquency*, ed. C. Winnicott, R. Shepherd, & M. Davis (pp. 13–14). London: Tavistock; New York: Methuen, 1984.

Winnicott, D. W., & Britton, C. (1944). The problem of homeless children. In: J. Kanter (Ed.), *Face to Face with Children: The Life and Work of Clare Winnicott* (pp. 97–111). London: Karnac, 2004.

Winnicott, D. W., & Britton, C. (1947). Residential management as treatment for difficult children. In: D. W. Winnicott, *Deprivation and Delinquency*, ed. C. Winnicott, R. Shepherd, & M. Davis (pp. 54–72). London: Tavistock; New York: Methuen, 1984.

Woolf, V. (1927). *To The Lighthouse*. London: Hogarth Press; Harmondsworth: Penguin, 1964, 2000.

Woolf, V. (1941). *Between The Acts*. London: Hogarth Press.

Wyatt-Brown, A. (1993). From the clinic to the classroom: D. W. Winnicott, James Britton, and the revolution in writing theory. In: P. Rudnytsky (Ed.), *Transitional Objects and Potential Spaces: Literary Uses of D. W. Winnicott* (pp. 292–305). New York: Columbia University Press.

Zac de Goldstein, R., Valenti de Greif, L., & Jallinsky, S. (Eds.) (1997). *Winnicott's Space. Encounters, No. 1*. Buenos Aires: Asociacion Psicoanalítica Argentina.

Zeanah, C. H., & Zeanah, P. D. (1989). Intergenerational transmission of maltreatment: Insights from attachment theory and research. *Psychiatry, 52*: 177–196.

Ziman, J. (1968). *Public Knowledge*. Cambridge: Cambridge University Press.

Ziman, J. (1978). *Reliable Knowledge*. Cambridge: Cambridge University Press.

Ziman, J. (2000). *Real Science: What It Is, and What It Means*. Cambridge: Cambridge University Press.

Zohar, D., & Marshall, I. (1994). *The Quantum Society: Mind, Physics, and a New Social Vision*. New York: Quill William Morrow.

Zohar, D., & Marshall, I. (2000). *Spiritual Intelligence: The Ultimate Intelligence*. London: Bloomsbury.

INDEX

AAI (Adult Attachment Interview), 122, 129, 176
Abraham, K., 132
Abram, J., 10, 11, 117
Acquarone, S., 122
Adams, K., 27, 159
ADHD (attention deficit hyperactivity disorder), 4
Adler, S., 153
Adshead, G., 118, 176
Adult Attachment Interview (AAI), 122, 129, 176
affect:
　attunement, 150, 154
　contagion phenomena, 173
affectionless character, 72, 83–86, 92–96, 154
　and hopefulness, 92
affectionless child, 94, 97
aggression, 178
　in group setting, 131–133
aggressor, identification with, 132
Ainsworth, M., 41, 69, 80, 112, 115–116, 139–140, 145, 148, 173, 176
Alexander, P. D., 176
Alexander postural technique, 29
Allen, J. G., 176
Allen, Lady, 183, 185
Allyn, G., 2, 37, 48, 118
Amado, G., 111
Amenhotep, 127
American Cultural Centre, Cairo, 222
Amsterdam International Psycho-Analytic Congress, 18
Anna Freud Centre, 122
Anna Freud Clinic, 28, 59, 165
antisocial tendency, 71, 83, 87–97, 99–100, 140
Antonovsky, A., 172
Arafat, F., 222
Arbors, The, 111
Arden, M., 122
Aron, L., 130
Association of Workers for Maladjusted Children, 119

attachment, 39, 75–76, 83, 96, 109–110, 128–130, 154–155, 174
  bonding, 4, 159, 171
  disorders, 150
  figure(s), 42, 128, 132, 165, 176
    mother as, 156
  to mother, 17
  patterns, 154, 164–165
  rating and classification, adult, 69
  research protocols, 102
  vs. sexuality, 31
  spectrum, primary, 17
  style, 69
    avoidant, 16, 60
    transference, 131
  theory, 31–32, 41, 50, 102–104, 122, 130–133, 135–136, 149, 151, 154, 166, 173
    clinical applications, 163–165
    definition, 117
attention deficit hyperactivity disorder (ADHD), 4
Axline, V., 58

Balbernie, R., 6, 107, 112
Balint, E., 28
Balint, M., 128, 129, 146
Barkin, L., 123
Beebe, B., 130, 159
Beintera, D., 159
Belsky, J., 176, 177
bereavement, 27, 103, 120, 129
Bertolini, M., 127, 150
Bettelheim, B., 58, 123
Beveridge, Lord, 98
Biebel, D., 3
Bion, W. R., 102
Blehar, M. C., 69, 102–103
"boarding out" children, 185, 188–189, 196, 198, 202
Bogey's Bar, 28
Bollas, C., 51
Bonaminio, V., 38, 43, 124, 140
Boston Children's Hospital, 108, 109

boundary violations, 18
Bourne, H., 162
Bowlby, J. (*passim*):
  and academia, 65–67
  ambition and attitude to authority, 64–65
  author's acquaintance/ supervision with, 14–17, 26–30
  bibliographic references, 10–11
  and British psychoanalysis, 119–125
  child development, contributions to, 3
  child and family psychiatry, 3
  Child Guidance Consultations, 72
  concepts of:
    attachment theory, 117
    and group dynamic situation, 131
  contributions of, 115–117, 148–150, 161–163, 171–227
  and Darwinian theory, 152–153
  delinquency, understanding of, 117–118
  dreams, 44
  dyslexia, 17
  and Freudian theory, 150–153
  good practice, 61–62
  influences on, 128–129, 131
    Darwin, 68, 128
    Freud, 68
  interests, 115
    ethology, 3, 16, 31–32, 102, 128, 131, 135–136, 153–156, 175
    ornithology, 16
    science, 45–47
  language of, 56–58, 124
  as lecturer and writer, 55–56
  legacy of, 129–130, 165–168, 173, 209–215
  life strategy, 3
  "parking" questions, 56, 104, 126
  personal appearance, 14, 35–36

personal history, 59–61, 74–75
  absent father, 16, 31
  mother, 60–61
personality, 36, 38–39
  avoidant attachment style, 16
postwar broadcasts, 64, 73, 100, 213
preventive psychiatry, 159–160
remembrances of, 30–32
on role of child psychiatrist, 160–161
scientific attitude of, 135–136, 141
seminars and training concerns, 27–30
as strategist, 151–152
training method:
  observation and research, 39–40
  and seminars, 104
use of the work of others, 58
and Winnicott, relationship between, 67–76, 142–150, 171
working method, 37
as writer, 125–127
Bowlby, R., 7, 9, 16–17, 47, 60, 67, 121, 131, 148
Bowlby, U., 131
Boynton, R., 217
Bradley, S. J., 154
Brave, A., 30
Brazelton, T. B., 129, 155, 164, 176
Bretherton, I., 129, 164, 176
Bridgeland, M., 6, 23, 107, 112, 201
Bridger, H., 111
British Psychoanalytical Society, 10, 41, 65, 68, 69, 71, 120–121, 138, 142–143, 147, 158
Britton, C.: *see* Winnicott (Britton), C.
Buelte, A., 165
Bühler, C., 129
Burn, M., 6, 28, 107, 112, 159, 218
Burt, C., 80, 85
Bütz, M. R., 116

Cairo High Institute of Social Work, 222

Call, J. D., 155, 164
Cambridge Evacuation Survey, 87, 192
Cambridge University, 74, 105
CAMHS (Child and Adolescent Mental Health Services), 173
CAPP (John Bowlby Centre for Attachment-Based Psychoanalytic Psychotherapy), 9, 129
caregivers, supportive environment for, 9
Carlson, E., 130, 176, 177
Casement, P. J., 38
Cassell Hospital therapeutic community, 111
castration, 220
CAT (Child Apperception Test), 28
Chamberlain, N., 61
chaos theory, 45, 116
Child and Adolescent Mental Health Services (CAMHS), 173
child analysis, five-times-a-week, 77–78
Child Apperception Test (CAT), 28
childcare legislation, in Britain, 212
Child Guidance Service, 194
Children Act:
  (1948), 179–207, 210–211
    and Curtis Report, 181–184
  (1989), 188
  (2004), 214
children's officer, 186–187, 189, 197–198, 201
Churchill, W., 17
Clancier, A., 19, 36, 43
"club dream", Winnicott's, 44
Coates, S., 2, 28, 31–32
Cohen, A., 207
Coleridge, S. T., 46
Collins, A. W., 176
communication:
  kinaesthetic motoric ways of, 24
  nonverbal, 122

community:
    paediatrics, 3
    therapy, 28
Community Therapeutic Day School, Lexington, Massachusetts, 108–111, 113
complexity theory, 45
"compulsive caretakers", 156, 165
consilience among disciplines, 3
containment, 113, 116, 158, 213–214
Controversial Discussions, 120
Cooper, J., 18, 217
Cooper, P. J., 155, 165
Cornell archives, 147
Cornell Medical Center, New York, 10
Cornell Medical School archives, 52
Cortina, M., 1, 176
Cotswold Community, 6, 107, 112
"cottage homes", 189, 194, 210
countertransference, 33
Cox, M., 25, 26, 57
Cramer, B., 129, 155, 164, 176
Crapanzano, V., 175, 176
creativity, 9, 38, 99, 136–137, 214
    magical, 137
    of salivation, 125, 218
Crittenden, P. M., 165, 176
cross-identification, 132
Crowcroft, A., 10
Curtis, M., 183
Curtis Commission, 64, 152, 173
Curtis Committee of Inquiry (1945–46), 6, 90, 142, 180, 184–206
cybernetics, 29, 126, 161

Dar El Ifta, 223
Darwin, C., 4, 17, 68, 74, 121, 139, 152–153, 173–174
Davis, J., 217
Davis, M. E. V., 24, 42, 123, 125, 130, 135, 140
day-dreaming, 138
death instinct, 135, 154
Decobert, S., 36

"defensive exclusion", 141
delinquency, 6, 71–100, 117, 144, 154, 182, 204, 210
    juvenile, 72–73, 76, 84–85, 92, 179, 210
    social dimension of, 97–227
delinquent tendency, 85
deMause, L., 29, 160
democracy, 8, 61, 171
Department of Education, 190
Department of Health and Social Services, 210
dependency needs, child's, 212
depressive anxiety, 93
depressive position, 95, 158, 169
deprivation, 6, 71–100, 115, 135, 144, 156, 165, 191–192, 196, 204–205
    definition of term, 94
    effects of, 87
    maternal, 90, 210
    vs. privation, 95–96, 108–109, 118
Deri, S., 124
de Vore, I., 29
Diamond, N., 117, 130, 139, 141, 149, 155, 176–177
Dicks, H. V., 14, 64, 103, 120
Di Renzo, M., 124
dissociation, 139, 141, 219
Dockar-Drysdale, B., 6, 28, 96–97, 107, 112, 159, 201
dream(s), 26, 27, 44–45, 59, 69, 106–107, 110, 126–128, 135, 137, 139–140, 168
    analysis, 59
    and fantasy, 66, 138–139, 174
    material, clinican's, 107
    significance of, 44
    Winnicott's:
        "club", 44
        "explosion of total destructiveness", 41–42, 46, 54, 177, 219–220
        quelque-chose doll, 138–139, 156

dreaming, 24, 138
drive theory, 130, 135
    Freudian, 150–151
DSM–IV, 69, 145
Durbin, E. F. M., 31, 63, 174
"duty to care", 179–207
    vs. "duty of care", 179

Education Act (1944), 182, 190, 201
EFT (emotional flooding technique), 150
Egeland, B., 128, 130, 176, 177
ego-psychology, 143
Egyptian Ministries of Health, Religion, Education, Security and Tourism, 222
Egyptian Psychiatric Federation, 222
Eibl-Eibesfeldt, I., 29, 46, 160–161
Eigen, M., 38, 125
El Azayam, A. G., 223
El Azayam Hospital, 222
electroconvulsive therapy, 62
Eliot, T. S., 11, 46, 174
Ellis, M., 112
embodiedness, 35
Emde, R. N., 155, 176, 177
EMDR (eye movement desensitization and reprocessing), 150
Emerson, P. E., 160
emotional flooding technique (EFT), 150
enuresis, 93, 194
environment/environmental factor, 76–83, 87, 109, 119, 120, 138, 143, 195
    early, 76
    facilitating, 195
    facilitative, 88, 112, 193
    good-enough, 155
    holding, 108, 111, 118, 195, 196, 197
    management of, 88, 108, 112
    maternal, 75, 89, 97, 107, 175
        holding, 107
    role of, 73, 74, 75, 83, 87, 88, 97, 116
    society as, 97
    therapeutic, 107, 108, 113, 119
environmental deficiency disease, 204
environmental disturbances, 97
environmental therapy, 90
Erickson, M. F., 128, 176
ethology, 3, 16, 31–32, 46, 102, 128, 131, 135–136, 152–156, 175
evacuation, 75–76, 84, 98–99, 142, 179, 181–182, 189, 191, 195, 197
    Cambridge Evacuation Survey, 87, 192
    evacuated children, 75, 84, 87, 140, 181, 192
    Oxfordshire Evacuation Programme, 87–88, 184
evolutionary biology, 32
eye movement desensitization and reprocessing (EMDR), 150
Ezriel, H., 28

Fairbairn, W. R. D., 49, 128, 129
"false self", 34, 66, 156, 170
    child, 96
"family group homes", 189, 196, 201, 210
fantasy, 49, 56, 59, 139–140, 146, 162, 168
    conscious, 32, 46, 116
    and dream, 66, 138, 174
    vs. fantasying, 125, 138
    life, 116
        children, 103
        clinician, 107
    and reality, 217, 220–221
    role of, 24
    unconscious, 25, 46, 146
father(s), 16, 171
    lack of, 32
    need for and role of, 17, 32
        in family unit, 195
    study on, 17
Fees, C., 6, 10–11, 111–112

Feltham Borstal, 112
feminism, 30, 100
Ferenczi, S., 130
Ferid, H., 30
Fielding, J., 125, 138, 140, 174
Figlio, K., 80, 135
"fit person", 206
Fitzgerald, H. E., 165
Flavell, J. H., 46, 141
Fleeson, J., 130, 177
"flight to sanity", 123
Follett, M. P., 136
Fonagy, P., 130, 149, 155, 165–167
Fordham, M., 54
Foreign Service of Egypt, 222
forensic paediatrics, 3
forensic psychiatry, 118
foster care/fostering, 89, 187, 189, 193–196, 210
Fraiburg, S., 165
Fraser, J. G., 161
free associations, 5, 163
Freud, A., 35, 57, 63, 102, 121, 132, 143, 145, 147, 161, 177
    and Bowlby, 58–59
    and Melanie Klein: Controversial Discussions, 120
    and Winnicott, 58–59
Freud, S., 4, 16, 24, 50, 123, 149–152, 158, 161, 204
    dream work, 220
    drive theory of, early, and Bowlby and Winnicott, 150–151
    influence on Bowlby, 68, 74, 80, 135, 152–153
        concepts rejected by, 79, 80–82, 126, 143, 144
    influence on Winnicott, 4, 46, 57–58, 68, 74, 121, 127, 151–153
Freudian drive theory, early, 150–151
Fromm, M. G., 38, 125
frozen characters, 118
frozen child(ren), 96, 97

fuzzy logic, 45

Gaddini, R. de, 54
Galenson, E., 155, 164
Garmezy, N., 134
Geneva, University of, School of Sciences, 141
Giannakoulas, A., 124–125, 127, 130, 140, 152, 161–163
Gillespie, C. H. C., 44, 46, 105
Gillespie, W., 50
Gleick, J., 45, 116
Glover, E., 71, 100
Godley, W., 18, 69
Goldfarb, W., 86
Goldman, D., 38
Goldstein, J., 63, 161
good-enough mother(ing), 109, 154, 158
good-enough parenting, 116
Gosling, R., 28
Goswami, A., 116, 138
Grand Mufti of Egypt, 222, 223
Green, A., 127, 151, 155
Green, M., 176
Greenacre, P., 54
Greenspan, S., 176–177
Gribben, J., 46, 116
Groarke, S., 18, 132, 167–170
Grolnik, S. A., 123, 127
Grosskurth, P., 57, 120, 147
Grossman, K., 17, 130
Grossman, K. E., 17, 130
guilt, 78, 93, 125, 144, 178
    absence of, 72, 84, 96

Hall, E. S., 39
Hamilton, V., 2, 43, 130, 163–164, 166, 171
Harel, P., 155, 177
Harlow, H. F., 29, 46, 102, 104, 160
Harlow, M. K., 29, 46, 160
Harris, T., 130
Harvard University, 6, 109

INDEX

Harwood, R. L., 154
HAS (Health Advisory Service) Report, 27, 159, 173
Hauptman, B., 2, 6, 10, 27, 28, 37, 101–113, 153, 159
health, 157–158
Health Advisory Service (HAS) Report, 27, 159, 173
Heard, D., 14, 37, 163, 177
Helmholzian physics, 135
Hermann, I., 128–129
Hernandez, M., 124, 127, 130, 140, 152, 161–163
Hesse, M., 69, 129
Hillside Hospital, Queens, NY, 101
Hinde, R. A., 29, 46, 153
HM Prisons services, 112
Holbrook, D., 23
Holland, R., 177
Holmes, J., 72, 117, 177
Holocaust, 15
Home Office, 112, 190
Hopkins, J., 2, 19, 130, 163–164, 166
Hopkins, L. B., 18–19, 60, 217
Horder, Lord, 140
Horney, K., 31
hospital, children in, 3, 152
Hunter, V., 72
Huxley, J., 29, 46, 153, 160
Hyatt-Williams, A., 102, 147

IAN (International Attachment Network), 1, 9, 177
I ASC-ASULHAH (Israeli Association for Social Care, Change and Solution of Conflicts), 226
ICD–10, 69, 145
identity formation, 131
illusion, 136–139, 145, 157, 162, 168, 170
    creative vs. destructive, 163
    history of, 138
    wish-fulfilling, 137
information theory, 29, 152, 161

instinct theory, 128
Institute of Psychoanalysis, 75
    Child Department, 78
    Training Committee, 100
Institute for the Scientific Treatment of Delinquency, 71
institutional child rearing, 104
"internal working models" of self, 130, 139, 141–142, 148, 151, 162, 164
International Attachment Network (IAN), 1, 9, 177
introjection, 77, 81
introjective identification, 132
inwardness, truths of, 23
IPA International Congress, Copenhagen (1967), 34
Irizarry, N. L., 154
Isaacs, S. S., 43, 63, 87
Isaacs Elmhurst, S., 147
Israeli Association for Social Care, Change and Solution of Conflicts (I ASC-ASULHAH), 226
Israeli Foreign Ministry, 222

Jackson, J., 24, 110, 140
Jacobson, E., 141
Jacobvitz, D. B., 17
James, B., 177
James, H., 46
James, M., 43, 57, 58
Jazid, G. A., 177
Jews, attitudes to, 62
John Bowlby Centre for Attachment-Based Psychoanalytic Psychotherapy (CAPP), 9, 10, 129
Johns, J., 150
Jones, E., 72
Jonson, B., 36
Jung, C. G., 54, 59, 177, 219
juvenile delinquency, 72–73, 76, 84–85, 92, 179, 210

Kahr, B., 7, 9, 58, 68, 118, 121, 147–148, 150, 153
Kalmanovitch, J., 19, 36, 43
Kanter, J., 19, 23, 99, 111–112, 143, 197, 207
Kardiner, A., 175
Karen, R., 57, 120–121, 125, 129, 135, 141, 143, 176, 177
Karnac, H., 10, 117
Kennell, J. H., 165
Kestenberg, J., 165, 177
Khan, M. M. R., 18, 35, 60, 69, 217
King, M., 63
King, P., 1, 7, 35, 75, 120, 143, 147, 158, 170
Klaus, M. H., 165
Klein, M., 30, 35, 41, 50, 71, 75, 80–82, 105, 127, 140, 145, 158, 174
  and A. Freud, Controversial Discussions, 120, 121
  and Bowlby, 57–59, 87
    supervision of, 68, 74
  and Winnicott, 58–59, 125
    supervision of, 68, 74
Kleinian theory, 21, 28, 55, 59, 64, 81–82, 102, 120, 132, 141, 143, 169
Kohut, H., 149, 151
Kosko, B., 45
Kraepelinian nosology, 4
Kretchmar, M. D., 17
Kreutzer, T., 176
Kristeva, J., 162

Lacan, J., 30
Lachmann, F., 130, 159
Laing, R. D., 28, 111
Lake, B., 177
Laschinger, B., 129
Lee, A. R., 28
leucotomy, 62
Levy, A., 130, 176
Levy, T. M., 177
libidinal ties, child's ability to form, 77

libido theory, 143
Lichtenberg, J. D., 126, 132
Lieberman, A. F., 176, 177
Liedloff, J., 160
Little, M. I., 61
Lomax-Simpson, J., 10, 111, 119
London Child Guidance Clinic, 77, 84
London School of Economics (LSE), 23, 24, 67, 99, 112, 147
"looked-after" child(ren), 6, 159, 163, 183, 200, 202, 212, 214
Lorenz, K., 29, 46, 153
loss, 15, 37, 94–95, 122, 155, 164, 173–176
  vs. absence, 95
  effects of, 3, 117, 126, 147
  fear of, 176, 195
  impact of, 116
  of mother, 86, 94, 145
  object, 144–146, 183
    effect of, 144, 146
  theory, 132
loving, 16, 84, 176, 205–206
LSE (London School of Economics), 23–24, 67, 99, 112, 147
Lubetsky, O., 177
Lyward, G. A., 6, 23, 28, 107, 112, 159, 218–219

MacCurdy, J. T., 153
Mahler, M. S., 132
Main, M., 69, 129, 177
Main, T., 111
maladjusted children, 28
Malan, D., 28, 121
Maltings School, 63
manic defence, 144
  against maternal depression, 60, 66
Maratos, J., 47, 149
Marris, P., 102, 153, 176
Marrone, M., 1, 60, 117, 119, 122, 130, 139, 141, 149, 155, 176–177
Marshall, I., 45, 116, 126
Maslow, A., 25, 154

masochism, 41
Massachusetts Mental Health Center, 108–109
maternal depression, 60
"maternal infatuation", 177
Matte-Blanco, I., 30
Maudsley Hospital, 120
Maxwell, J. C., 105
McDougall, J., 54
McDougall, K., 112
McDougall, W., 46, 153
mechanisms of defence, 58
mental health care, primary, 117
mentalization, 130, 149, 166, 167
Messenger House Trust, 10
  homes, 111
Middlemore, M., 47, 159
Mill, J. S., 46
Miller, A., 31
Miller, D., 14–15, 27, 40, 102, 112, 218
Miller, E., 28, 75–76, 142
Miller, J. G., 154
Milner, M., 11, 19, 25–26, 38, 60–62, 136–138, 163
Minuchin, S., 28
mirror, mother's face as, 33, 107, 109, 167
Mitchell, S. A., 130
Molino, A., 127, 175
Mollon, P., 130, 150–151, 177
Monckton, Sir W., 183
  Report, 1945, 183
"monistic idealism", 116
Moore, K., 177
Moretti, M. M., 177
Morgenthal, G., 27, 159, 163
Morris, D., 16, 160
mourning, 3, 15, 116, 122, 129, 143–145
Mulberry Bush School, 28, 96, 100, 107, 112, 201
Münsterberger, W., 123
Murray, H., 14, 64, 111, 120
Murray, L., 155, 165

Nagan, W., 222–223
National Health Service (NHS), 98, 173
  Act (1946), 182
National Institute of Mental Health, 108–109
Nazism, attitudes to, 63
neurosciences, 4
  contributions to, 3
Neve, M., 19, 46, 60
Nezworski, T., 176, 177
NHS (National Health Service), 98, 173
  Act (1946), 182
Nichtern. S., 101, 102
Nicolis, G., 45
noosphere, 46

object:
  relating, 41, 131, 138, 219
    vs. use of an object, 42, 55, 123, 130, 171, 177
  use, 133
Object Relations Technique, 28
ocnophils, 129
Ogden, T. H., 38, 51, 57, 123, 125, 127, 168
omnipotence, 42, 169, 219
  psychic, imaginary, 34
O'Neill, D., 183, 189
O'Neill, T., 183, 189
Orbach, S., 130
Orlans, M., 177
Osborn, E., 28
Osofsky, J., 165
Oxfordshire Evacuation Programme, 87–88, 184

Paddington Green Hospital, 48, 52
Padel, J., 121, 174, 175
Palestinian Red Crescent Association/Hospital, 222
Pally, R., 122
Panksepp, J., 3, 4

Parkes, C. M., 14, 37, 102–103, 129, 153, 176
Parsons, M., 25
Pearlman, L. A., 173
Pearson, J., 41, 162
Pena, S., 19
Peper Harrow, 111
perinatal paediatrics, 3
PETT (Planned Environment Therapy Trust) archives, 10, 119, 218
Pfäfflin, F., 118, 176
phantasy:
   life, 81
   unconscious, 32, 116, 169, 177
Phillips, A., 127, 138
Phillipson, H., 28
philobats, 129
Piaget, J., 46, 141
Pitt-Aikens, T., 112
Planned Environment Therapy Trust (PETT) Archive, 10, 119, 218
play, 22
   role of, 24
pleasure principle, 143
Pollock, G., 177
Pontalis, J. B., 57, 124
Poor Law Institution, Bicester, 88
Popper, K., 45, 46, 102, 104, 134
postnatal depression, 165
potential space, 46, 52, 124, 130
Powell, E., 52
Prechtl, H., 159
preventive psychiatry, 3, 8, 27–28, 116, 159
   and politics, 62–64, 222–227
Pribram, K. H., 46, 151
Prigogine, I., 45
primary home experience, 195
primary maternal preoccupation, 90, 177
Priory Gate school, 28
privation, vs. deprivation, 95–96, 108–109, 118
projection, 63, 77, 81, 169

transferential, 132
projective identification, 132
   reciprocal, 25
psychiatric classification, 3
psychiatry, preventive, 3, 8, 27–28, 116, 159
   and politics, 62–64, 222–227
psychoanalysis, Bowlby's and Winnicott's contributions to, 161–171
Purnell, C., 129

Q-camps/Hawkspur, 112
   supplements, 6
quantum theory, 45, 116
Quine, W. V., 106

Raphael-Leff, J., 45
Rayner, E., 112
reality:
   external:
      acceptance of, 162, 167
      and inner world, 42, 54, 74, 81–82, 116–117, 134, 138, 144, 166–167
      loss of contact with, 145
   and fantasy, 220–221
   nature of, 3, 46
   principle, 66, 146, 169
   psychic, 137–139, 167
   testing, 82
   transitional, 46
"real self", 33, 66, 156
reception centres, 192–193
Reeves, C., 2, 6–9, 28, 35, 64, 71–100, 112, 116–117, 135, 159, 179–207, 209–215
reflective function, 149
regression, therapeutic uses of, 171
repression, 139, 141
research methodology, 29, 103, 161
residential hostels, 93, 184
Rholes, W. S., 176–177
Rice, A. K., 28, 107

Rickman, J., 75
Ricoeur, P., 175
Riviere, J., 68, 74–75, 79–83, 87, 120, 143
Roazen, P., 19, 121, 123, 127
Robertson, James, 102–103, 146, 156, 177
Robertson, Joyce, 102–103, 146, 156, 177
Rodman, F. R., 43, 49, 62, 75, 79, 82, 117, 143, 167
role:
    differentiation, 131
    reversal, 132, 165
Rose, M., 111
Rothschild, B., 130
Royal College of Psychiatrists, 67
Rudnytsky, P., 9, 19, 149–150
Rustin, M., 134, 141
Rutter, M., 84
Rycroft, C., 13, 18, 41, 68, 121, 122, 127, 138, 149, 162

Saakvitne, K. W., 173
Sable, P., 176–177
sadism, 41
Sameroff, A. J., 155, 176–177
Sampson, O., 201
Sandler, A.-M., 18
Sandler, J., 49
Sarah Lawrence College, Bronxville, New York, 177
Schacht, L., 38
Schaffer, H. R., 160
Schaller, G. B., 160
Schmideberg, M., 71
Schmidt-Neven, R., 165
Scholes, M., 176
Schore, A. N., 4, 122, 130, 149–150, 154–155, 159, 177
Schrödinger's cat, 45
Schur, M., 143
Schwartz, J., 129
Segal, H., 102, 132, 158

selfobjects, 116
Senn, M. J. E., 74
separation, 37, 106, 122, 176, 192, 220
    and attachment, 96, 103
    and loss, 132, 155, 173–175
    of child from mother, 77, 83–85, 192
    early, 72, 76–77, 85–87, 89–90, 135
    long-term, 93
    effects of, 3, 117
    –individuation, 132, 166
    theory, 39
    traumatic, 26
Shakespeare, W., 36, 46
Sharpe, E. F., 26, 43, 45
Shaw, O. L., 28, 107
Shoah, 15
Siegel, D. J., 176–177
Simpson, J. A., 176–177
Smith, B. L., 38, 125
Smuts, A., 89, 120
social engineering, 8
Social Services Act:
    (1971), 210
    (1972), 210
social theory, 29
Sofer, C., 28, 65, 161
Solnit, A., 63, 161
Solomon, J., 129, 177
Southgate, J., 30, 32, 37, 39, 126, 141, 176
spatula game, 140, 165
Spero, M. H., 59, 156
Spitz, R., 86, 129, 143
"split-off intellectual functioning", 123
Spruiell, V., 116
Spurling, L., 157, 158
squiggle(s), 103, 110
Squiggle Association, Winnicott Memorial Lecture, 60
Squiggle Foundation, 10
Squiggle game, 107, 110

Squiggle Seminars, 52, 112
Sroufe, L. A., 128, 130, 164, 176–177
Stanford University, 14, 57, 65
stealing, 84, 93
    as sign of hope, 91–92, 142, 157
Steele, H., 69, 122, 128–129, 149, 177
Steele, M., 69, 130
Steiner, R., 75, 120
Stern, D. N., 129–130, 154–155, 159, 164–165
Stevenson-Hinde, J., 102, 153, 176
Stoller, R., 217
Strachey, J., 38, 59, 74, 127, 156
"structuration of exteriority", 168–170
subjective creation and destruction, necessity of, 162
Summerhill School, 28, 159
superego development, 49, 91
Sutherland, J., 28, 119, 129, 218
symbolism, 24
symbolization, 65, 126, 162
systems theory, 4

Tagore, R., 46, 52
Target, M., 130, 149, 166–168, 176–177
TAT (Thematic Apperception Test), 28
Tavistock Clinic, 14–15, 21, 27–29, 40, 45, 50, 53, 59, 64–65, 102–104, 120, 129, 135
    Adolescent Unit, 15, 102
    Departments of Child, Adolescent, and Adult Psychiatry, 27, 159
    Department for Children and Parents, 14, 100
Tavistock Institute, 28, 67, 120, 129, 142
    –Leicester University Group Relations courses, 66
Tavistock School for Family Psychiatry and Community Mental Health, 14, 20
Taylor Robinson, H., 125
Teilhard de Chardin, P., 46

TFT (thought flooding technique), 150
Thematic Apperception Test (TAT), 28
theory of everything (TOE), 116
therapeutic community schools, 28, 89
therapeutic unit, residential, 100
Thielgaard, A., 57
thinking, 24
Thomson Salo, F., 122, 155
thought flooding technique (TFT), 150
Tinbergen, E. A., 29, 46, 153, 161
Tinbergen, N., 29, 46, 102, 104, 153, 160
Tizard, J. P., 35, 52, 55
Tod, R., 75
transference, 157, 171
    attacks, 131
    -based interpretation, 151
    –countertransference interactions, 33, 130
    negative, 131, 133, 177
    sustaining of, 78
transitional area(s), 44, 130
transitional object(s), 69, 75, 99, 123, 138, 156, 169
transitional reality, 46
transitional space, 46, 53
Trevarthen, C., 177
Trist, E. L., 14, 28, 64, 111, 120, 161
Trowell, J., 63
"true self", 34, 123, 156, 170
Turner, J., 138
Turquet, P., 28
Tutté, J. C., 3
Tuttman, S., 141
Tyson, R. J., 155, 164

unconscious fantasy, 25
"unit status", 127, 213
"unthinkable anxieties", 49

Valent, P., 154

van Dijken, S., 10, 27, 60, 74, 100
violence, 142, 196
　human propensity for, 42
　social pathology of, 225
von Frisch, K., 29, 46, 160

Wall, S., 69, 102–103
War Office Officer Selection Board, 194
Washington Institute for the Victims of Trauma, 222
Waters, E., 69, 102–103, 128, 130, 177
Weinfield, N. S., 177
Weiss, R. S., 177
Wellcome Trust Archives, London, 10
Weston, D., 69, 129
White, K., 27, 129–130, 159, 173
WHO (World Health Organization), 8, 64, 86, 89, 99, 103, 141, 143, 148, 172–173, 203, 207
Wilbur, K., 116
Williams, R., 27, 159, 173
Willoughby, R., 18
Wills, D., 6, 87, 107, 112–113, 119
Wilson, M. K., 46, 153
Wilson, P., 29
Wingfield, R., 129
Winnicott, A., 11, 19, 37, 53, 61, 62
Winnicott (Britton), C., 7, 18, 44, 52, 67, 88–89, 99, 123, 128, 138, 140–141, 147, 156, 177
　biographical comments on Winnicott, 11, 20, 22, 35, 46, 48–49, 59, 60, 118, 127, 157
　independent contributions of, 112
　relationship with Winnicott, 19, 49
　　and mutual influence, 111
　wartime work, 119, 184, 189
　work on welfare of children, 173, 180–207
　work with residential, therapeutic, and educational communities, 10, 19, 88

Winnicott, D. W. (*passim*):
　ability to surprise and to trigger "turning points", 7, 20–22
　and academia, 65–67
　aesthetic imperative, 57
　ambition and attitude to authority, 64–65
　appearance, 35–36
　author's acquaintance with, 17–26
　bibliographic references, 10–11
　and Bowlby:
　　criticism of, 5, 40, 68, 142–150, 171
　　relationship between, 67–71, 71–76, 142–150, 171
　and British psychoanalysis, 119–125
　child development, contributions to, 3
　child and family psychiatry, 3
　concepts of, and group dynamic situation, 131–133
　contributions of, 115–117, 148–150, 156–157, 161–163, 171–227
　creativity of, 52–54, 111
　and Darwinian theory, 152–153
　delinquency, understanding of, 117–118
　doodles, sketches, paintings, 52
　dreams:
　　"club", 44
　　"explosion of total destructiveness", 41–42, 46, 54, 177, 219–220
　　quelque-chose doll, 138–139, 156
　eccentricity, 35, 50–51
　and Freudian theory, 150–153
　good practice, 48–50, 61–62
　on health, 157–158
　influences on, 127–128
　　Darwin, 68
　　Freud, 68, 127
　interests, 115–117
　　in philosophy of science, 45–46

Winnicott, D. W. (*continued*):
  kindness to strangers, 48
  language of, 56–58, 123–125
  as lecturer and writer, 55–56, 105–107
  legacy of, 209–215
  life strategy, 3
  mother of, 60–61
  mutative metaphors, 57
  nonverbal communication of, 22
  personal history, 59–61, 74–75
    oedipal issues, 158
  personality, 24–25, 36, 106
    maturity and being childlike, 22–24
    playfulness, 22, 25–26, 35, 38–39
    "self-ablative" tendencies, 127
  playing with meaning, 43–45
  poetry of, 128
  preventive psychiatry, 159–160
  on psychoanalysis vs. psychotherapy, 118–119
  reaction to criticism, 41–42, 55
  relationship with colleagues, 49
  salient comments, 20
  scientific attitude, 42–43, 133–134, 136
  "structuration of exteriority", 168–170
  as supervisor, 32–35
  as theoretician, 151–152
  "turning-point", 49
  use of the work of others, 58
  wartime broadcasts, 8, 23, 64, 65, 73, 100, 112, 124, 213
  work of:
    cross-referencing, 170–171
    developments from, 165–168, 174
    working method, 37–38
  as writer, 125–127
Winnicott, V., 124
Woolf, V., 46, 138
Woolliscroft, K., 1
World Federation of Islamic Psychiatrists, 222, 223
World Federation of Mental Health, 222
World Health Organization (WHO), 8, 64, 86, 89, 99, 103, 141, 143, 148, 172–173, 203, 207
Wyatt-Brown, A., 150

Young, R., 80, 135

Ziegler, E., 27, 159
Ziman, J., 46, 126, 134
Zohar, D., 45, 116, 126